BUSTED! is the true story of Martyn Pritchard's
life as an undercover detective.

The events he relates here all happened,
but some of the names and locations have been
altered to protect a number of serving police officers,
some of their informants, a few innocent people caught
up in the drugs scene and others – perhaps not so
innocent – who were never convicted.

CONTENTS

Introduction

The scruffy, long-haired hippy with his torn jeans, combat jacket and rucksack, was new on the scene. He looked the part, spoke the lingo and played the guitar, looking for a dealer who would supply 'some weed' at the right price. Martyn Pritchard was actually a drugs squad detective, working undercover, sleeping rough, on loan to Wiltshire Police and aiming to trap a pusher who was branching out.

When Martyn had been accepted in the local pubs and squats, he was offered "really good acid, 10,000 tabs if you want, £30 a thou". With those words began Operation Julie, still the world's biggest drugs bust.

A cottage industry in Cambridge, turning out a little recreational acid for friends, soon expanded and eventually took on the status of a multinational corporation, with a global supply network. This only collapsed when 800 detectives made 120 coordinated arrests – and the masterminds were gaoled for a total of 214 years.

That sudden lack of supply meant that overnight, the street price for acid tabs rose from £1 to £8.

Busted, first published in 1978, was a biography of Detective Sergeant Martyn Pritchard's five-and-a-half years working undercover. It's a story of risk and bravery, worth retelling and bringing up-to-date to remind us how, from those early beginnings, the global drugs scene developed.

Chapter One

Prior to Day One

Edward Laxton: Long before Martyn Pritchard joined the police, which was three years prior to the huge Thames Valley force being formed, the drugs problem in Oxford was notorious. The university city had hit the headlines for all the wrong reasons when Joshua Macmillan – grandson of the recent Prime Minister, Harold Macmillan – died in 1965 of a heroin overdose.

Hundreds of the university's 11,000 undergraduates were indulging in all sorts of drugs – cocaine was not yet in vogue, but good quality cannabis was in great demand, amphetamine pills were plentiful and 'acid' parties were getting more popular as LSD tabs became cheaper. But hard drugs were rare.

Joshua Macmillan was probably the first Oxford celebrity killed by his drugs habit. He was certainly not the last. He was a member of the well-known publishing family. Father Maurice was a leading Tory MP and grandfather Harold had left No 10 Downing Street only two years earlier, in 1963, following the Profumo Scandal.

He grew up at Highgrove, now the family home of Prince Charles and the Duchess of Cornwall, and followed his father to Eton and then to Balliol College. In the university city – home for the Inspector Morse TV series – the drugs scene was wild. The Criminal Investigation Department within the then Oxford City police force, had a specialist drugs squad before Scotland Yard.

In mid-1966 I arrived on this scene, as The Daily Mirror's staff reporter, working from home to cover the Thames Valley. I was soon to meet, again and again, Detective Sergeant Mick Strutt, who ran the drugs squad. He was a chubby, rosy-faced, bubbly character who often found the time to persuade one of his squad's victims to try a spell of re-hab, and to personally recommend them for a place in a specialist unit.

At that time the university had its own official enforcers, the bowler-hatted 'bulldogs' who were out-and-about trying to maintain some semblance of order – the university's own private police force. But they were well-known and easily identified to the rowdier and less-disciplined students...

The campus of the 38 colleges was virtually sacrosanct, with town police officers never venturing into any of the colleges or the university's buildings and properties. The bulldogs were not disbanded until 2003.

The drugs squad was in operation for five years before Martyn Pritchard joined them, consisting of five men and a young woman. Pritchard was born in 1947 in Wales and brought up in Reading, where he went to school and gained seven 'O' levels, but still failed with his application to join the police cadets. He was too small.

He became an apprentice engineer, worked for an oil company in Norway for a year, and finally joined the force at the age of 21. He was still too small – by a quarter of an inch – but 'stretched' that necessary fraction at his medical. Thames Valley Police had just been formed from an amalgamation of the two small forces of Reading and Oxford with the three county constabularies of Berkshire, Buckinghamshire and Oxfordshire.

No other force in the country has such a diverse 'patch' to operate on, not even the Met in London. It covered an area from the perimeter of Heathrow Airport, through Windsor, Ascot, Oxford, Chequers, Pinewood Studios and Broadmoor. Some 130 Members of Parliament had a temporary or permanent home in the Thames Valley, the UK's richest stretch of real estate, from the picturesque banks of the River Thames to the newer homes of Milton Keynes. This would soon be Martyn Pritchard's patch from his base in Oxford.

After two years on the beat and nine months in CID, a vacancy for the drugs squad came up early in 1972. Only volunteers were considered for this squad and there were 49 applicants. Martyn's usual good luck took care of that problem. After a tip-off he made his first drugs arrest two days before the police board considered the applications. He got the job.

Day One

Martyn Pritchard: I started life in the drugs squad with a bollocking. On my first morning I knocked on the door of this little office, which overlooked the prisoners' exercise yard at the police station, almost bang in the middle of the city. I had just cleared out my locker in the CID office along the hall and I knew this was going to be something different.

The door burst open, a big hand came out and yanked me inside.

"In future, don't be so bloody formal and don't call me sergeant."

That was Mick Strutt. He ran Oxford's drugs squad for years, a great character who became a great friend. But that morning I wasn't too keen. I had never been in there before. The office was a mess, five desks and a couple of phones, way-out posters all over the walls, names and phone numbers scrawled everywhere, stacks of papers and books.

The posters were great. A nude girl on a motor bike, a moody drawing of Jimi Hendrix, and another saying, 'Just because you are paranoid doesn't mean they are not after you.' That was my favourite. In between the posters were official medical pictures of drugs and junkie equipment, and chemical descriptions.

There was one completely clear desk, which was obviously mine. The last bloke had emptied it before he left, but I never got the chance to go anywhere near it.

Mick was immaculate – he was even wearing a waistcoat – a total contrast to the other two blokes in the office. I knew them by sight and they looked worn out and filthy dirty as they wrote up their notes after a busy weekend. I knew the drugs squad usually looked scruffy, but I was just starting and didn't want to overdo it on my first morning, so I was wearing a suit and tie.

"You call me Mick in here and out there." He was off again, "Get back home and take that bloody fancy dress off, get down the town and grab some gossip."

There was no settling-in, no one pointed to a drawer for my notebooks and stuff, no introduction to new colleagues and drugs squad procedures. Nothing. I was going red, the other two were grinning and Mick was talking so fast… The phone rang and he snatched up the receiver.

"Speak man," he said, and suddenly he was as nice as pie, beautiful accent, smiling down the phone. Then he cupped his hand over the mouthpiece, "Go on, piss off," he hissed. "There's no junkies in here. The work is out there, find some."

And as I was leaving, bemused and a bit angry, he called through the door, "Ring in, Martyn, let us know if you're still alive."

That was my introduction to the drugs squad. A shock, but the lesson was right there. It's different, an extension of CID, a branch of the police force. Sure, the same rules apply and so do the wages. But it's like living and working in another world.

Drugs squad was all about information. There was no crime sheet with a complaint on it. Who would complain? So, Mick Strutt hit me with this distinction straight off. And psychologically the crafty old devil made me so mad and started me wondering what the hell this was all about. But it really was the best introduction.

It was information that helped me get on the squad. Just before my interview board a contact in the university dropped one on me. "Don't suppose you're interested in drugs, Martyn?"

I put him right and he told me all about a guy in Oxford who was known as Bernie the Bolt [a reference to the prop man on the 1970s' popular TV game show The Golden Shot]. According to my informant, Bernie was pushing a lot of hash and kept his supplies hidden in his airing cupboard, inside the insulating jacket round the hot water tank.

He lived right in the students' quarter, in Great Clarendon Street. I was already on CID so I spent a bit of time round there for a couple of days and found out Bernie was also a great womaniser. He was tall, black-haired and supposed to be a student, but always had plenty of money and a steady stream of birds coming back to his flat.

Bernie Juhasz he was called. When we hit his place he had 9lbs of cannabis stashed away. In 1972 that much cannabis was worth about two grand, a fair old bust for the provinces in those days.

Not only did I bust Bernie, I got him deported. He was an Aussie and not supposed to be in the country. He wasn't a street dealer, very much a middleman, and he kept records just like running a straight business. So, a few names of his customers came to light, the smaller pushers.

My informant was a businessman, too. I didn't know it then, but his motive in talking to me was to get Bernie out of the way and take over his operation. Certainly, the info he gave me was spot on. When we went in, Bernie was in the middle of weighing up some of his supplies. I made sure Detective Constable Pritchard was the arresting officer, and by coincidence it was all sewn up two days before my board interview for the drugs squad. Wallop. The other 48 applicants came joint second.

So now the job was for real and I was on my way home to get geared up and start work. In those early days, as I soon discovered, it was enough to let your hair down, pull on some old jeans and worry beads, and you were accepted. Later on, the hippies, pushers and everyone on the drugs scene knew the undercover coppers were there. And they were looking for us.

Many a time I have been in situations, particularly at music festivals, where they play a game called 'Spot the Pig'. Once I was recognised and had a close escape, but usually I helped them play.

And I have seen a few innocent folk get a good kicking for looking like a copper.

The longer I worked undercover, the more difficult life became. The jobs grew bigger and more important. To ensure a conviction I would have to provide evidence and then go to court. As you come out in the open more and more, people get to know you and it gets a real sweat.

There's no point pretending I was brave. I was always on edge, a bit nervous and worried. It was murder walking into a room and meeting strangers. I may know 300, possibly more, people on the drugs scene. But there's a thousand, probably three thousand, who know me. And when you meet someone you don't recognise, there is always the chance they will recognise you.

It's not enough just to look like a hippy: long hair, unshaven, faded denim, you must have dirt under your fingernails, holes in your socks and tatty old underwear. If you kip down in someone's pad, the white brightness of your underwear would dazzle them. That's not how they look and, mister, you have to be the same. So, it's dirty, you smell, your hair's unwashed for a couple of months, but that's how it is.

It becomes a total way of life, not just the working hours. For instance, you have to stay slim. You never see a chubby junkie. They're skinny because they are on drugs, but I wasn't. So, I had to cut down on my appetite and my beer consumption, look skinny to maintain my cover. I put on two stones, no trouble, soon after I finished undercover work.

I smoked cigarettes before I joined the drugs squad, but now I had to roll my own, because that's what they do. Half-a-dozen times the customers tried me out to see if I could roll a joint. I used to practise at home, so I did it really well. I had to do a lot of things I wasn't taught at police college. And often the rule book went out the window. In fact, there is only one rule: get on with the job.

Some of the senior officers, especially the uniform men, thought we were cowboys. They hadn't grown up with drugs. They thought it was all a joke and the drugs squad was the biggest joke of all. But attitudes changed – gradually.

One thing was always working against us, and it got up their noses permanently. According to the books, we were clearing up virtually 100 per cent of all drugs offences. The only minuses were the occasional cases we lost at court.

That was nonsense, of course. Think of all the drugs deals we never heard about! But they didn't become part of police statistics because no one made out a form CID 1A, a crime complaint. They weren't crimes as far as the hippies were concerned! We never even recorded the dealings we witnessed as we kept observation, waiting for the more important and bigger raids.

The bust, on the other hand, would go down in writing. We got a conviction and it was automatically a plus on our crime rate. So, on paper we always looked very good. And we mostly got guilty pleas to our charges because we were right there at the time of the offence, or we caught them with the stuff in their pockets.

When I joined the drugs squad, we were still building an entire mode of police operations. When fraud squads were invented, policemen were sent to college to become accountants, bright young men, conventional police officers.

But our college was out there on the street, right in the middle of the drugs scene. And there was nothing conventional about us. It was like we had 'dropped out' of the police service but were still getting paid.

The job took over my life to such an extent that when I was chatting up a new girlfriend and started on about myself, all sorts of details from my undercover identity would tumble out. I got the two characters muddled up – Martyn the copper and Martyn the hippy.

I used to shake myself, "Hey, man, think straight, this is the real life." It was like I played at being a copper, and worked at being a hippy. Really, I had three identities: the copper, the hippy drugs-dealer and a third one tailored to fit the bill. It all depended on the chick and the circumstances when I met her.

Some birds wouldn't want to know a copper at any price, others would be impressed, especially by a detective on hush-hush work. But on certain operations I wouldn't show out to anyone I didn't know, male or female.

So, I used to have this shadowy background, never letting on too much about how I earned a living. That was the easiest way, because my undercover life was so full of lies, I couldn't keep up with too many lies off-duty as well.

Name as well. For a while, to everyone, absolutely everyone, I was Martin Poole, dealer, ex-guitar player, painter and decorator, drop-out, anything but copper.

One of the biggest problems was my Mum. I told her what I was doing but she didn't really understand because I looked, talked and smelled like a hippy. And all the neighbours felt sorry for her. "Three lovely daughters, shame about your son," they would say.

There was no way she could ever let on what I was really doing, that much she did understand. Everyone thought I had dropped out, so I had to slip home after dark and leave the house very quickly. But wow, you should have heard my Mum later on, five years bottling up her pride, so she really let loose. Wrote to everybody and showed the newspaper cuttings when the Operation Julie team went to court. "My son Martyn, he set all that going." She was so proud.

I suppose it was difficult for her for a long while. She knew I had to look like a tramp, but at least I should look like a clean tramp. That was her theory. And one time that really gave me trouble. In the middle of the 1975 Watchfield music festival, near Swindon, when I was living on-site in my little tent and doing my own thing, I had to come home for my sister's wedding.

I asked formal permission from the bosses and they said no. The work I was doing was too important and it was too dangerous to send in anyone else. Charming! So, on the Saturday, I jumped in the car and buggered off.

Now I needed to return looking exactly the same for two reasons – the customers and the guvnors. When I got home I dumped all my gear in the corner, brushed my hair and beard out a bit decent and put on a suit, collar and tie, buttonhole, the lot. And off I went to church.

I think the family were quite pleased to see me there. At the same time, I think they were quite relieved when I refused to line up for any wedding photographs. No pictures, too big a risk. But trust Mum! Despite all the confusion at the house that morning, everyone getting ready for the ceremony, she had found time to wash all my gear.

She didn't ask me. Put it all in the washing machine, then the drier and finally ironed it. Everything, jeans, jumper, T-shirt, even my combat jacket. When everyone went off to the reception, I had one glass of champers and zoomed home to go back to work.

I found all my gear laid out in my room. Who knows how she found time, but there it was, all spotless. I went mad. She had done this before but not quite so thoroughly and never at such a bad time.

As I put it on layer by layer I went out in the garden and rolled around in the grass and dirt. If the neighbours felt sorry for my Mum before, they would have cried for her if they'd witnessed all this.

I thrashed around getting the creases in and rubbing the dirt on, but it still wasn't right. So, I went in and grabbed the dust-bag out of the Hoover, took it back to the garden and tipped it over my head. And off I went back to Watchfield.

Now I am off the job, I have been able to tell Mum there were quite a few dangerous moments, and explain why on some of our raids, guns were issued to us. I couldn't tell her before, not while I was still working. One time she was so upset she even phoned up one of the senior officers and asked him outright, "What are you doing with my son Martyn?"

I'll tell you how it happened. It was the end of a trial at Reading and the Daily Mirror wanted a picture of me, the copper who had lived in a commune and busted a Moroccan cannabis mob. We have always been Mirror readers in my family, but I couldn't let them take a photo – I had two undercover jobs going at the time.

Instead, the Mirror used a cut-out of DC Pritchard, back to camera, looking like he was about to enter this commune. The story was all over the paper, front page and centre spread, but when Mum read it she went up the wall. Even from the back of me, she recognised the stance of her only son.

She couldn't get hold of me, and after reading the story three times, she phoned headquarters and, as I said, demanded to speak to a senior officer. "Your son is doing a very important job, Mrs Pritchard, and he has the full protection of the police force at all times," she was told.

Where was that senior officer on my very first morning on the drugs squad? The instruction was, "Ring in, let us know if you're still alive." And that wasn't a complete joke. At times you really were on your own.

On that very job which upset my Mum, a tail of five police cars, with at least a dozen coppers on board, lost me on the way to a big drugs deal. As a result, I sat in the back of a motor with a load of drugs in my lap and four bloody big West Indians surrounding me. One of them had a knife at my throat for 25 minutes.

Full protection? Forget it.

Chapter Two

Preparing for the End of the World

Edward Laxton: Without realising exactly who he was, it was at the Moroccan cannabis case at Reading Crown Court that I first came across Martyn Pritchard. I was in the Press Box, he in the Witness Box. A very good story, the evidence traced masses of high-quality drugs back to the foothills of the Atlas Mountains, to the tenanted estates owned by King Hassan ll, and all told in fine detail to the judge and jury.

The team of pushers and smugglers on trial had been moving cannabis oil and huge quantities of concentrated cannabis resin, which was in great demand at inflated prices in America. Mid-trial, the Mirror news desk agreed that I should go to Morocco – if you don't try you don't get – so photographer Eric Piper and I flew to Tangier, hired a car and drove up into the mountain range. Next stop the Sahara Desert.

We were hardly expecting the country's ruler to come out and pose for us, but we very nearly came back empty-handed. Well, I did – but Eric had a picture of a police posse surrounding our car, refusing to move a heavy chain across the road, with big arrowheads that would puncture the tyres on a 10-ton truck. The King's guard!

We learned the Moroccan embassy in London was sending back daily reports to the capital, Rabat, of developments in the Reading court case. We also discovered how the King's tenants walked slowly through the hundreds of plants each morning, brushing their coarse leather aprons among the stems, flowers and foliage, to collect residue from the glands of each plant. They would stop to brush off the 'harvest' from their aprons, to be compressed into bricks of cannabis resin, a simple but more refined form of hashish – this was all good background in readiness for my end-of-trial stories.

This was Martyn's biggest case so far and he had to give evidence to make certain of the guilty verdicts. The trial lasted three weeks. Back from Morocco, Eric and I persuaded Martyn to allow the rear-view pictures. They actually made the story more dramatic, especially with the agreed explanation for hiding his face, that there was a price on his head.

Reporters covering court cases don't spend all their time in the Press Box. Much more can often be learned in the pub next door or over the road, people to talk to, and listen to. Somewhere during that trial – though certainly not from Martyn – I picked up a few clues to another yarn, and another plot of cannabis plants, at the safari park out at Longleat. And that led to another meeting with the undercover hippy copper.

The End of the World

Martyn Pritchard: I wasn't very pleased with myself. I couldn't wait to join the police force. Then I couldn't wait to get out of uniform. Then I couldn't wait to move off CID to the drugs squad (DS). But what had I got myself into now?

I wanted DS, I volunteered and worked my ticket to get in, but this was so different. In every other branch of police work you get shown the ropes, you go to training school and courses. Nothing comes completely new. Now I was floundering, out on my own and looking anything but a policeman.

Don't get me wrong. I'd wanted to get out of uniform, to special-ise, use my loaf and all that, but I had enjoyed myself and had a good time for two years in Abingdon as a bobby. Well, it certainly had its moments.

The first one came two weeks after I passed out of training, when I went to my first domestic. Nasty quarrel, neighbours report noises and raised voices, and we answer the three nines call.

I am 21. The customer is in his late forties, living in this very seedy council house, with dirt and grease on the walls. It turns out he has been married 22 years, has three kids, and I am supposed to sort out his family problems. Keep them happy, that's official advice. Be light-hearted, make them laugh and see everything less seriously.

"I've just killed my wife and the children," he announces.

"Oh really?"

"I am not going to tell you where they are."

"No reason why you should."

"There's no point. The world is going to end tomorrow."

"I hope not, it's my day off."

I think it was the flippancy that threw him. He suddenly pulled a bloody great carving knife from under his dressing gown and went for me. I smacked him, then put a chair across his shoulders and he went down. I had just sat on him when a sergeant from a back-up car arrived at the kitchen door and shouted, "Leave him alone, constable, don't touch him."

That was before he saw the knife. Then the customer's missus burst into the room, and the kids. We called a doctor to get him committed to a special hospital on a three-day order.

When we reached the hospital the sergeant and I got out together – and chummy locked himself in the police car. I had to bust the windscreen with my truncheon, crawl in and get him out.

"I have to report I was forced to break into a police car to apprehend a prisoner…" That's how my incident report began.

Another time I wrote off a Panda car. Well, I was blocking a getaway car from a robbery. It crashed and we recovered the money and three semi-conscious members of the gang. I felt 200ft tall.

I radioed for two breakdown vehicles.

"Why do you want two?"

"Both cars are write-offs, sarge."

"Both cars? I'll send an inspector."

The inspector arrived, had a look at my car and the skid marks and radioed for a superintendent. 50ft tall.

We make the statements and measure the road and two weeks later a full inquiry was ordered. Just after that, my Panda and a little old lady's car collide, and I am charged with careless driving. I am 5ft 7 and three-quarter inches exactly and wishing I had never stretched that extra quarter to get into the bloody police force.

Fortunately, I got an absolute discharge in court, but that is still a conviction. So, I've got a record after six months in the force, just for doing my duty.

I suppose the funniest and certainly the most outlandish incident I got mixed up with has to be the cattle trucks. I'm just waiting for a night shift to end, sitting in the car and having a quiet smoke in a lay-by at Kingston Bagpuize, outside Oxford. A lorry driver pulls in and tells me about a terrible accident just down the road.

It's terrible weather and I get there to find one lorry is on its side, the other right over on the roof. There are cattle inside making a dreadful din and a driver staggering around with blood all over his face. "Send an ambulance and heavy breakdown," I tell control. "Might need fire service and definitely some help."

I start talking to one of the drivers. "My wife's in the cab. She's eight and a half months pregnant and thinks her waters have broken," he says.

Bloody marvellous. It's snowing and eerie with just my blue light flashing.

"Send a doctor, send everything. Warn maternity," I radio.

His wife is not in the cab. She has been thrown through the windscreen and is lying on the ground – not badly hurt, just a few cuts but nothing broken.

"What do you mean, her waters have broken?"

"It means the baby's coming," she says.

"What, now?"

"Yes, officer. I'm sorry, I'm sure it's definitely coming."

"Don't worry, love, the hospital is only 10 minutes from here."

Five minutes later, the baby is well on the way. So are the ambulance, the doctor, the vet, the fire brigade and the patrol cars. But at Kingston Bagpuize PC Pritchard is all on his own. And scared bloody stiff.

The back-up services arrive just after the baby. It's a girl. Fortunately, I don't have to do a thing, the baby arrives under her own steam, and perfectly okay. I just watch, totally amazed, the husband is flabbergasted and so am I.

Then the vet won't go in the cattle truck on his own. The other coppers all take two paces back and it seems I'm elected.

It turns out there are very valuable bulls inside, on the way to an artificial insemination centre. But they are tied up and not very happy being chucked about in the crash. Straw and shit are all over the place when we get inside.

We block off the road with various vehicles and start turning the bulls into what looks like an empty field by the roadside. Two are still in the lorry when I fall over and see a bloody great head and horns coming straight at me. I have no idea what's happening, I think the bull is more frightened than I am. Anyway, we both come out of that truck at 90 miles an hour.

Then the local farmer rolls up and tells us our bulls – *our* bulls, mind you – are fighting with his horses. Oh Christ, it was a real mess! But that was then, this is now.

And right now, I'm in another mess. Drugs Squad is supposed to be specialised, but there's no instructor to tell you what to do. No one wants to know me. "Go on. Piss off and get some information." And that's that.

During Day Two I started coming to my senses. When I phoned in, everyone was nice and cheerful. Day Three was the same. Yet as far as I could see, I wasn't doing much more than wander around. Then that evening, Mick Strutt told me to drop into the office the following morning.

"Where have you been, dear boy?" he asked when I turned up. "What have you learned? Who did you meet? What great knowledge have you acquired?" He was always like that.

I told him all the pubs I had been to, and the college hang outs in Oxford I'd visited. I only had four or five names of people I'd talked to and a couple of snippets I'd picked up, nothing at all. But as it turned out, I had done all the right things, all that could be expected from a beginner.

For the next five hours I had an insight into the sort of life I was going to lead. Mick Strutt was a great teacher. Anyone less like a hippy you could not imagine, but he knew the drugs world inside out and backwards.

He was balding, on the tubby side, nice grey suit. I have never seen anyone look so comfortable in a waistcoat. He was articulate, nearly always used three words where one would do, and very sharp. He got everyone to do exactly what he wanted.

Mick was only a sergeant but his 20 years' experience was his real qualification. It didn't matter whether he was dealing with lawyers, doctors or chief superintendents, Mick charmed them and conned them and they all performed accordingly.

What a lesson it turned out to be. "Marijuana was discovered 5000 years ago. The leaves of the plant have an odd number. It is the most widely-used drug in the world and it also revels in more names... pot, grass, hash, hemp, weed, dope, ganja, skunk, Mary Jane, the list goes on, dear boy.

"Cocaine is called coke, Cecil, happy dust, heaven dust, gold dust.

'Stimulants, amphetamines, commonly known as pep pills,

directly affect the central nervous system."

That morning he talked non-stop. This was the briefing I needed.

"All your colleagues are out. I arranged that because you have a lot to learn in a short time. Here are some books, they will take you a month to read and digest, they will give you the background to all the drugs which will come within your province.

"Here is my own private exhibition so that you can see what they all look like."

And Mick opened a wooden cabinet with all these pills and powders neatly laid out and labelled. Heroin for shooting with a syringe, all kinds of pep pills, cocaine for sniffing, LSD for tripping, and the various forms of cannabis for smoking.

Then he went over the paperwork involved in DS work and the procedures usually followed on raids: sending samples for analysis, claiming expenses, obtaining search warrants, what to look for on a raid, interrogation techniques.

"Now let me introduce you to the safe. The combination has been changed. That always happens when someone like your predecessor leaves the drugs squad. Only serving members of the drugs squad know this combination. This is where you keep all seizures."

The green safe was in one corner, diagonally opposite Mick's desk. Then he spelt out all the temptations facing DS detectives.

"Pushers, especially the big boys, will try to buy you. Not only to escape one particular arrest but to gain more permanent protection. They have access to lots of money, easy money. They will suggest you bust them for an ounce of cannabis instead of the four pounds you have just found.

"They will tell you that way no one gets hurt. You still have a conviction. What harm will it do? Who else will know? You will know, Martyn, and eventually, so will I. In this room we have to trust each other but don't ever drop the name of your contacts in here, just in case of accidental slip-ups later.

"Certain small sums of money are available from time to time as a reward for information, these are rare occasions, but never buy your informants with drugs you have seized elsewhere.

"Always try to work out for yourself why your informant has tipped you off. There are any number of reasons, but few solid citizens exist on the drugs scene. They don't talk to you out of the goodness of their hearts, there is usually a hidden reason.

"Jealousy is the most common cause, they want someone out of circulation so they can move in and pinch his business. That means your informant is dealing himself. And, Martyn, no one is sacred. You will bust your informants, if and when you catch them at it.

"Funnily enough, they will respect you for it. No one has time for a mug. Play it straight with everyone on the drugs scene and you will make fewer enemies than you imagine."

Mick Strutt went on and on and it was fascinating. Then he showed me the disguises cupboard, just inside the door. There was a short white coat and a stethoscope. Most people will talk to a doctor far easier than they will talk to a policeman.

There was also a gas board uniform in there and the jacket and hat of an electricity board meter reader. But we had to throw those out, they scared the younger generation even more than the drugs squad. Lots of people on the drug scene would take out an 'overdraft' from their meter or by-pass the bloody thing altogether and get their energy free.

So, if you turn up at the door wearing one of those uniforms, they are far more worried than just being confronted with a straight drugs bust.

Then Mick talked to me about working undercover.

"Not everyone can do it, not everyone wants to, but that is where the big busts come from. I have watched the drugs scene grow and grow in this city, in this country. It's for real now. It's not students' kicks any more. The villains have moved in, drugs are big money.

"Give it a whirl, Martyn, see how you get on."

We talked about preparing an undercover identity.

"I am not telling you not to carry your warrant card. Every police officer should carry his warrant card at all times. But there are certain things you will find an embarrassment to have in your pockets, especially if they are searched at any time." And he winked.

So, there was rule number one straight out the window. No warrant card.

"You will have to learn to roll your own cigarettes, no one smokes straights where you're going. You will have to drink with them. Unfortunately, I have to tell you the out-of-pocket allowance for such drinks is only six pounds a month. Unless you want to ask the barman for a receipt when it's your round."

He went on to tell me how to spot the drug users, what to look for on a raid, and how to build up the evidence and strengthen your case.

A cannabis cigarette, a joint, has a filter called a roach. Almost anything can be used as a roach but the most common item is a piece of card torn from the corner of a Rizla packet of cigarette papers, chewed a bit then put in the end of the joint. So, anyone with a ripped Rizla packet is probably on the scene.

If you find a set of scales to measure small weights in a house, they are for measuring out hash. Ten to one the owner will say he weighs envelopes because he writes to lots of friends abroad. So, look in his address book – there will be two overseas addresses at most. And that book may contain names you know from the local drugs scene.

A blackened knife or razor blade means he has heated it and made it easier to cut through slabs of cannabis resin. Reams of cling film or small plastic bags mean he is probably a supplier. They are for wrapping up his deals.

He is almost sure to have a Social Security book. They call it SS money. Outside loads of houses in Oxford, 'SS' used to be scrawled, just like the old Nazi sign. There were posters saying 'Know your rights' and 'Are you aware what you can claim for?' Inside were our customers.

Next Mick Strutt explained about videoing our customers. If you ask a suspect about his calls at such-and-such a house, he may deny it. Produce the shots of him leaving that house and he often collapses and tells you everything. We never needed to produce the films in court.

"I want to talk to you a bit more about informants," says Mick. "It is always safer for you to let me know, just me, that you are using an informant who has come up with this or that bit of gossip.

"They will often try to set you up and you may need more than merely your word against theirs if a complaint follows a set-up. On the other hand, an informant may be trying to work two officers and that gets dangerous. You don't have to give me his proper name, use a special nickname and tell him or her they can always leave a message at this office in that name.

"If you are out but we know you have confidence in that inform-ant, we will go and swear a warrant and state that we fully believe in the info we have, then do a bust.

"Informants are important. Show you trust them. Pass on little bits of gossip about the police, about me if you like. Say I'm a bastard, say I wouldn't pass your expenses, anything like that, which would get you into trouble if it got back here.

"They will be proud you have taken them into your confidence. It's all a matter of psychology, and when you work out why they are informing – and they all have a reason – you'll be able to play them even better."

Mick turned to using pocket books and giving evidence. "Stick to the script, Martyn, don't try to make anything up. If you don't know something, say so or tell the court you have forgotten. Remember the officer who follows you into the witness box.

"Defence lawyers will ask if you prepared your notes with other officers. Tell them 'Yes, for the purposes of accuracy and in the interest of justice'.

"When you get a client back here for questioning, do your homework first. See if we know him here. What's his address, Rochdale? Right then, ring Rochdale nick and see if the local police collator can tell you anything about him.

"Then go over your own ground, what you know. And face-to-face, impress him with all this knowledge. He will think the world is falling on top of him."

Mick was tremendous. He threw me in at the deep end first, then nursed me and trained me. But, however much teaching you get, nothing beats personal experience. In fact, I soon realised drama school would have provided a better training ground for working undercover than any police college. I was an actor, no question, playing the part of a hippy or a junkie.

I couldn't be one of them. At night I would go home to a bed with clean sheets. There were at least two square meals on most days, and I carried on watching sport on television, drinking with my mates in the police club bar, and playing rugby.

I was a fairly normal young bloke in his early twenties. The only thing I had in common with the customers was music. So, I had to act the part.

And sometimes my performance had to last for days and nights at a time.

Chapter Three

Learning the Tricks of the Trade

Edward Laxton: Working undercover within a fringe community that indulged in drugs, Martyn Pritchard had to remain inconspicuous, avoid the barber and the razor, stay slim, don the same casual clothing. And gradually, his day-to-day, permanent undercover role became part of his personality.

The disguised detective had to be a good actor, becoming identified with the role he was playing. So, Martyn used to find himself sitting on the floor in casual company, among friends or at home with his family, as if he was at 'work' in a hippy commune. In fact, eventually he found squatting on the floor more comfortable than sitting in a conventional armchair.

He needed to fit in and soon found his old combat jacket was snugger than anything else in his wardrobe. His conversational style changed too, many drug-scene phrases remaining in his everyday vocabulary.

Martyn trapped drugs dealers and tricked them, but he never set them up. He used his wit against their cunning, his courage against their greed, his authority against their abuse of the law. But he maintained a certain integrity and that, apart from many other reasons, ruled out 'planting' or 'fitting-up' his clients.

Drugs have found their way into pockets and handbags, ashtrays and hiding places, without their owners' knowledge. Police officers have taken the view, 'This will make up for all the other times they got away.' That is planting.

To make the evidence even more damning, a piece of cannabis resin is produced in court wrapped in part of a page from a magazine. The rest of that magazine and the torn page are also produced, and police say they were found at the accused's home. The pieces of paper fit together perfectly. That is fitting-up.

If you invent evidence there is no challenge, no sense of winning, no detection. It is an illegal and sinister police practice, but it happens. Martyn had to use his own judgment. It was impossible to work as an undercover detective and not break the rules. But he was never 'bent'. The vast majority of the people he arrested pleaded guilty. Lots of them later became his friends.

Tricks of the Trade

Martyn Pritchard: Every actor needs to look the part he is playing. For me, the hair and clothes were easy and obvious. But how about the pockets, the car, the little tell-tale signs – the props, if you like – for my act?

The first thing, before I put on any clothes at all, I used a touch of scent. Patchouli oil is an Indian aromatic lotion extracted from a plant and it gives off a scent just like cannabis. That was a must. I used to buy it in those arty-crafty shops and I would smell as though I had been smoking a joint. I always kept a bottle handy.

It was no good telling everyone "I'm a hippy." They had to make that assumption for themselves. And if they also assumed I was on the scene using drugs, I had succeeded. But in case they were suspicious of me and had a chance to go through my clothes, I kept the ticket stubs from a recent concert and a letter or two with a reference to drugs in my pocket.

Friends of mine in America and Norway were under instructions to pencil in my name and address on envelopes when they wrote to me. I would rub that out, put in my alias and insert a fake letter which contained phrases like, 'Thanks for that green acid, it was great,' or 'Remember Jake Green, he's just been busted for supplying coke.'

In the car I usually kept the remains of two or three packets of Rizla cigarette papers, plus half a tin of Old Holborn tobacco in the glove compartment and maybe a postcard I had sent myself from Majorca – again with a drugs reference on it. I also kept a yellowing bail form in there showing I had been busted in Manchester for possession with intent to supply 500 acid tabs.

Most people I encountered on the drugs scene were nosy bastards. They won't ask too many questions, but they poked around everyone else's possessions. So, we used to put things there for them to find, and that way add to the character we were portraying. I used to keep my guitar in the car, plus a couple of records and the mouthpiece of a hookah, the Arab hubbly-bubbly pipe, down by the gear lever.

If I had someone in my car for the first time, I would stop and make a phone call. Leave him on his own and, sure enough, he would have a nose around my gear. You could tell by leaving things at certain angles on the seats, in the door pockets or the glove compartment.

Of course, as well as putting things in the car, we had to make sure certain other things were taken out — like payslips or notebooks or anything with an identifiable phone number. We used to check each others' cars.

And the story had to be right. From the police in Manchester, where I was supposed to have been arrested and bailed, I found out the procedure they adopted, what passages led to the cells, what time they served breakfast, just in case someone tried to test me out.

The ultimate prop for my act was a phoney file put in the Criminal Records Office, complete with false name, my fingerprints and details of two previous convictions, including the 500 acid tabs. It's not difficult for an outsider with the right contacts to run a check through the Criminal Records Office, as long as he has a name and date of birth. I had to change my file a couple of times when I switched to a new phoney name. But I kept the same birthday, my real birthday, so I wouldn't forget.

I used to keep my contacts book with all my phone numbers in the car. But I would add one to all the numbers except the noughts and nines. So, 14179 would be 25289.

We used to question each other about our identities and every time we switched from real life to the alias, we would recap on the situation, mentally ticking everything off, and then go through our pockets and car to make sure everything was kosher.

Most of these ideas were passed on by other members of the Oxford drugs squad (DS). And there were plenty of tricks to learn, too.

No one, absolutely no one in CID likes paperwork. And there's plenty of this in the DS. A list of the samples for analysis alone might include scales, knives (for cutting up drugs), paper wrappings, ashtrays, pipes, clothing, letters, as well as the drugs themselves.

You have to watch your colleagues. Because if one beats you to the draw during interrogation and says, "Now, Mr Pritchard will tell you *why* you are being charged." Or maybe he would suddenly say, "If you have cautioned the prisoner, you can charge him now, Mr Pritchard." That means only one thing – you have just collected the paperwork for that job.

But before you got that far along the road, there were tricks to remember at the time of a bust and, again, when you got prisoners back to the nick for questioning. They were traps more than tricks. Any detective or lawyer will tell you that in all areas of crime, the villains do more to convict themselves by what they say, what questions they answer and statements they make, in the 48 hours following arrest.

You can often peg that back to four hours. It is amazing the effect a cell, isolated detention, will have on most people. You don't have to make any promises about helping them or not opposing bail. Most have no stomach for the battle that is about to start between the two of you, once the questioning begins.

You, the detective, are on home ground; they are in the wrong and in trouble. And they always think you know much more than you really do. No one has to answer questions, and you make that quite clear when you issue the caution.

And if they agree to answer a few questions, you say, "Listen, it could go even better for you if you make a statement. The court might think I have had to drag it out of you if I put in a Q&A form, listing questions and answers with my report. But it's entirely up to you, your choice."

If there's a woman involved with a fella you arrest, and she is back at the police station as well, similarly locked up, the bloke will often suddenly become very noble and start in, "Officer, if I tell you everything, will Annie be able to go home tonight?"

So, you always take the ladies along after a bust and make sure they are escorted away to the cells first. Now, a lot of folks might think this isn't very fair, but that's crap.

Why should we fight crime with our hands tied behind our backs? On the other side of the interview table is a fella prepared to lie through his teeth, and it's his fault, not yours, that he's been busted.

These traps are often in a prisoner's interest. When you get to court with a customer who's been helpful, his lawyer will ask you in the box, "Will you tell the court whether or not my client obstructed your inquiries?"

Lawyer and client are fully prepared to seize an advantage like that, and many a time I have been called by the defence to explain in detail exactly how we were helped by the defendant. It usually reduces the fine or the sentence, too. They're only human on the bench.

Traps when interrogating the less helpful customers are also important. Let's take a hypothetical case. We bust a flat where we know the two occupants have been pushing dope. There are six of us and four fellas inside. The visitors have small quantities of cannabis in their pockets, which they have just purchased.

There are two customers to be charged with possession. But it's the other two guys we're after. So, my mates will take the first two into another room for a chat while the rest of us start to search. I find a letter in a drawer, read it and get all four together in one room. It might go like this.

Me: "Who is Little John?"

One of the occupants: "I am."

"Oh good. And who is Barry?"

No answer from anyone. I produce the letter. "This is addressed to Little John. Is that you?"

"It must be."

"So who is Barry? He signed the letter."

"I don't know."

"Yes, you do, you supplied him with hash."

"That's not true."

"Lying bastard. It says so here."

"Where does it say that?"

"Oh, so you've read this letter?"

"Well, it was addressed to me."

"Do you usually get letters from people you don't know?"

Silence.

"People who know your nickname is Little John and know your address and know you can supply them with hash?"

"Where does it say I supply hash?"

"Barry writes asking for more smoke and if he wants more, there must have been some originally. And what else does smoke mean if it's not hash. You're not running a bloody tobacconist's, are you?"

Silence again.

"Right, take him back, he's busted for supplying and that letter is exhibit MP1."

You make that sound like an order to a colleague, very officious and aggressive. The exhibit now carries my initials MP and is the first one in the case so far.

Now that's a bit of a shaker for the other three. Two of them are really facing less serious charges of possession, but you start hinting at everyone being involved in supplying drugs. The difference is between a simple fine for possession in front of the magistrates and prison from a judge at Crown Court for supplying.

In Oxford we always sent suppliers for trial at Crown Court and that was well known. So, you frighten them. "Where were you two going with this stuff?"

"Nowhere, it was for us."

"Do you think we're daft? We've been watching this place, we have seen you calling before."

"Only once, honestly."

"Oh yes, and what was that for?"

"The hash. Same as this lot."

"You only came here to score?"

"Yes, honestly. It was just for us."

"So, they were supplying you from here?"

"Yes." And more silence.

Now the fourth guy, the other occupant of the flat, can see the admission and the letter add up to a case against Little John for supplying. So now he's not going to feel too badly about opening his mouth as we've got him cold anyway.

And when we put all this to Little John back at the nick, he's not going to be happy carrying the can and he'll land his flatmate right in it as well. That breed always rat on each other, believe me.

You see, once the bust is made, the people you have to bear in mind are the magistrates, the judge, the jury. I know the customers are guilty. Now I have to prove it with good evidence to gain a conviction. And the evidence has to spell out exactly what the guilty people were up to. That way the sentence or fine is more likely to match the offence.

If you do the job properly, when you come to prepare the prosecution report and put in the statements, the Q&A forms, list of exhibits, your own evidence and details of observation, defence lawyers may well recognise there is no room for a not guilty plea. You get a hands-up admission with no aggravation, and save a lot of time.

Let's take another example. A guy has been arrested and is down below in the cells awaiting questioning. Among the items recovered from his flat at the time of arrest, are: a list of names with figures indicating weights and prices; resinous substance suspected of being controlled drug cannabis resin; plastic bags; scales; £240 in notes; and on you go with a number of exhibits called 'drugs paraphernalia'.

Now that little lot is going to impress the court. But how big a supplier is he?

Question and answer routine with the prisoner will run like this.

"How long have you lived at this address?"

"Six weeks."

"You seem to have acquired lots of friends in that time."

"No, I let my friends know I had moved."

"What, over 100 of them?"

"No, just a few."

"How many?"

"Just a few, say a dozen or fifteen."

"We have kept observation for the last six days and more than a hundred people, 108 to be accurate, have called at your flat. Were they friends?"

"No, visitors."

"But you have just told us you changed your address. Yet all these people knew where to call to visit you."

Now all this will go into the file for the court and the judge will read it. Very simply, you have already established three things that will impress him. He will know the drugs squad wasn't keeping observation just for laughs. One hundred and eight callers in six days mean this fella is doing a lot of dealing. And, despite the change of address, they knew where to go. So, he's been at it for quite a while.

"Did you supply all these people with drugs?"

"No, definitely not. I don't supply drugs."

"Oh? Well this is quite a size, this cannabis resin we found in the bread bin."

"It's not so big."

"Well, how would you describe it – large, substantial, commercial?"

He doesn't want to cough and admit his guilt, so you can keep scoring points with phrases like that. And, remember, he hasn't denied the 108 callers.

"I smoke a lot," he says.

"What, this much? Come on!"

"Well, I have a few friends. I told you that."

"So, your friends come round and join you for a smoke, is that it?"

"Yes, that's it."

"So, you allow your premises to be used for smoking cannabis. Did you know that's an offence?"

And you've got him on the run.

"Do you have a job?"

"No, I'm unemployed just now."

"When were you last employed?"

"Two months ago."

"So, you're living on Social Security?"

"That isn't a crime."

"But do the officials know you've got £240, the money we found in the bread bin with the cannabis?"

That's going to earn him some bird because nothing gets up a judge's nose more than someone living on Social Security with a nest egg provided by drug dealing. Matey is going down.

You can see how it can often pay for the customers to cooperate.

This bloke could have refused to answer questions, written out a voluntary statement and probably got himself a lighter sentence. But this way, we were able to impress the judge by the wording of our questions. What we said was more important than what he said.

Mind you, if anyone did make a voluntary statement, and we were writing it out in longhand for them, we would make deliberate spelling mistakes. When the customer read it through, before signing at the bottom of each page he would spot the mistakes, make the correction and initial it.

So, if in court he denied making the statement, claimed it was made under duress and all that old cobblers, we could point to these kindly corrections of a simple copper's errors. That proved he was volunteering his help, in more ways than one.

There were tons of tricks. We arrested plenty of unemployed gents who suddenly got a job just before their case came up. They were making a new start in life, their solicitors said. Perhaps the court would take pity and give them a chance. A load of bull.

Not much you can do about that, but they would also get a haircut and a suit. We could see what was coming. So just before the case, perhaps the night before, we would go out in the town and talk to some of the people who knew them.

"You know old so and so? He comes up tomorrow, poor bugger. His brief has told him to put his hands up, but he's scared stiff he's going down. He could do with a bit of support tomorrow."

Next morning, he would be standing there in the dock all clean and impressive. And crowding into the court, nodding to him and smiling, would be a load of scruffy weirdos. That usually spoiled his chance of getting off lightly.

Then there's the notebook catch. Say the defendant has pleaded not guilty. If we had something really juicy in our notebook that we couldn't put in as evidence because it came from an informant, we would deliberately struggle in the witness box, pretending to have problems reading our notebook.

The defence lawyer or the magistrates might well ask to see your notebook. Perhaps the judge would direct that the notes and the particular page be shown to the jury. Ideal!

In there would be written say, "Prisoner denies he ever dealt in acid but informant insists he deals 500 regular, every month."

So, they would see something we couldn't introduce in court ourselves because it was hearsay and we couldn't possibly put up our informant to give evidence.

We got up to all sorts of tricks on busts. There were not many pads where we were frequent callers but a few big houses in Oxford were involved full-time with drugs. They were mostly squats. Their owners went abroad and left the places empty. Then the hippies and drop-outs moved in and lived rent-free.

The electricity, gas and water would get turned off, but that didn't matter to them. And every room would soon be in a mess. The only care taken by the new occupants was over keeping the law out.

There would be a couple of safety chains and three or four bolts on front and back doors. When we raided the place they would have ample time to hide the gear or throw it over the wall. We had two options: use the universal key – that's what we call the sledgehammer – or break in quietly.

The first way would still mean a time lag. The second is only legal if the occupants prevent entry. When you raid and have a search warrant you are supposed to knock and announce your presence. But nowhere does it say you have to shout. So, we used to tap on the door lightly and whisper, "Open up. Drugs Squad. This is a raid." Then we used to try and break in. One of us would go through a kitchen window perhaps, or one on a first-floor landing, with a jemmy. Then he would creep down to the front door, draw all the bolts and chains and let the rest of the team in.

"How did you get in?" someone would start yelling and

screaming.

"The front door was left open." And that would bring on their paranoia. There was a snitch in the house, they thought, and it all helped our cause.

Well, we were hitting one place all the time, and our guvnor got mad about having us shin over a 10ft wall, which used to sway like crazy. He decided to do something about that front door.

On the next raid, while about 10 or a dozen of us kept everyone out of the way with searches and questioning, the guvnor and two of the lads unscrewed all the bolts and went to work with metal cutters on the screws.

When they put everything back, each screw was only a quarter of an inch long. Next time we hit that place, which was exactly four days later, we rammed the door and it flew in.

That was just to teach the occupants a lesson, show them we could get in. They never found out about the screws, because afterwards, we replaced the ones we had sawn off. Luckily, they were new bolts, so there was no paint or anything to worry about.

At less well protected houses, we would ask the occupants to empty their pockets and then take everyone into another room. One of the lads would sprint down to a key shop right opposite Oxford nick, and get copies cut for our future needs.

Sometimes we did a good job just by starting a rumour. My first Christmas on the squad was a laugh. The overtime rates were so high for public holidays that headquarters always refused permission for us to work.

All the squad got out on the town in the two or three days before Christmas, moaning like the clappers to their contacts.

"What do you think of that bastard Strutt? He's absolutely wrecked our Christmas. He's lined up three busts for Christmas Eve, six for Christmas Day and another seven for Boxing Day."

The news went around the town like wildfire. We had visions of all the junkies and dealers pouring their gear down the toilet or digging hidey holes out in the freezing countryside, and laughed ourselves silly at our party.

After Christmas we were bad news. "You rotten bastards. No one got hit and a fortune went down the drains." We heard the same story a dozen times.

We also had ways of dealing with leery sods on the scene who gave us a bad time, taking the piss whenever we walked into a bar. Any member of the public getting a mouthful like that would walk over and belt the guy. But we were police officers. On or off duty we were subject to discipline and that wasn't allowed.

But when you had a good bust, the news would soon get around. Within an hour, everyone on the drugs scene in Oxford knew what house had been raided, who was inside and how much stuff was found.

As soon as we got things cleared up, we would all go out for a drink. It was an ego trip for us, let them know we were very pleased to be on the winning side once more. If you ran into one of these cynical sods, absolutely ideal.

"Hello, Cyril, my old mate. Here, have a drink."

Carry over a pint to the surprised gent and give him a little wink, and someone was bound to wonder if he was the grass for that night's job. Honestly, I have seen blokes get that treatment and when the penny drops, they literally run out of the pub.

One night, Mick Strutt opened his wallet and there was about a £100 inside. I think he was going on leave and had his holiday money, but he asked at the bar, "Has anyone seen Wilson? I've got something for him." He tried to leave a tenner behind the bar, but the licensee protested, "No, no, I don't want it."

And the lad that Mick had mentioned, Wilson, who had been very saucy and made life difficult as well as uncomfortable for us, he got a nasty smacking a couple of days later.

Of course, we were always bad news in the pubs – if not with the drinking customers, certainly with the landlords. If we went in alone or just with one mate, no one took much notice. But if the squad walked in, five or six of us, we could clear a bar in five minutes. Even this could work to our advantage.

"You rotten sods. We had a really good night building up. I was taking a stack of bread." That was the licensee speaking. And just to keep us out, or sometimes to keep on our side, he would pass on some useful bits of information.

I had lots to learn at first, but I was able to learn fast. For in 1972, when I started, there were lots of drugs on the go in Oxford, and I was soon working in Reading, Slough and Aylesbury, and then in the Midlands, the South Coast, London and the West Country as well.

We did pretty well in Oxford, though not in the university, which was a closed shop, and the drugs were always being moved around. Even if your information was only a day or two old, it was usually too late. I once took out a search warrant for 'Oxford University' in general, without specifying any one of the 30-odd colleges, after talking sweetly to the magistrates.

It didn't get me anywhere, though. I couldn't catch up with that hash consignment. I knew who was involved but couldn't nail them. Win some, lose some, but we always drew the line at fitting-up any of our clients. You take a few chances and a few liberties, but we never planted any drugs.

Looking back, I guess the most important ingredient for the undercover role is 'bottle'. When your courage goes, your arse, your 'bottle and glass', falls out. If you're undercover you have to push your luck, and if your bottle goes, that's the end of that operation. You've got to be relaxed and confident, listen to what's being said, watch what's happening, keep analysing what's important. No point worrying about being exposed as a copper.

And all this needs 'bottle'. There may be dangerous consequences if the undercover detective is discovered. I used to make a mental note of escape routes in any new situation, even second-storey windows, honestly.

But there wasn't too much danger around Oxford University. That place was a law unto itself, in a world of its own. They had their own statutes, which ignore English law, once you're inside the college walls. For instance, a bobby could not wear his helmet anywhere on university property.

You had to take off your helmet as soon as you entered any college, and that's one of the first things the governors told you when you join the police in Oxford. Students were told they could knock a bobby's helmet off if they saw him wearing one, anywhere inside university boundaries.

They had their own police force, the 'bulldogs', and their own discipline. The college deans didn't want to know about trouble, so a lot of upper-class trendies went scot-free.

Chapter Four

Grass by Many Other Names

Edward Laxton: There are even more names for marijuana than Martyn Pritchard was told at his initial teach-in. Texas Tea, Indian Hay, jive and straw, are a few more, all terms for the so-called soft drug that derives from the plant Cannabis Sativa, its Latin title.

Grass is the name usually given to chopped-up pieces of the leaves, stem or stalk of the actual plant. They can be smoked on their own or mixed with ordinary tobacco.

This produces a milder smoke than a reefer (or a joint) made with tobacco and the scrapings from a block of cannabis resin. The blocks themselves are a more concentrated form of the same drug and are easier to smuggle.

The effect on the smoker is the same, no matter how the drug is taken. He experiences a 'high', a sense of well-being, euphoria and excitement all mixed together. Hence, even more names – giggles-smoke, happy-bush and locoweed.

The police recognise yet another kind of grass: the informant, snout, snitch or contact. His or her reasons for 'informing' are many and varied. These people are essential in all kinds of detective work, but they are so rare... unless they become insiders and almost personal friends of the drugs squad coppers.

Hardly surprising, the police informants' fund is rarely used by the drugs squad. Modest payments like £5 are normal. Martyn's highest payment was £30, and the most he could ever remember being paid out by the squad was £100.

When he purchased drugs – he often needed to do so to maintain his undercover identity – refunds were claimed on expenses if they had not been previously authorised. For big deals, detectives often used their own money. It was quicker and did not involve lengthy paperwork or internal 'aggro' within the force.

Informants are rarely pleasant characters, but they are necessary. A detective must know how far he can use his grass, whether he can trust his information, how he can protect him. And he must also sort out in his own mind why the informer wants to talk.

The Other Kind of Grass

Martyn Pritchard: Although Oxford University caused us problems, we did well with the dealers in the city, who were supplying many of the students. We put in a lot of work to build up a tight network of grasses, but we also picked up gossip from a variety of sources... and for a variety of reasons.

I'll start with 20 Plantation Road, a house where we had regular tip-offs – and which we busted – repeatedly. We must have hit that place at least 50 times over the years. It's where I started my undercover career.

I totally blew it that first time. Inexperience, nervousness, anxiety, they all contributed, and bang went my cover straightaway.

Mick Strutt had pointed me at this team of three in the house doing acid, some of it bad. There was Bruno, who was no saint, believe me, a little Scots feller called Mac and another guy called Johnnie. Some kids were getting some very nasty trips and we had several leads going back to Bruno and his two mates. But we had to catch them at it.

Then early one Saturday morning a young nurse was picked up in Port Meadow, a huge common down by the river. She was on a diabolical trip, naked and eating cow-pats. Mick ordered a special investigation. Once more the finger pointed to Bruno and No. 20 Plantation Road.

We had a conference and decided to put a newcomer to the

squad – me – in there. We already held camera shots of everyone staying at this house, taken from a car about 40 yards away with a telephoto lens. My introduction was through a pub. They all drank in the Victoria, or the 'Vicky Arms' in Jericho, not far from the house.

No. 20 was a squat with about 40 fellers and girls living there, if you can call it living. I think the owner was staying somewhere in the Far East. By the time he found out that a load of squatters had taken over his house, he must have decided that to get it re-possessed would cost too much trouble and expense. In any case, another bunch would probably have moved in immediately afterwards.

It was like a fortress at the front and back doors. But the garden was a rubbish tip, at least 2ft deep in paper, rags, rotten food, tin cans, everything. No one had thought of buying a dustbin, in any case they would have needed half a dozen, so everything went out the back window into the garden. The smell was dreadful.

And it was nearly as bad inside the house. There was hardly any furniture, just a load of mattresses, blankets, sleeping bags, rucksacks and cases.

There was also an army of cats living there, mostly in the basement, and people were sleeping about four to a room on the three floors above. Their only common interest was drugs, any and all kinds.

Imagine living without water, electricity and gas. It was cold and dirty, the cooking was done on camping equipment. Total income amounted to 30-odd quid a week each from social security, and the money mostly disappeared in a cloud of cannabis smoke or an eight-hour acid trip. What was left went in the pub. A great life.

But the pub was where I did my business and got started with Bruno and the others. The Vicky Arms was a hippy boozer, psychedelic posters on the walls, dim lights. It had a great jukebox with Dylan, Jimi Hendrix, Pink Floyd, Led Zeppelin, all music like that, no straight pop. Not many straight customers either in those days.

The music scene was one of the things I had going for me. I knew their kind of music as well as they did. I used to play bass guitar in a Reading group called The Thousand and One. And music did the trick for me in there. People accepted me because I knew what I was talking about.

To be honest, I never looked like a copper, not even in uniform. Skinny, short, driving a beaten-up old Volkswagen. My hair wasn't really long at that stage so I wore a headband, which made me look freakish, and a pair of John Lennon glasses with clear lenses.

I put some thought into my appearance, or lack of it, and it worked. I went back to Bruno and Johnnie's place on a couple of nights, and in a while the talk got round to dope. There was a lot of smoking, all joints naturally, but I was blowing not inhaling mine, like Mick Strutt had showed me. And it looked real.

I was there two more times before I was asked whether I wanted to score. "Yeah, man. I'm hanging on to £250 but my regular hash supplier hasn't been round lately. If I can't find him, we can deal. OK?"

"How about acid?" asks Bruno.

"Great. Even better. Do you do acid?"

"We can do you 1000 tabs for £230."

"I don't need that much. I mean, I don't use it too often, but I have a couple of connections. Say 500 tabs, that would be cool."

"Sure, 500 tabs then. We'll say £120. Okay?"

"Sure thing, Bruno. When do we do it?"

"We'll let you know. You gonna be around?"

Now this was on a Thursday night. The pattern of work on the drugs squad was: Monday and Tuesday paperwork after the previous weekend's busts; Wednesday and Thursday out getting info; Friday and Saturday doing busts. Not much doing on Sundays.

I didn't know how soon I would score the acid, but when I went into work next morning all excited, I chatted things over with Mick.

"He's going to do it soon," the guvnor reckoned. "He maybe trusts you, but he doesn't know whether you talk around in the town, and the longer he leaves it, the more things can go wrong."

So, we left it that I would hang on with this mob, and if I needed help that night or Saturday, plenty of the drugs squad boys would be around.

I went home and got some money ready, about 20 quid of my own. Then I carefully cut up sheets from an old telephone directory with a razor blade, making them the same size as pound notes. I made a thick wad, with real notes at both ends, stuffed it inside an envelope and put it in the back of a wallet.

That night I popped in for a couple of quick drinks at the Vicky Arms, just to show my face. I arrived early and started drinking draught lager. Soon the beer was flowing, and I realised I was getting pissed. The music on the jukebox was great and I was really enjoying myself, forgetting about work and the police force.

The three fellers and a couple of girls in the set-up were there. Suddenly, Bruno says, "You wanna score? We'll do it now."

"You mean now?"

"Right now."

"I haven't got the bread."

"Can you get it?"

"Sure. Be back in 10 minutes."

"Go with him, Mac. Take my car."

It happened as quick as that. They obviously didn't realise I was a copper, but they didn't want to take any chances with a newcomer, so they sprung everything fast. That's why I had a minder while I fetched the cash. They were careful, but they wanted my money.

I sobered up and drove home. I pulled up well short of my flat in Oxford and made my watcher wait in the car. Inside, I grabbed the phone. Both extensions in the drugs squad office were engaged and I panicked.

"Cut one of them off, this is very urgent," I told the police operator. Mick came to the phone and I told him I thought the acid would be at their pad in Plantation Road and suggested they raid the house 10 minutes after I went in. I rushed back outside, and back to the pub. Then I showed Bruno the wallet. That was usual practice – I would show the money but hang on to it. If he was satisfied I had enough bread, he would show me the drugs whenever he decided.

I could examine them and make sure it was the real stuff, and once I was satisfied we would make the exchange. This was done to avoid rip-offs.

I was sure the boys were somewhere around outside the pub as we left to go back to the house to do the deal. I thought there would be some hassle but, just in case, I left the money in the car before we went in.

To my surprise, Bruno produced the gear as soon as we were in the house. I told him I'd left the cash in the motor.

"Why did you do that?" said Bruno, all suspicious.

"Well, you could still rip me off. I wanted to see the acid." I knew exactly when the boys would arrive. When a copper says 10 minutes, he doesn't mean 9 minutes and 55 seconds. But 10 minutes is a long time under those circumstances and I couldn't chance Bruno finding £100 worth of telephone numbers and flushing the LSD down the toilet. And I might get my head kicked in as well. So, I kept talking.

"Hang on, I'm bursting with all that lager inside me. Then I'll get the money."

"OK, OK. But this is no rip-off. Get the bread."

"Listen, Bruno, if that acid is good, can we deal regular?"

"Sure, but we only deal when I say so. Right?"

"Right man. That's cool."

He was getting nervous, but the chances were Mac had nosed around in my car and he would probably calm everyone down while I was out of the room. When I went back into the house I left the front door open. The drugs squad boys were right behind me.

I got busted as well and taken back to the nick, but it was all too obvious. It all came together too neatly at the house, and the word was soon out. My cover was blown on my first solo operation.

A week later Strumpet, the underground paper in Oxford, came out with the news: *Watch out for this man, he's just joined the DS [drugs squad] in town.* And they carried my full description with some details of the bust, the pub and the house.

Overall, I suppose things worked out reasonably well. Bruno got a year on account of his previous, and the other guys got heavy fines. I learned a good few lessons and gained some confidence. At least I had proved to myself I could get in, I could deal and spiel with the customers.

It taught me I needed to be more careful, more prepared, learn a bit more about timing and keep my bottle. And definitely watch the booze intake.

As I said earlier, 20 Plantation Road held great attractions for us. We busted two or three dozen other houses in that area, but for us No. 20 was top of the pops, permanently. It became so regular, I'm sure dealers used it because they figured we would think no one could be daft enough to work from there any more. It was a double con.

The houses in that part of Oxford were all around 50 years old, much bigger inside than they looked. There were two or three squats, and the rest were let as flats or bedsits. There weren't many regular students staying there, mostly college hangers-on, a lot of drop-outs from other universities who enjoyed the Oxford scene.

On one of our busts at No. 20 we had some info insisting we check the bathroom at the top. Normally drug users weren't interested in washing, and usually the water board had turned the supply off.

We went along and I was first in. I made sure none of the occupants went near that bathroom. Then I opened the door and went inside. Some bastard had replaced the second of the three steps down into the room with cardboard, and I went flying as it collapsed under me.

Remember, hippies and junkies do a lot of nicking from each other, and this was an anti-theft device. It would have told the dealer, who lived in the room next door as it turned out, that someone was in there who shouldn't have been. We also learned our information was dead right. The bath had been altered. It was built up on a plinth about a foot high. And underneath we found a false compartment.

That little hole was full of about five or 6000 quids' worth of gear – raw opium, cannabis resin, a stack of pills, heroin, needles and syringes. It was like a miniature junkie warehouse. We collected perfect fingerprints from each bag and their owner went to prison for two years. And I bet he enjoyed better living conditions inside than he had at that house.

Another good source of information was girlfriends. That saying about hell hath no fury is dead right. If a drugs dealer breaks up with his chick, he had better watch out. The chances are she will squeal, and we weren't too fussy how the information arrived.

Mind you, a bloke will do the same thing and for the same reason. Take Brinny, for example. He was keen on a chick who left him and went over to a guy he soon learned to hate. Her new man was Philip, plenty of bread and only slightly known to us.

I picked up Brinny in the middle of Oxford one night, purely on the off-chance. I knew he was a speed dealer and, sure enough, he had an ounce on him. He faced a charge of possession or possession with intent to supply, which is much more serious. And an ounce is a lot of speed, too much for personal consumption.

But I was ready to trade with Brinny and charge him with the lesser offence. So, he gave me the information on his ex-girlfriend's new man, the well-heeled Philip, who lived just off the Cowley Road. He was into heroin, and the very next day he was due to pick up £2000 worth of smack in London.

We kept Brinny in the cells, partly for his own protection but mainly in case he got pangs of conscience and told the other side we knew about the heroin. Then we staked out Philip's house in Hendred Street.

Brinny told us our man drove a new white Peugeot and would probably be alone. Just before six o'clock in the evening a white Peugeot rolled up and we hit the car. Wrong bloody motor. While we were still discovering our mistake, another white Peugeot arrived, and when the driver saw all the action, he kept going.

A distinct lack of success. But we had a new team to watch. Philip didn't grab his luck and get out of the business. He kept going, and a month later some of the lads on the squad nicked him in full possession of about £700 worth of heroin. And who was on his arm? Brinny's ex-lady love – who got pulled in as well.

After she was released, Brinny apologised and told her he gave us the original information but didn't mean to get her busted as well. She told her man and Brinny got himself a good hiding for nothing. That's love for you.

Mick Strutt had warned me about the crafty buggers who talk because they want to increase their own turnover and profits. When they tip you off, it's because they want a rival off the street so that they can pinch his business.

I proved that, purely by accident, with Frankie, one of my snouts. He gave me the names of three fellers, information that a new consignment was arriving soon, and an address. The following afternoon Frankie phoned and said the stuff had arrived and the three clients were almost sure to be doing their weights that evening.

We bust this house but it was absolutely clean, and the occupants didn't fit the bill. I roared round to my informant's place and practically fell through the door. There he was with the scales out, doing up his own deals of hash. I went berserk.

"You bastard. You deliver a bum steer like that to get us out of the way and do your own thing." And I went for him. I was almost very physical.

"That was good info, honestly, Martyn," he whimpered. "Yeah? Well, there was no gear, no three fellers. We bust the place and left full of apologies."

He went red, then green. He was pig sick.

"Anyway, you're nicked. Get all your stuff out or I'll tear this place apart," I said.

This unplanned bust was a very good one. Frankie was preparing half-a-pint of hash oil, the first consignment we had seen in Oxford, when I rushed into his place.

Hash oil is very concentrated cannabis. It's thick, like treacle, so it's mixed with ether to thin it down. The mixture is poured over ordinary tobacco, the ether evaporates, and you are left with tobacco impregnated with hash. It's much stronger than straight hash, a really heavy smoke.

As I gathered up his stuff, Frankie kept shaking his head.

"I can't understand what happened, I know it was definitely on. I daren't tell you how, I just know."

"I suppose you gave me the right address?"

"Oh no!" he groaned. "What colour was the front door?"

"I don't know, green I think, a sort of dirty green."

"What? You should have busted a house with a pink door, bright pink, and pink window frames."

And when we drove round there, he had given me No. 54 instead of 64. So, after I dropped my man into a cell, we went back and bust the place with the pink door. Our Frankie was right, his info was kosher. They were doing up their deals when we went in, and we had two good busts for the price of one.

And Frankie admitted to me in the cells that he was hoping to move this team and grab their business with his new hash oil.

"At least he didn't have to worry about anyone in the other

set-up suspecting him of grassing. After all, he was busted as well. And they all went down for a few months inside.

Another night we had a good bit of information from a regular grass about three pushers in a house in Walton Street, in the middle of Oxford. When we bust the place and found all their gear, one of them got really nasty.

"We know who shopped us. He'll get paid out all right," he told me.

"I didn't need information to catch you lot, we've been watching tricks here. You got too cocky, too obvious."

"Then why didn't you bust that bastard Henry?"

"Henry who?"

"Come off it. He got his gear same time as us. How come only we got busted? Because you bastards did a deal and left him out."

Suddenly I cottoned on. "You mean Henry, who lives up at Headington?"

"You know bloody well who I mean. And I'm going to get the bastard, don't worry."

"You're wrong, man, but thanks for the info," I said.

We tore back to the nick and went up to Headington, on the outskirts of Oxford. We sat outside Henry's place until everyone was in bed. Meanwhile, one of the boys collected a warrant, and we hit the pad at about one in the morning. Sure enough, Henry had some of the same gear, but he was no grass. The other feller was talking out of turn, and when he saw Henry in the exercise yard next morning, he was sick. And so was Henry.

One of the other boys on the squad got a tip-off that was very embarrassing for me. I was living in Abingdon at the time, on a nice new housing estate. He was told there was a cannabis 'farm' in a house somewhere near me, but he didn't have an exact address. Great!

Then we got into winter and one very cold night we had a light snowfall and all the pavements, trees and roofs were covered in white – except one, and that was only four doors from where I was staying. The roof was clear, a black space in a big white expanse. We soon found out why.

I reported this strange phenomenon as soon as I got in and we all came to the same conclusion. We raided my neighbour's pad and found 470 cannabis plants in neat rows in the loft. It was an amazing set-up. The roof was lined with oven tin-foil to keep the loft warm and reflect light and heat from the special bulbs they had fitted. All the plant pots were on proper matting to hold the moisture, and the feller farming them had even rigged up a watering system.

The warmth had melted the snow and frost and chummy was waiting patiently for harvest-time. However, all his plants were removed and destroyed and he was lucky to get only four months. And all the time he was inside, I was the butt of a lot of humour at the nick, living four doors from a cannabis farm.

As I've said, information comes in lots of ways. Someone might decide to do all his buddies a good turn and shop them. We might help a person like that to get a bed and some treatment in hospital. Then when he comes out, he wants to repay the favour.

One feller I knew on the scene used to have long chats with me. He had two cons going but I never busted him. He would talk about his rich girlfriend who had dropped out of university and was a bit immature. Her parents didn't know she was finished at college and made her an allowance of £100 a week, plus car and clothes.

One night he and the girlfriend had a giant row and she took an overdose. He didn't know what to do so he put through a call to me. Luckily, I was still at the drugs squad office. The girl was rushed to the Radcliffe Infirmary, the big Oxford hospital, and I had a word with one or two people up there who agreed to keep it quiet for her sake. The Radcliffe in those days always had about 10 beds treating patients who had overdosed, either purposely or accidentally.

So, her parents never found out, and my man was forever grateful. He never fed me any of his friends, but he must have had a lot of enemies.

On a lighter note, a pal of mine once had the weirdest bit of information I ever heard, and I went on the bust with him. His man explained that the customer kept his stash of cocaine in a plastic bag under the sand at the bottom of a tropical fish tank.

We can't go straight to the tank in case he guesses where our information has come from. So, we mooch around his pad looking in likely places, and finally, with me leaning against this huge tank, my mate says, "Try in there, Martyn, that would be a good place to hide the gear."

I take my jacket off and start rolling up my sleeve. Just as I'm reaching inside, the feller hollers, "Don't do that. You bastards will do me for assaulting a police officer."

We just blink at him.

"One of those fish is a piranha. It's only a baby, but it will definitely go for you."

And there is this four-inch long, man-eating fish. Fantastic! What a guard for a drugs stash.

"I fancy there's some gear in there. Either you get it out or I will. And if that fish bites me, you'll get done for inciting an assault, believe me," I said. And very sheepishly, he gets all the cocaine out.

It didn't amount to much, but he got a £100 fine for his pains. Funnily enough, the fish didn't have a go at him.

The piranha wasn't the only animal we had to deal with. Quite often when you are following up information, you know where to look but mustn't give your informant away. That's where dogs come in handy.

I know they are supposed to be very good at nosing out drugs once they have been trained, but that's not what I found.

Usually you guided the dog to the area where your informant said the drugs were kept – for instance, inside a stereo speaker or an oven – and made that the excuse for rummaging around.

We had a dog over at Sulhamstead, near Newbury, and it was hopeless. On one bust the damn thing jumped up on an old dresser and went mad about something in a glass dish. Bugger me, we found 150 acid tabs in the dish. But goodness knows what attracted the dog, because LSD is colourless, tasteless and odourless. Its paws were also resting on a drawer, and inside we found 4lbs of cannabis resin. This had been completely ignored, and the dog should have sniffed that as soon as it got into the room.

Of course, not all information was good. Sometimes it was deliberately bad. If you make an enemy on drugs squad work, one way he can get even is to set you up. That happened on one job, when we got two bits of info. The first was about another house in Walton Street, in Oxford, where a couple were marked down as dealers. We had a few brushes with them and made life for them a little too hot.

So they had someone else feed some gossip to us about a party, a smoke-up at their pad… very interesting. The party was on a Friday night and we recognised lots of names who were supposed to be going along.

The day before the party, and the raid we had planned, I got a phone call. I recognised the voice on the other end. "You're going to bust Fergie's place," it said.

"Are we?"

"I reckon you will. Tomorrow night."

"Go on, tell me more."

"Take care, that's all."

"What do you mean, take care?"

"Just take care. Don't go charging in there."

"Listen, I know who's speaking, I've got the voice. Spell it out."

"Take care, Martyn. Have a look under the mat. Don't go

charging in there."

And that was it.

We made the raid as planned. The party was going on upstairs and we crept in very carefully. The front door wasn't locked. We looked under the mat as we came in and the floorboards were sawn through. When we lifted them up we found that these bastards had put blocks of wood down in the cavity, with six inch nails sticking up.

No way could we prove anything against anybody. And there was no hash upstairs. But we had a serious talk with Fergie and his chick, and put the word about in Oxford. A month later, they were gone. No one would talk to them, let alone deal with them. Life was too uncomfortable.

Sometimes we were plain lucky. We were busting a little cottage just outside Oxford one Saturday afternoon and half-way through our search the phone rang. Before anyone else could move I picked it up and got the shock of my life.

"Is that Martin?" said a voice.

"Yeah, this is Martyn."

"OK if I bring the stuff round?"

"Sure. How long will you be?"

"About 10 minutes, OK?"

I couldn't be sure what he was talking about, but I had a fair idea. There were five blokes and a chick at the cottage, and no one would admit to either being or knowing any Martin. But sure enough, this gent rolled up 10 minutes later and I bagged him. Four ounces of cannabis in his pocket. He's nicked.

These grasses, plus a little bit of luck, helped us enormously. But occasionally we got information we didn't want. One night I was in the office and a guy phoned to say, "If you want Bundle, do him now. He's got half an ounce on him at the Crown in Jericho."

"How do you know?"

"It's in his pocket, right-hand pocket of his jacket."

"How do you know."

I mean, it was a strange tip to pick up just like that. And I had to be absolutely sure before I could pull a bust inside a hippy pub or just outside it.

"I know, that's all. I'm telling you it's there."

"But how do you know?" I was insistent.

"Because I bloody well put it there."

"And why would you do a thing like that?"

"Because he's screwing my sister. OK?"

Nice one! But I told the guy that even if he had the best reason in the world, we wouldn't do anything.

"Why? It's a good bust."

"No, it's not. We don't do business that way." And I didn't touch him.

A couple of weeks later, probably because I told my colleagues and they chatted about it, Bundle heard about this. One night he came over in another pub to say thank you. He didn't give me any information, he was just grateful. But he talked, and people on the scene liked the story. And they knew we were straight.

Chapter Five

Overseas... But Over Here

Edward Laxton: Martyn Pritchard's base while he was on the drugs squad was always Oxford. His desk was opposite the door in the small first-floor office of the police station of St Aldates, almost in the centre of the university city.

It was forever busy, and always demanding his time in between the operations that took him to other towns, other counties and other police force areas. Strangely, his Oxford responsibilities also took him into what was virtually another land – yet still in the same county.

Thames Valley police takes in the towns of Witney, Banbury, Bicester and Abingdon. Martyn and one other drugs squad officer were assigned to keep a 'watchful eye' on these towns and the area round them.

And between Bicester and Oxford lay what was United States Air Force Upper Heyford (USAF left after the Cold War), a huge base with three tactical squadrons, some of America's most up-to-date wartime weaponry, and 10,000 of her citizens.

Upper Heyford had its drugs problems too. Many local people, including some magistrates who handed out stiffer penalties to the airmen than they gave English offenders in similar cases, thought the Americans were bringing in drugs and spreading the habit around the base and nearby communities.

But this was rarely true. English suppliers fed the air force junkies, and it was those dealers who attracted the attention of Martyn Pritchard and the drugs squad. Under the Visiting Forces Act, the Thames Valley police had official jurisdiction. They busted airmen who were found in possession, but they were more interested in the pushers who were coining the substantial profits to be made from selling to the American buyers.

The USAF Upper Heyford base was a piece of America in the heart of the Oxfordshire countryside. For Martyn it was a work place… and sometimes a playground.

Little America

Martyn Pritchard: There was one informant I haven't told you about, and he was probably the best of the lot. Ned Kelly I called him. He was a sergeant in the United States Air Force, on the big base at Upper Heyford, not far from Oxford. Two of us, Tim Todd and I, were given the place as part of our territory.

Drive down a quiet, pretty country road, turn through the gates and you were suddenly in the middle of the United States. The base was a Little America: the food, beer, cars, accents, baseball – and a lot of drugs. With all of the airmen's dependants, there were about 10,000 Yanks there, but our main target wasn't the Americans using drugs. We wanted their English suppliers.

These used to take their payment in kind rather than cash, the duty-free booze and cigarettes Americans could buy so cheaply on the base. That way both sides were happy. The pushers were getting better value than their drugs would normally earn and the Yanks were buying the stuff a lot cheaper than they were used to at home.

We had terrific co-operation from their Office of Special Investigation and from the base commander, Colonel 'Mac', who was later transferred to Korea. He told us, "You don't need search warrants here. If you have good reason and you want to bust our doors down, you do that. They are my doors and if you do your work and stop these drugs getting on to the base, you will be doing me and Uncle Sam a service."

We usually carried our warrants, but one night we burst into an airman's room and he nearly started a riot. We knew he was on the drugs scene, on and off the base. So, we took a couple of USAF police with us and we found some grass in a fire extinguisher housing just outside his room.

"You bastards planted it," he hollered, and after we finished searching he contacted the guard room and signed a complaints form. Then he demanded that the commanding officer go over and examine everything.

The next day we were asked to go back to the base, where we were told an amazing story. Apparently, after we left, this airman had gone out, got drunk and taken a young English girl back to his room.

The colonel arrived at his office early in the morning, as he always did, saw the complaint, called up the military police and charged straight over to the quarters of the airman, who told him we had thrown all his gear round the room and planted the cannabis.

Colonel 'Mac' said the room looked tidy. Then he opened the wardrobe. Out stepped the English girl, naked and very embarrassed. And what do you think this airman said? "The Thames Valley drugs squad must have planted her as well. I've never seen this chick before."

The colonel was so furious, he wanted him off base and sent back to America to be dealt with. He called us back that morning to ask if we had any objections in view of a possible arrest. We told the colonel there was no case – the drugs were found outside the bloke's room. So, this guy was on his way back to the States that very same day. But the story had a tragic ending. Just 48 hours later he died in a road crash.

Just after that, Ned Kelly started feeding us info. It started after we busted his room-mate and found a dirty pipe that had obviously been used for hash smoking. The pipe belonged to Ned, but we couldn't take that any further. We simply had no proof.

Ned, on the other hand, thought we were doing him a favour, and a couple of days later I got a phone call in the office. Ned identified himself and told me he would be hitch-hiking along the Bicester road in exactly one hour. I picked him up and began one of the most successful liaisons I ever had with an informant.

Ned's motive was unusual. He wanted to join the police force when he went home and got out of the service. He thought I could give him a testimonial, saying how useful he had been. I wrote him a letter after he left England and cited a few cases, but I never heard from him again. But for nearly two years while he was over here he fed me some fantastic gossip.

Apart from the British supplies at Upper Heyford, some drugs did come in from the States. Fortunately, the air force had well-trained dogs that used to sniff all the mail and incoming goods, and they found a fair amount of the stuff being smuggled in.

Ned kept giving us the names of guys in the base Field Maintenance Squadron, labourers on the base, who looked after hangars, runways and buildings. I suppose there were 250 of them and we must have busted two or three dozen on separate small possession charges.

Then Ned heard about a big new supply of hash, arriving in time to kick off a big July Fourth smoking party. At 5am a few days before the Independence Day celebrations, 70 coppers busted the entire maintenance squadron. Every man jack was arrested in an operation involving all the drugs squad, the Thames Valley Police support group, the local CID and some uniform officers.

First, we found a few small amounts of drugs in rooms, which gave us half-a-dozen possession charges. Then came the jackpot – coke and acid as well as cannabis, hidden all over the place. They had stashed it away in the communal areas, like the showers and toilets, the lounges and TV rooms, so we couldn't prove who owned it.

A later tip-off from Ned concerned another fella on the base who he reckoned was responsible for a lot of heroin. This guy lived up near Brackley with a schoolteacher from the base. She was a cracker, really gorgeous. We bust him at home and he wouldn't say a word. He was very scared, but not so much of us. He kept hinting that he would be in trouble from his suppliers.

We didn't find any drugs at first, but inside a bag in his loft we came across the worst pornographic pictures I have ever seen. A lot of them had this fella in some dreadful poses with women and all sorts of gear.

He flapped when we produced them and begged us not to show his girlfriend. I told him she would defnitely find out if he didn't talk. He sat down and just stared at the floor thinking about it for a good 15 minutes. "I guess you had better tell her. I daren't talk to you guys, I'll be dead," he said at last.

I believed him. Man, he was that scared. Then we discovered a fair quantity of cannabis done up in deals in his airing cupboard, and we bust him on that. He might have been into something bigger but he wasn't going to cough, and I didn't have the heart to show his girlfriend all those terrible pictures. So, we missed the suppliers.

We were always busy round the base, but our work was spiced up with a lot of recreation. We often ate there in the clubs, which sold a big steak for under a pound. You might have been in a New York restaurant or a nightclub. The waiters and barmen were all dressed up, and some of the airmen going on to a party or dance would come in wearing tuxedos. The drinks were Manhattans and Martinis – it was all very different from busting sordid squats down the road.

These were the all-ranks and NCO clubs, The Yard and the Rod and Gun. Ironically, the officers' club was an imitation English country pub, all timber and horse brasses.

One guy, a big pusher, gave us a real run-around. Funnily

enough, he wasn't American or an airman, and when he went to prison for four years, it had nothing to do with drugs. He was a Nigerian called 'Sweet Pea' and every time we bust him, he was clean. Eventually, Colonel 'Mac' put out a notice, like an old-time Western reward poster, with a photograph and a warning: *This man is banned from USAF Upper Heyford.*

He worked out of London, had a lot of very heavy form, and according to Ned, he could supply everything.

Well, one night Sweet Pea came out of the Rod and Gun Club and saw two of my mates, so he made a run for it. They grabbed him and found he was clean of drugs. But he had a couple of bags with some duty-free booze. The Americans handed him over to our Customs. Because of his previous form he collected four years for breaking the excise laws.

To most people at Heyford, we were 'the man' and they treated us very well. We were never jeered at or harassed if we went up there for an evening out, not like we were in some of the Oxford pubs. They sometimes had strippers and go-go dancers at their clubs – until the base padre put a stop to all that – and a lot of English women in there were little more than hookers. Mind you, some were good informants.

Following a series of tips from Ned, we were able to bust the base security guards. They were giants, and they were aching to find out where we were getting the news. Ned was nearly always spot on, but he had plenty of scope because there were always drugs about.

Many airmen had picked up the hard drugs habit in Vietnam, where they were plentiful and cheap. Back in the US they would have had to pay a thousand dollars a week for their supplies.

The American forces started health and welfare checks to keep ahead of the problem. They would take a sniffer dog around the barrack blocks to go through the rooms and make a physical search as well.

When they found drugs, the guys concerned were never charged but put straight on to a rehabilitation course, which reminded them of the evils and dangers of drug abuse. And, of course, their card was marked for the future.

There was another check called the 'Gold Flow', their nickname for urine analysis. Practically every week they would grab fellas at random – "You, you and you" – and take samples. Positive results qualified the owners for the same rehabilitation course, as their water would show up any cocaine, heroin or speed.

These tests had a double bonus for the air force. They identified the users and also let the authorities know if the level of drug abuse was rising.

For a while I had an American girlfriend, who helped the doctors on the Gold Flow. That was very useful, because she gave me (quite unofficially, of course) the names on the positive samples. So, I had a very definite idea of who was on the scene.

Alternatively, if I had some information about a suspect I would feed the name to the OSI, the Office of Special Investigation. One way or another, it would be arranged that the person should be picked for the Gold Flow. That way I could check out my suspicions and also find out whether my informants were on the level.

We kept a lot of people on their toes. On one occasion, a chef proved positive on the urine check. A month later, we bust him in his kitchen at about six in the morning as he started work. He was so amazed he took us straight to his stash.

Then he cooked me a great breakfast of steak and eggs before I took him back to Oxford and charged him. I never busted anyone too soon after their test, in case our little ruse became obvious. But the story of that early morning bust soon swept round the base and must have worried a lot of people.

With information like this, and Ned constantly reporting in, life on the base became a lot easier. Without tip-offs, searches were a risky bet. A lot of the airmen kept their stuff hidden away inside expensive hi-fi equipment. Those guys thought nothing of paying a thousand quid for a pair of really good speakers. And the innocent ones wouldn't take kindly to having their speakers ruined!

But if you had Ned's information, plus the knowledge that the owner had recently pissed a positive sample on the Gold Flow, you could take a chance on spoiling his equipment. If there were drugs inside, the gear was finished, for the magistrates would later make out a destruction order for anything contaminated with drugs.

We worked quite closely with the base police. Gene Walker, our contact with the OSI knew a lot about drugs. He had worked undercover himself in the States. So, it was great to work together.

If the American police ever found somebody in possession of a fair quantity of drugs, they used to call us in. When we arrived it would be like a hold-up scene. They would have their guns out, holding them with both hands on the butt, pointing them straight at their prisoners. Everybody would be frozen to the spot. That's the official term, they 'freeze the area'.

I'm sure the customers were relieved when we took over.

Most of them would answer our first question with, "I stand on Miranda." This was a reference to American law, following a famous case a few years ago. They didn't want to make a statement unless an attorney was there. But we used to tell them, "You're in England now, sunshine, it's different."

It wasn't that much different, but usually this reply would unnerve them and out would pour exactly what you wanted. And they often used to get their pals in trouble too. We got a lot of coughs, and some of the guys we busted went away in the States for as long as four or five years.

But in the two years I worked around the base, we never busted an officer. Yet the guy we called 'The Judge', a lawyer in their Judge Advocate's Office, told us that quite a few of their younger officers got hooked in Vietnam. Over there, he said, they were often losing as many men to heroin as they were to the enemy. They were on such chemically pure supplies that their bodies couldn't take it.

Another failure was the day we arrived for a bust and found everyone on War Alert for one of their strategic exercises. Some guys had gas masks on, everyone had guns out, and planes were circling the base. I began to think that our time had come – the tannoys were screaming, "We are in imminent danger of attack from enemy forces." A drugs raid was impossible, so we just went home!

That exercise was something Ned Kelly hadn't told us about, but when it came to drugs, he was right on the ball. I used to make sure he got his expenses, a few pounds at a time, and he always scrawled a signature on my official receipt – 'M. Mouse.' Actually, I knew his real name at one time, but I called him Ned for so long and so often, I forgot it.

Just before he went home, he gave me some beautiful information. One of these Yank airmen named Rodgers lived in a huge country house outside Bicester. He told everyone he had rented it cheap, but according to Ned, he ran a very big drugs operation. He was doing hash, acid, speed, smack, the lot. But you couldn't get near his house without being seen, and he always kept doors barred and windows locked.

Tim and I decided to look around the place one night and studied an Ordnance Survey map in preparation. Off we went across country and we were nearly up to the house when I sank into water. I thought it might be a mud hole until I started stepping around and found it was all water. We had found a small river that wasn't marked on the OS map.

Obviously, this sort of approach was useless. We had a re-think and got permission to go along to Kidlington Aerodrome, just outside Oxford, and hire a helicopter. It cost £75 an hour, but it was easier than trying to get an hour's paid overtime. We flew over the house, and while we were taking some aerial pictures, Rodgers came out and we got him on film.

Two nights later, we took a team cross country and hit the house fast. I'll never forget it – we burst in and the TV was on playing the Z Cars theme music.

Our customer was in a little office doing up some hash deals. When he finally coughed, he showed us his stash in a wooden box in the garden, close to a tree I particularly remembered from our first foray. It was about 10ft from where I stood knee deep in this bloody river. Mr Rodgers went to gaol for four years.

Chapter Six

Getting Busted As Well

Edward Laxton: Many of us make friends through work, and several young people on the drugs scene became good mates of Martyn Pritchard, including some who met him officially when they were under interrogation, on the wrong side of the law.

He remembered these young men and women more kindly than a few of the other characters who crossed his path, the ones he calls 'the real nasty bastards'. To catch some of these individuals he was prepared to get busted himself, to go into the cells as a prisoner for a few hours or overnight if necessary.

This would protect his cover and behind bars he might pick up more information. There were never any half-measures, he was arrested in the same manner as the real customers. If he put up a fight the police involved would use 'sufficient force' to arrest him. Usually on a raid only a couple of officers knew his true identity.

Afterwards, at the police station, Martyn was 'processed' like anyone else, searched and documented, briefly questioned and placed in detention. When it was his turn for interrogation, he was taken away like all the others to an interview room. But inside he held a debriefing session with colleagues. Then he was bailed and served with the same papers as everyone else.

Occasionally when Martyn was busted, he could disappear from that particular scene without any of the victims of his undercover role ever knowing he was a policeman or that he was responsible for their downfall. But if the customers pleaded not guilty at their subsequent trial, Martyn had to break his cover and give evidence.

Many of the pushers and dealers he caught could not and would not believe he was 'the fuzz', because he did his work so well. When they finally accepted the truth, it could mean trouble for an innocent third person whom Martyn had used to get alongside his target.

Busted

Martyn Pritchard: I spent several nights in the cells during my drugs squad career. I had to get busted myself just to keep up the act, and my overnight stays usually happened when I was trying to nail the nasty bastards.

Any time behind bars is always horrible, even though I was pleased to be helping put criminals away. The really unpleasant ones knew what they were doing and were into drugs purely for the cash – big money and easy money.

A lot of the kids, the punk pushers and hippies who moved a bit of gear to pay for their own habit, were just weak characters who got caught up.

But 'Sweet Pea', the Nigerian at the American air base, he was evil. And another fella, Skinny Morgan down in Gloucester, was in the same class. Skinny ran a West Indian club, a shebeen, and in the early Seventies, that place gave the local law a lot of headaches.

Their local drugs squad were well-known, especially by the clients of that shebeen. We were asked to go down there and get inside – not easy, because they didn't cater for white clubbers, but this was another challenge, something different. And Dave Snell and I were looking forward to it.

But the night before we went down there we heard that one of their coppers had been knifed on a previous raid. We never found out the truth about that stabbing, but there was nothing much we could do about it. We had to play our own game.

Our buddy Vince Castle from the local drugs squad briefed us when we arrived and produced two radios. "The chief says you must wear these whenever you go inside the club. He insists."

"Absolutely not on, Vince. We're volunteers and we have to be allowed to call the shots."

"It's supposed to be for your own protection."

"And what happens if we get in and they find the electrics? They'll play football with us while we're yelling in the mikes and your lads are trying to get in and save us. Forget it."

Vince knew the score, he was a great copper. But he had had to pass on his chief's instructions.

We left the radios, but the Gloucester lads were obviously worried about our future health. And I will give them this – when the bust happened it was the one of the best. Vince organised it so well that I got on the end of the strongest punch in the county and wound up in the cells again!

A shebeen is an illegal gambling, boozing and dancing club, a bawdy house in other words. It's licensed for nothing but it's doing everything. Our shebeen was all this and threw in the drugs as well.

Skinny Morgan ran it with a white chick, not a very nice lady. Down in the basement was a dance hall, if you could call it that, and in the corner a sort of bar where everything cost 50p. Two little girls, about 12 and 13, dispensed all the drinks. I think they were Skinny's daughters.

There were cards and dice, and someone ran a book on the horses. Girls were available, like the rooms on three floors upstairs. You could smell the dope as soon as you walked in, the sweet scent of cannabis wafted around that old Victorian house, which had clearly seen better times.

Up the road was a pub whose customers were all Caribbean. A lot of them used to drift on to the shebeen. So, Dave and I started up there.

We had all the gear on, naturally, and we shelled out a lot of bread and got boozing with a little Jamaican guy, an older fella of about 50, who knew everyone. When the pub closed we got the invite. "Come on, man, I know where we can drink."

No kidding. Apart from Skinny's missus, who resented us, we were the only white faces in there, among about 100 customers. Later on, three or four white girls appeared from upstairs.

Dave and I had a great time that night. We figured we might as well enter into the spirit of the thing and enjoy ourselves – confining our activities to the basement, I might add.

The action started when a huge bloke, who'd been hovering over me, pointed at a girl. "Why don't you dance with her?"

"No thanks, mate, I'll just watch."

"She's my sister."

"OK, I'll dance then."

She very obviously wasn't his sister, but he had made up his mind. And he was a pretty menacing bloke. So I danced almost non-stop for about three hours and kept clocking the customers, the layout, all the windows and doors, ready to draw a sketch map for a raid, and a quick emergency exit if necessary.

Naturally, after a night like that we had to go back. We went in again via the pub and our little old Jamaican mate, and angled ourselves towards one of their more permanent clients. Vince had told us he was a dealer. We had seen his portfolio and spotted him the time before.

We scored a bit of ganja or weed, and later that night he offered us 4lbs of the same stuff. Setting up the deal wasn't difficult. Our performance in the pub ensured that everyone knew money was no problem. Not that we actually carried much cash on us, but we appeared to be free spenders.

We pretended not to be too interested at first, but he pressed us and we agreed to be in the club Saturday week. I think we fixed a price of £750 for his grass.

When we staggered out of the club we had to go straight to a debriefing session with Vince Castle. That was no chore. There was always plenty of black coffee in the nick and often some takea-way spare ribs and chips.

Vince was well pleased with us. We figured one raid might close down this shebeen permanently, so we organised a good team. The pusher was going to be there to be taken. We could also finger a few characters and testify what we had seen going on inside.

Vince produced the pictures and put a name to various blokes and a couple of girls. We penned in the captions, detailing their activities at the club – gamblers, pimps, pushers and prostitutes. That was for future use by the local law, but our target was the club itself, including Skinny Morgan and the major pusher.

When Saturday night came around we got a nasty shock. Before Dave and I left the nick, well in advance of the raiding party, we saw a message from a patrol on the M5 motorway. Our man with the 4lbs of grass had been nicked in a routine stop-and-search when he'd stopped for petrol at a service station. He was on his way from Birmingham to meet us in the shebeen and do the deal. Never mind.

But when Dave and I got inside the club, we couldn't believe our eyes. There were three or four newly-painted signs saying: *Restricted goods are not allowed on these premises.*

We couldn't make it out. Was this a show that they were trying to clean-up the place? Didn't matter much, the entire shebeen was illegal. They could hardly call their nightly activities impromptu parties.

When the bust happens, it's very, very fast. I'm on the dance floor doing the reggae like I invented it, and suddenly I'm arm in arm with a blue uniform. Again, we're the only two white men in there. Vince could have told the team the two honkies would be coppers, but I'll give him his due, it was better to keep it quiet.

There are maybe 100 customers doing their thing when about 120 coppers charge in on the bust. They're organised in teams and cordon off 10 customers in one corner, a dozen in the middle, a few more over there. And only one punch is thrown… at me.

There are knives and bits of dope on the floor, small packets of grass, as our customers turn out their pockets to avoid getting done for possession of illegal drugs or offensive weapons. That's always happening on big raids.

I'm lined up against the wall and a SOCO, a scenes-of-crime officer, has his camera going snap, snap, snap. That's useful because when it comes to court, they might deny I have ever visited the club. But one look at the picture of Dave Snell and me, dressed in all our finery, and the jury are happy.

The camera also catches a perfect shot of me about to get a smack for a bit of cheek. A big uniform fella, about 6ft high and just as wide, says to me, "What do you do?"

"I'm self employed."

"What does that mean?"

"I do a bit of this and a bit of that."

"A bit of what? Don't get lippy."

"What day was it yesterday?"

"Friday, why?"

"Well, I was doing a bit of that on Friday and I'm doing a bit of this today."

Crack! The punch catches me smack under the left side of my jaw, takes me off my feet and dumps me on the deck about 10ft away.

It's a hell of a good punch and certainly impresses the customers. When I try to move my jaw, I think it's broken. I can see Dave Snell grinning as I'm pulled up on my feet and put back in the line-up against the wall.

The Gloucester lads take over a room upstairs and use it as an office to process everyone. About 25 customers and Skinny Morgan are bussed back to the nick and we're passengers with them.

So, I go inside again with the clients in the cells, to try and pick up more info about the club and drugs deals – and also to protect our little drinking friend from Jamaica. Vince Castle left me down there for four hours, just for a laugh, claimed he had forgotten all about me because he was so busy. But I vowed to get my own back for the stunt if the chance arrived. It did, and I had the last laugh.

What wasn't so funny was the fate of our little mate who unwittingly gave us the original introduction. We thought his clubmates wouldn't take it kindly when they found out the sort of guests he had introduced.

We were right. We couldn't get a guilty plea, so Dave and I had to show up and give evidence. Skinny Morgan went inside, the shebeen put the shutters up – and the little feller got his head kicked in a few days later.

You might think I would consider that big copper who bopped me was a nasty bastard as well. But it was my fault. I overdid the lip and got too saucy. Coppers are only human and that club had brought them too much grief. Anyway, I never saw him again, but he must have found out I was on his side and I bet he felt worse about that punch than I did.

I've heard of very few blows struck by policemen, and violence was never our bag on the drugs squad. It's usually the customers who hit out. Dave Snell and I were on another shebeen raid in Reading, where the timing was a bit off. The opposition kicked so many corners off us before our lot arrived, I had pain and bruises for well over a week.

We met another 'nasty' on a job in Brighton, and he was crafty with it. A magazine carried a very full account of the drugs scene that operated out of a seaside pub, and the Chief Constable of Sussex got very uptight.

His own drugs squad was very well known, so we were sent down to move in again. When their guys met Bob Buckley and me as planned, in a lay-by outside town, they could not believe we were Old Bill. Bob had gone really strong, wearing earrings and a hair-ribbon.

There were loads of punk dealers in the pub, coming in and scoring from just one guy, who took the bread but let his lady carry the gear and pass it from her handbag to the small-time pushers. We were in that pub every night for nearly a week before we set up the busts, and we had a very neat operation.

Outside the pub was a strong team of coppers, with a few young fellas in civvies who weren't on the drugs squad. We had a bleep device in the pub and when we pressed the button it signalled outside for one of these coppers to come in.

Then we would get up really close to a client and turn the handle of our beer glass to point right at him, or her, so there could be no mistake. Chances were they had only come in to score, have a quick drink and go out. And there they met their doom.

One by one they were getting knocked off as soon as they stepped outside – the copper we had signalled to was waiting for them to leave. The customers inside the pub had no idea this was going on. Some of them, who were known and identified by the Brighton drugs squad as they were leaving, were allowed to go home with their gear. Then their pads were raided.

On those house busts the local force pulled in a lot of home-grown grass from windowboxes. Many cannabis plants were thriving in the Sussex sunshine.

When the pub closed it was my turn to get busted. There were no bleep signals by now, I just walked out of the pub and got nicked. It must have been the way I looked, or maybe this uniform bobby who lifted me felt he had missed all the fun and fancied his luck.

There was no point in making a fuss, though this bust was entirely unscripted and unnecessary, just a mistake. Back at the nick, I told the station sergeant to check with someone upstairs and have a car waiting to get me back to the squad, which was now assembling for a conference in a car park near the pub.

Altogether, I suppose they must have busted a couple of dozen customers. We certainly broke up the scene in that pub.

Unfortunately, we had very little on the number one pusher, nothing that could be turned into evidence. I didn't like the way he was using everybody for his own ends, including his lady. But you can't win them all.

And sometimes you blow out when you think you're winning. On one occasion we had another nasty character and plenty of evidence to put him down for a long time. And he walked away – no, he ran away laughing, all the way to the Far East when a court gave him bail.

He had his girl performing for him, too. We were working with Customs and Excise on that case. This fella lived in High Wycombe. I can't name him because he has never appeared for trial. He had a perfect system for smuggling in heroin and, funnily enough, we only caught him because of a post office workers' dispute.

He used a neat system. He had a lot of cards and documents with phoney identities – a trade union card, a driving licence, a student card, a credit card and lots of things like that, all in different names. He used to produce them at post offices to 'prove' his identity, and collect parcels sent there for him marked 'Poste Restante'.

His lass came from Thailand and she travelled back and forth. To do their smuggling, she would go home and send him a stream of parcels, care of the post offices at Amersham, High Wycombe, Marlow or Bourne End. These were all in Buckinghamshire where he could pick them up easily.

She knew which name to use for each post office and he would produce one of his fake identity cards to claim the parcel. In each package was a Chinese, Malayan or Thai doll, the sort in national costume that folks collect. All very innocent if any customs officer looked inside. Piped down the fluting of the corrugated cardboard packaging inside the parcels, was the white stuff – pure heroin.

The girl sent off parcels from Bangkok to half a dozen post offices, one at a time, with a decent gap in between. But union trouble at the main sorting office this end delayed delivery. A customs bloke noticed five similar size parcels, all marked 'Poste Restante' for towns in the same county, but addressed to different names.

He decided to have a good look and hit the heroin, no trouble. Next day the sixth parcel arrived and a customs investigation branch operation was under way. We were called in because the drugs dealer was on our ground.

The parcels were emptied and re-wrapped for him to collect and all the post offices were staked out. I was at Amersham, but our man made his first call at Marlow and got nicked. We found the documents and cards relating to the names on the parcels at his home, plus a load of forgery equipment.

But for my money, Customs charged him too quickly. After that, questioning becomes difficult, nigh impossible according to the law. So, a lot of ends in this country were left untouched, although it was obvious there was too much heroin – £550,000 worth on our bust alone – for a small organisation to be moving.

No one was more surprised than matey himself when he got £6,000 bail. He laughed himself all the way out of the country and disappeared.

Another bunch I really couldn't stand were the buggers who kept syringes hidden in their pockets. Before we did a body search, we always asked if they had one, especially if we suspected the client was on the hard stuff.

The last thing in the world any of us wanted was to have a needle stick into a finger or run up inside a nail, and I have known that to happen. The pain has nothing to do with it – the germs on the needle always worried us.

Hepatitis, the clap and all sorts of diseases and blood disorders get passed on by junkies' syringes. I used to ask the question this way, "Are you sure I'm not going to find a syringe? If I do, whether it sticks in me or not, I shall get really nasty, OK?"

That usually did the trick if they hadn't handed it over in the first place. I was lucky but some of my mates got pricked.

There were plenty of other things to worry about on searches, too. The sort of people we were dealing with would hide their drugs anywhere and everywhere. In the early days they concealed them in the hollowed-out legs of Oriental or Arabic tables, taped them under their armpits, or stuffed them into Afro hairstyles. But these became well-known. So, they found some better places.

I'll never forget one night at Oxford when one of our girls, quite new on the squad, was told to search a chick we had just picked up. Mick Strutt, the guvnor, had definite information she was carrying some gear.

Our girl couldn't find anything, and she was almost in tears when Mick sent her back into the room for the fourth time to keep on searching.

"Wait a minute," says Mick, "I've just thought of something." He disappeared and came back with a pair of rubber gloves. "Sorry, my dear, you will have to search her really thoroughly." She found the drugs in a place where only a woman could have hidden them...

A fella once pulled a similar trick — well, I say almost. Customs at Harwich pulled him in on his way back from Holland, after we tipped them off, and again we had very definite information that he was carrying. It was supposed to be concentrated speed.

They found nothing and called us. Mick was insistent with them, as he always was when he was sure of the info. Matey boy had the powder, all right. It was pure amphetamine sulphate in a small plastic bag taped right up behind his testicles.

He either had some finer feelings or he just didn't trust them, because he asked if he could please remove the sticking plaster himself. I think we might have saved him the trouble and ripped it off in one go.

On the run from Morocco, the smugglers used false compartments welded inside petrol tanks to smuggle hash oil. But their neatest trick was to put the oil into a condom, swallow it and pass it after they went through Customs. The oil was so concentrated that even such a small amount was worth hundreds of pounds.

They used shaving cream cans and aerosols with false tops, the bases of dog kennels – they imported the dogs as well as the drugs – and cans of pineapple with a special compartment in the middle, so that both ends contained fruit. And there must be plenty of smuggling tricks that haven't been discovered yet.

I've told you about the 'nasty bastards' of the drugs world. Well, we had 'heavies' on our side – not physical, but sinister enough to persuade the customers into co-operating.

One of my early jobs involved working with Scotland Yard's Flying Squad, and the guvnor of the team that came down to Oxford was Tony Poole, a detective inspector with a lot of experience who became a great mate.

He could be as heavy as any villain and the mob he came down to bust were a right bunch of crooks. He needed our local knowledge, so we joined the Sweeney for a night. The opposition were into everything: drugs, forged bankers' drafts, fraud and robbery. They had connections in Turin, Beirut and Marseilles.

What were they doing in Oxford? Well, every organisation like that needs a front, especially if they are involved in import and export, in other words, smuggling. Their front was a male boutique in Oxford.

The villains included a Canadian who was a professional hitman and always carried a .38 Smith & Wesson; a London 'financier' who had worked with the Kray twins; and a rally driver who handled their cars and bits-and-pieces. The ideal business front was run by two other fellas in Oxford's historic High Street.

Nearly all their gear was imported: Italian shoes, Swedish trousers, Portuguese shirts, Israeli leatherwear, so they travelled legitimately, but carried on their illegal dealings at the same time. Eventually, they all went down for long stretches, but we could never prove anything relating to drugs.

Anyway, their big guy operating on our manor used the name Rodriguez and lived at Woodstock, not far from Oxford. He posed sometimes as a Spaniard and other times as a Mexican, but he was actually Italian. Other gang members lived in Bicester, Banbury and Bampton.

The Sweeney's interest centred on a load of blank traveller's cheques, apparently nicked at London Airport, on route with Pan Am Airways from Los Angeles to Paris. This mob were forging high-denomination amounts on the cheques, including the secret codes used by the bank that issued them.

Although it was a small American bank, the cheques were accepted by American Express, so there was no trouble getting them changed at hotels, airports and big stores almost anywhere in the world.

Rodriguez had cashed one at a Lebanese hotel. The bloke who paid him out took down his phoney passport number but also noted his car registration. He drove around in a big chocolate-coloured Vauxhall Ventora, and that's how the Yard picked up the trail to his beautiful flat in Woodstock.

Interpol had put together a lot of intelligence. The gang were suspected of cashing these forged traveller's cheques and using the money for drugs. They were shipping a lot of heroin from Marseilles to the States and quietly making a fortune. There was plenty more background in London on their earlier activities, which had always been impossible to prove.

Tony Poole told us all this within about half-an-hour that evening. We looked over the Oxford shop and immediately organised a raid for Woodstock. We knew they were pretty big villains, so a smooth entry was called for here.

It was well after midnight when we got to the flat. Mick Strutt banged on the door, frantically. Not surprisingly, Rodriguez, who was living there with a very high-class English bird, would not open up.

"What do you want? Who is it?"

Now, Mick knew Rodriguez slightly, so he had to use a little ploy.

"It's de Gas Board, man," he says, in a great West Indian voice.

"The what?

"De Gas Board. We is looking for a leak, man, you gotta open up real urgent."

"There's no gas in this flat."

"I don' care 'bout dat, man. De gas pipes run right under dese flats and everybody's got to get out."

The door opens then and five of us go in like racehorses. Mick stands back at the door and I hear him say to Rodriguez, "Sorry about that, dear boy, it's the Flying Squad, actually."

Inside was magic. There was a draughtsman's board over at the window with all the gear – but not for drawing plans. This guy was making simple little plates for his forgeries out of tin-foil cartons like the ones you get at a Chinese takeaway.

He had a collection of minute tools and a small hammer for putting secret codes on to the traveller's cheques to validate them and verify the amounts he had also printed in.

Even in his dressing gown, Rodriguez looked immaculate. He was about 30, very slim and dark, obviously Latin. You could smell his aftershave 20 yards away. He was very proper, very charming, but a right devil underneath.

He stood in the middle of the room while we searched the flat. Apart from the forging equipment, we found some documents, good enough to impress a jury.

"I am saying nothing, inspector," said Rodriguez.

Tony Poole looked at him. That copper put the fear of God in me, and I was on the same side. "This stuff here is doing all the talking. You shut your face and speak when you're spoken to, understand?"

We took Rodriguez to a cell and then there were more raids

to get the others in. The Canadian hitman turned really nasty. Luckily, he was in bed with his chick when the Flying Squad burst in without any formalities such as knocking first. He went straight for the wardrobe where his weapon was hidden, and was knocked clear across the room before he got halfway from the bed.

Rodriguez was put in a cell where he could see all the others arriving. One by one the rest were taken out for questioning, but Tony Poole didn't go near him. It didn't take him long to work out that his mates might be telling a version of the story that wouldn't do him any good. So, Rodriguez was glad when Tony finally sent down to the cells for him.

All that team went inside, except the London financier. But the funny thing was this: the two English fellas who worked for Rodriguez were ripping him off something rotten. They were moving loads of this expensive clothing out of the Oxford boutique they were running for him and stocking a shop they had bought in Banbury.

Unfortunately, we nicked them a few days before they were due to open. When we told them that their boss might like to hear about their private enterprise, they couldn't stop talking as well.

Arrest is a great purgative for the conscience, but they all kept very quiet about drugs. We suspected they were dealing with very heavy people in Marseilles and the States.

Eventually, we found that Vauxhall Ventora parked up on some wasteground and had it stripped down at an Oxford garage. Under the wheel arches, two secret panels had been welded into place and then covered with undersea! again.

There were no traces of drugs inside, but we sent some particles away for analysis, just in case. They came back identified as camel dung, so the car had certainly been in the Middle East.

Chapter Seven

Palming, Popping and Tripping

Edward Laxton: Living and working undercover on the drugs scene brought many problems. One of the greatest for the young police officers was how to avoid arousing suspicion while not using drugs themselves.

Martyn Pritchard practised 'palming' pills by using children's sweets, Jelly Tots or Smarties. At a party or in a pub he would appear to swallow a few drugs, but having palmed the pills, they went straight into his pocket.

Martyn smoked cigarettes before joining the drugs squad, but from April 1972 he had to get used to rolling and smoking his own. Few on the drugs scene smoked 'tailor-mades' or 'straight' cigarettes. But how could he actually avoid smoking reefers, joints, love weeds, Texas Tea or giggle sticks?

His skill was once challenged in court. He denied joining hippies in a smoke-up, and demonstrated in the witness box a trick he had used dozens of times. He blew on the joint and made the end glow as if he was drawing in the smoke. While everyone else was getting high, the young detective was at work.

There was always the risk at a really heavy smoke-up of getting a secondary 'high' from all the marijuana fumes in the air, but this was never strong enough to make him lose reasoning.

Acid was a little easier. Just as he would pretend to be high on hash, Martyn would palm the LSD tab and feign a trip. If everyone around him was tripping-out, they would soon be too far gone for Martyn to worry about his acting prowess.

He turned down many a sniff of cocaine by saying, "That's not my bag." The same reason was usually accepted if heroin was offered – even junkies have some respect for those who want to avoid getting addicted to hard drugs.

However, Martyn was well aware that the time might arrive when he was put on the spot among the users and pushers of heroin or 'H', smack, snow, junk, white stuff or joy powder. That moment arrived in an over-heated flat in North London.

A Girl Named Maria

Martyn Pritchard: I missed out on a party one Saturday in November 1974 and spent the night behind bars instead. There was a fair amount of pills and hash on the go in Aylesbury at that time and someone had just introduced a drop of the hard stuff – heroin. The local drugs squad knew the 'H' was linked through London to a girl named Maria.

She was 19, a funny-looking girl, short and thin, red hair and very exaggerated eye make-up, a pretty face but absolutely no figure. Maria was intelligent and looked almost innocent, until she started talking about drugs. Then her expression changed, it became hard, very hard, for someone so young. Her drugs form started at 14, she had convictions and at this time, was still on probation.

None of this meant a thing to her, she was really bad. A whole string of young kids thought Maria was great. And some of them were ill, man. There were a couple of attempted suicides, a bad breakdown case and a few who were on their way to getting hooked. They were all just teenagers.

I first heard about Maria at squad conferences and we all recognised we needed to get someone inside the set-up. But she was a cagey cow and that was not going to be easy. Two previous boyfriends had died from drugs or drugs-associated illnesses. Now she was kicking around with this evil bastard, Chris. Then one of the drugs squad lads knocked off her bloke.

He was picked up in Aylesbury wandering around and absolutely spaced out. He knew all their drugs squad lads, so the idea was to put me in the cells with him and take it from there. That night I was at a party and I got a message to call Aylesbury nick. I shot back home, got some dirty gear on and drove over. I was going to spend the next 12 hours with a junkie, behind bars.

The uniform lads kicked me in the same cell as Chris. Actually, it was the same one where, for many weeks, the Aylesbury police kept more than £300,000 recovered from the Great Train Robbery. But that didn't impress me, not that night.

Chris was like a kite, arrested on suspicion, only suspicion, of possessing drugs. His clothes were clean, but you can get done for possession if drugs are found in your urine. So, they wanted a sample from Chris.

About midnight he starts to get with it and I tell him I'm in for possession, too. All night long they keep trying to get him to pee, but he can't. He's been on morphine and that screws your guts up so that peeing is nigh impossible. We start chatting and I keep reminding him, "If you feel like pissing, do it in your trousers now. Don't give a sample."

There is no point in sending Chris up on a urine possession job and have him cop a fine. He is key to that little team around Maria.

"I'm clean as well, man," I tell him. "They are doing my car and my pad. Two days ago I would have been in trouble, but not now."

"Have you got form?"

I nod. "I reckon we're in trouble, man. They'll do us for something."

But I keep encouraging him. I'm telling him right, too. No uniform shift is going to take over on Sunday morning and allow two prisoners who are both clean to stay in the cells. We chat all night and by about eight o'clock, when the station sergeant comes down to the cells, we're mates.

"You can either wait for breakfast, or go now."

And we both jump up, follow him, sign for our gear and clear off. I made a meet with Chris for the following night and I was in. This had been such a problem for so long, and suddenly it was as easy as that.

On Monday morning I went across to see the lads in Aylesbury and get updated about their scene. That night Maria, Chris and I all met in the Rockwood pub.

"You can lay on some dope then?"

They're the first words she speaks.

"How much for a quarter of an ounce?"

"From my bloke, a fiver," I tell her.

"That's regular, as long as it's good stuff."

Junkie or not, Maria is very sharp. She got seven or eight 'O' levels at her grammar school.

We go to another pub, the Saracen's Head, and all the time she is probing. She is also coming on strong with the body, keeps rubbing herself against my shoulder and thigh. Chris might just as well go home. But he puts up with all this and Maria starts talking about wheels. This is her problem.

"I can score 'H' if I can get up to London. Can you take me?"

"Sure. Whenever you want to go."

"This Saturday. I'm right out, but I daren't go on the train. The pigs watch the station. I'll go inside if they pull me again."

"Right. Saturday it is then."

"Let's meet Wednesday. Just us," she whispers. Now she fancies me – which is very good in one respect but not very nice in another. I make the meet, in the Saracen's Head again on the Wednesday. I filed a note on everything that had happened so far – a two-hour conversation all about drugs. Bloody good job I did too!

The boys offered a silent watch this time, but I kept everyone away. There's just Maria and me up at the bar. Chris comes in later and stays in the corner. He is under orders.

I get the body treatment and the old come-on again, so I tell her, "Listen, I'm all for it but I've got a dose. It's up to you. Otherwise, leave it out 'cos it's not doing me any good." Not the first time I had used that excuse.

She buys the story and gets back to business. And we arrange the trip to the Smoke, just her and me. I wonder if she will keep her distance, all day together? I bloody well hope so. The job means a lot to me, but bedding a hopped-up junkie who has probably got a dose herself was beyond the call of duty as far as I was concerned.

Now we've got off the subject of sex, talk of drugs is about all done, so we turn to music. I can hold my own there. We pass a pleasant hour and Maria is very impressed with the pop chat.

Suddenly she remembers I was supposed to score some dope for her. And she is very sharp again. I've got my story ready. "Look, luv, don't think I'm bad luck. My man was busted on Saturday. I phoned him and he told me to stay well away."

"Dead right," she says. "Those bastards will screw anyone. If you get planted, what can you do?"

"Yeah. Couple of my mates have found themselves with a pocketful on the way to the nick."

"Know what I want to do? I wanna set them up. I've given it a lot of thought and it's not difficult, believe me."

So now we spend a good hour talking about setting-up fellas on the drugs squad, particularly my mate, Phil Gell. She had a lot of hate in her heart, that lady, and Phil was too good at his job for her liking.

She had a plan. Her little team were going to flood the drugs squad and Aylesbury nick with a lot of duff info about drugs. They would have to do a few busts because the gossip they were going to be fed would be that good.

And every time anyone was busted, they would complain. They would allege harassment, planting at their pads, getting fitted-up in the station, beatings, verbals, the lot. They would sod up the system, because so much time would be wasted answering all these complaints.

Eventually, she reckons the entire Aylesbury drugs squad would have to be investigated and probably broken up. Several of her mates were all for the idea and she was going to brief them all the way.

But she had something special for Phil Gell. Maria was going to tip him off and have a quiet meet down by the graveyard in the town. There was a stack of dealing going on at that spot in those days.

When they met, late at night – her friends would make sure Phil was on his tod – she was going to scratch his face and tear her own clothing, then make an official complaint that he had sexually assaulted her.

Believe me, that would have gone very badly for Phil. You might be innocent until proved guilty outside, but it works the other way in the job. You have to prove your own innocence and a complaint like that is ugly, really bad news. I put in a report on this the very next day and privately warned Phil to watch his back. But I needed to watch my own as well.

Because what happened on the Saturday is something I will never forget. I only knew we were going to London. Maria said she knew the house and would guide me there. She didn't know the address, but it was in Stamford Hill, North London.

I had to accept that and arranged three tail vehicles with six of the lads. I picked her up in my blue Cortina in the morning, outside the Rockwood pub. She gave the directions from the start and she took us a long way round, on to the M1 and then along the North Circular Road.

She lets on in the car that the stuff she is scoring from a couple of registered addicts is Physeptone [a trademark of methadone]. It's a heroin substitute prescribed by doctors to treat addicted patients.

I guess this was another case of over-prescribing – the addicts sell off what they don't need and use the money to buy the real stuff.

Maria tells me she uses Physeptone herself.

"It's not as good as smack and the trouble is I need plenty to get high. But as long as I can sell the rest at a profit and cover my own stuff, it's OK."

"Smack has never been my scene. Is it that good?"

"It's great but it's expensive and you've got to know the dealer. There's plenty of bad stuff around. Phy is cheaper and easier to score."

She was right there. We knew all about Phy and how it was getting on to the market through too many doctors over-prescribing. Honestly, that's how it was, and especially in London.

Physeptone was just like a pre-med, the jab you get before an operation. That's supposed to be the effect, you just float and feel very relaxed and happy. The trouble is it makes your mouth go very dry. Your tongue feels fat and you can't swallow.

While she goes into all this I switch on our little experiment in the car. We were always playing about with mikes and tapes and all sorts of gear to improve our operation. When you're driving, it's not easy to remember everything being said – names and address- es, and all the details that add to your information.

So, this time, two days before the trip to London, we had worked on the car in Oxford and rigged a mike behind the sun-visor on my side, an on-off switch beside my seat and the rest of the gear hidden in the back.

The idea was to keep her talking and keep transmitting, so the lads behind could get it all down. The recordings weren't bad, as it turned out. By now we were well round the North Circular and running into very heavy traffic.

The boys were still there, changing places with each other. They had tailed us well, but it was easy because she wasn't driving and constantly looking in the mirror.

All this traffic at Saturday lunchtime seemed strange until I suddenly realised they were football supporters. Tottenham Hotspur were at home and in no time I lost the tail. All three cars disappeared.

This was scary. I didn't know what I was going into, or who we were meeting. The lads were meant to be staking out the house. And they would move in if they saw me walk past a window, which meant trouble was brewing, or if they saw me rushing out of the house.

Well, they wouldn't be doing that now, baby. Quick decision. Maria is small business for a London team. They shouldn't be too heavy. After all, they're registered addicts and because of that, they're drawing attention to themselves. I'll go it alone.

She directs me to a house in Filey Avenue. We stop and Maria says, "Listen, let me get you a couple of phials. You'd really love it."

"How much?"

"Four quid."

I give her a fiver and she gets out. A girl lets her in and a couple of minutes later, Maria comes to the doorstep and beckons, "It's OK, Martin."

Inside the house she introduces the addicts, Billy and Sheila. Billy's a bad-looking bugger with the shakes in both hands. He could be dangerous, looks a bit freaky. If they don't know what they are doing, his type can be worse than real heavies.

The flat isn't bad for a junkie-pad, but still awful. We're in a front room on the first floor. It's very warm, but that's usual. They always feel the cold and would rather spend money on electricity or gas than food. It's steamy, like a launderette. Paper is bubbling off the walls and the windows are streaming.

I assume Billy and Sheila live together. They're both on social security and apparently he does a fair bit of business pushing in Piccadilly. But he's warned Maria off there in case she gets ripped off.

Folks don't realise what goes on in the drugs world, particularly with the hard stuff. Pushers break down the pure heroin and mix it with milk powder or sugar, talcum powder, bicarbonate of soda – even brick dust. Junkies can buy a mix as low as one-to-five or even one-to-six.

This is often what kills them. They switch suppliers and get a bag of pure, or nearly pure, heroin. But their system is used to a much weaker mixture, and they don't realise the change in quality and inject the same quantity of powder. Suddenly, the body gets a jolt and can't handle it.

That's one way they go. Another is the diseases junkies pick up from their dirty works – the syringes and needles. Their weak constitutions can't take too much.

"There's nothing here," says Billy. "We've got to get the script at the chemist's. Can you run us down in the car?"

It's only half a mile away, the Boots chemist at Stamford Hill, and we're soon back at the pad. Maria is itching to shoot some of this Physeptone. She wants 20 phials, but the gent can't do that much.

"I can do 17, OK?"

"OK, OK, but I want to do three now. Got any works?"

The mere sight of those drugs has turned her on. But she can't find a vein. She breaks open three phials of the Physeptone, loads the syringe and has another go. I'm sitting on the floor watching all this.

First the left arm, then the right. She is getting really impatient and jumpy. She's perched on a big bed with brass rails in the corner. She's pinching her skin and holding the works between her knees.

"Come on, someone, give me a hand."

Billy obliges. He finds a vein at the top of her left arm and injects the drugs. Billy and Sheila take their turn. Then he holds out the works to me.

"You gonna shoot, man?"

There is blood coming off the needle. Some of Maria's, some of his and some of Sheila's. It's dripping off the end and onto my jeans as he holds it over me.

"Come on, man, enjoy yourself." It's my moment of truth.

"Listen, it's not my bag. And I've got wheels. We're driving back tonight, could be a bad scene," I say.

And he wipes the works under his arm and puts everything up on the mantelpiece.

Then Sheila says, "Let's have a cup of tea."

I am knocked out, it's like a weird dream. These three have all had a fix. Spurs are playing up the road. Meanwhile, my mates are prowling around trying to find me, I hope. I've been persuaded before, softer drugs, but for the first time in my life someone just tried to get me to use the needle. I am very keyed up, nervous, and a bit scared. And suddenly, it's time for tea!

Calm as you please. Don't these people realise? No, they don't. Drugs mean nothing to them.

Maria gets off the bed and settles down in my lap on the floor. I can't notice any appreciable difference in her. She's a bit more relaxed, and now she's getting all lovey-dovey again.

Billy remembers the money and Maria counts out 30 quid, two fivers and the rest in ones, which she had obviously collected the night before.

She drinks her tea and we all start talking about the drugs scene in London, the Piccadilly pushers, the latest gossip. It's obvious that Billy is doing more and more business from the house.

"I make less money, but there's less chance of getting busted," he says. Mmmm, that's what you think, Billy.

Maria asks me whether I can run her up to Billy twice a week. Everyone is happy and we split. She puts the prescription box, with the 14 phials inside, in her handbag. And in the car she gives me my pound change.

"I'll keep the two phials I scored for you until we get back to Aylesbury."

"Listen, keep them. You didn't score as much as you wanted."

"No, no. They're for you and it's your car we're using. If you don't shoot, sell the stuff and cover the petrol. I'll just hang on to them until we get home in case we're stopped by the pigs. Only one of us gets busted then. We hope."

"How many will you sell?"

"I don't know yet. I've got to give Chris three. I'll need some more but I'm pretty skint and I need to cover my own stuff, so I'll move as much as I can."

"What price do you sell for?"

"Depends how much I've scored. Three quid a phial, usually. Depends how much they need."

"Who are the customers?"

She shuts up and I apologise quickly. I thought she might be high and off guard.

"'No, don't answer that, I don't want to know. What I meant was, are they all on hard drugs or do they only use it occasionally?"

"I've got about 20 friends who regularly use the stuff," she says, and she is relaxed again.

"Well, they can't all shoot three phials, that's nine quid a fix."

"No, some of them take off on only one. But they can get high on a big bottle of cough mixture. They're lucky. Three are not enough to get me high now, I'll need more on Wednesday."

"Aren't you scared of getting hooked?"

"Not really. I don't want to get addicted and I certainly wouldn't register, that's the end. I reckon I can handle it."

As we drive along, I'm much more relaxed. The boys are there again. The tail vehicles cruised the streets for nearly three hours until they found my car. Now they're following us home.

At a garage selling cheap petrol outside Aylesbury, just off the London Road, we pull up and I flash my lights twice. It's the signal.

We drive into town and Maria puts the two phials in my pocket. Then she pulls a syringe and needle from her handbag and puts them in the glove compartment.

"You'll need the works, luvver."

"Yeah, thanks."

"Next week, after we see Billy, I should be able to score some acid. Do you fancy that?"

"Great. That's more in my line."

"See you Wednesday," says Maria, and gives me a kiss before she gets out of the car at the Hen and Chickens roundabout.

I shall see you on Monday, my pretty, I think to myself. See you in court, and you will really hate the pigs.

Wrong. Dead wrong. The next time would be 11 months later. But I didn't know that as she crossed the road, and in the mirror I could see the boys pick her up.

She was bailed at the nick and 24 hours later she was on the trot and disappeared in London.

We heard on the grapevine she met up with Chris and they concocted a defence. They were going to claim I originally supplied them with the quarter ounce of cannabis at our first meeting and supplied the money for the Physeptone before we went to London.

As I told you, I made a full note straightaway of everything that was said, everything that happened, at our first and second meetings.

When she asked me for the money in London, we were outside the addicts' house. It was quite spontaneous, and I had to cough up to go along with the image. I was happy but not comfortable. It was going to look pretty squalid in court. But it never came to that. For Chris was Maria's third boyfriend to depart this world.

He died from pneumonia. A set of works was found by his bed and plenty of needle evidence on his arms. He was too weak to fight the illness.

An arrest warrant for Maria was granted and she was finally nicked in London, trying to cop some tablets from a chemist on a forged prescription.

When she finally came up in the Crown Court at Aylesbury, most of the fight had gone. She was in the dock and I was in the witness box. Maria wouldn't look at me. Not once.

She pleaded guilty to possession and supplying drugs to me. She got borstal. Billy and Sheila were done in London for supplying but didn't answer bail.

Maria's disappearance made a big difference to the scene around Aylesbury. She was quite a girl, and I'll never forget that job, although it only ran a week. And the most vivid memory was the blood on that junkie's needle as my turn came to shoot some works.

Chapter Eight

The Free Music Festival

Edward Laxton: The 1960s was the decade that made sure music would never be the same again. Pop music – the Beatles, the Liverpool sound, the Rolling Stones – had arrived. And towards the end of that decade, the music festival was also established.

This was an added dimension to the concert tours that successful groups were undertaking in Britain, America and Europe. At massive open-air shows, thousands and thousands of fans listened to solo singers and bands. Then gradually the shows grew into three-day festivals.

We saw the start of Glastonbury in 1970, a small event that has grown to the biggest open-air festival in the world, where 175,000+ fans gather over five days. The world of pop music has undoubtedly been responsible to some degree for spreading the drugs cult. And the festivals have played their part.

A bunch of hippies in London, heavily into the drugs scene, came up with a novel idea. Led by a character who called himself the Reverend Father F...! they chose a prime site for their People's Free Festival.

Not any old spare stretch of meadowland or well-known but worn-out venue. They were determined to set up in Windsor Great Park, right there just beyond the famous castle, just beyond the Queen's back garden at her weekend retreat.

So, two kinds of music festival emerged – the traditional show, well-organised, with popular groups and good music, where orderly fans paid for their entertainment. And the Free Festival, a show that was not so well-organised, where nobody gave a damn, where there was a lot of drugs, a lot of inferior music, and no one paid.

No one, that is, except the folks whose rates and taxes paid for the massive policing, clearing-up operations and damage to property.

The organised shows were usually happy and noisy affairs, colourful and brash. Free Festivals could be dirty, drab and unsavoury events, more the victims of bad planning than the uncontrollable enthusiasm of the fans. They also became part and parcel of the drugs scene, attracting the activities of the pushers, the users and, naturally, the drugs squad detectives.

In the Queen's Back Garden

Martyn Pritchard: A number of conferences were held to discuss tactics at festivals from 1972 onwards. Everyone was involved – the Home Office, our top brass, the drugs squad. For everyone except the drugs squad it was a matter of keeping the peace in the areas around the festival site, making sure these so-called 'long-haired weirdos' behaved themselves outside the perimeter.

But inside, where we had to graft, the top brass didn't want to know. For uniform branch, that was the place of the great unwashed. And if you had volunteered to go and work among that lot, you were off your head.

This will give you a clue to how little appreciation there was at the top for the drugs squad's work, how little they knew about fighting drugs at ground level and getting stuck in where it mattered.

We figured these two- and three-day long festivals needed special treatment. The kids were rolling up with sleeping bags and tents, organising themselves for living on-site for days at a time. So we had to do the same.

Really and truly, a lot of ordinary folks with office jobs and maybe fairly mundane lives were grabbing an opportunity for some weekend festival fun.

I put in for permission to buy a tent and some cooking gear. Back came a memo from headquarters: *Report to Sulhamstead for this equipment.* This was the force training school, near Newbury.

They were waiting for me, with instructors ready to demonstrate the quickest and most efficient way to pitch this particular model. Don't forget to slacken the guy ropes at night and tighten them up in the mornings. You can imagine how that routine would go down with the neighbouring hippies who, as often as not, walked away when the festival ended and left their tents behind.

I thought the tent they were using was just for a demonstration – it had bloody great big blue letters on it saying TV [Thames Valley] Police Cadets. "No, no, no, officer. That's your tent. They are all the same," they replied.

What a marvellous reception I'd get in one of those! If they couldn't issue me with something more discreet, I would buy my own. After all, it was my neck.

And that's what I did, a little orange pup-tent. And that was bad enough because it was brand new and looked it, but at least I was ready to go camping. I had a red patch sewn on the side, so my mates could distinguish the tent and find me easily. They might need me and, man, I might need them… in a hurry.

The Free Festivals were a big problem. They were nothing more nor less than junkie conventions. The hippies might not have wanted them to turn out that way, but it was bound to happen.

We went to one of the early Glastonbury festivals in 1972, just after I joined the drugs squad, to have a look round and see what was going on. We weren't working, merely observing. The local force ruled the site a no-go area for their lads and we watched a fella pushing drugs like I had never seen. He had a big baker's tray with a canvas strap around his neck.

All his stuff was laid out. Uppers and downers, black bombers, speed, I mean a dozen different amphets [amphetamines], and blue and green microdots, Moroccan cannabis, Lebanese Gold and Mexican hash. And he was knocking it all out fast.

There was nothing we could do. We just watched, fascinated,

and all of us memorised a bloody big blue tattoo on his right arm. But we never saw that gent again. A year later, we had the first Free Festival at Windsor. There were more coppers than hippies. We outnumbered them about four to one.

Our people were so worried, it became an overkill. I don't blame them because we had no idea how it would turn out or how many people would turn up. Even the law about freedom in the Great Park was a bit confusing – and this is the Queen's back garden.

The first day, just before the August Bank Holiday, there were nearly 200 of us and – despite all the publicity – about 10 of them, just the organisers. We did manoeuvres all day, displacement of men for the moment the action began.

It never did, not that year. About 40 or 50 fans turned up on foot, the rest were turned back at the station. Uniform chased the ones who did get there all over Windsor Great Park. They couldn't settle down and the bands didn't know where to go because there was no designated stage area.

But the following year, they were ready. They had a lot going for them, as the Crown Commissioners, who control the park, were persuaded into granting permission, and the Home Office thought it would be a good idea. Everyone was anxious to back off any confrontation.

Now there's a world of difference between the properly organised music festival and the free ones. At Reading, for instance, in the early days it cost £5 or £6 to go in for the three days and, apart from the drugs, there was less trouble than when Manchester United play away.

That was a very colourful scene. The Welsh hippies would have a dragon flag out and the communes displayed their own banners. There were a few great signs, very funny, and some terrific bands.

They had their own security men on the site and lots of them were off-duty Met coppers from London, picking up a day or two's pay as stewards and helping to control the crowds. Very unofficial that. You're not supposed to take on any other work if you're in the job, but these guys were ideal. Just the way they stood, their 'presence' did the trick.

Of course, there were drugs at Reading, but there was spontaneous fun, too. Anyone could go along and drop out for a day or a weekend, with no aggro, some good music and excitement.

Windsor was altogether different. There was a foot-high metal rail along the edge of the Cavalry Ground, which we used to call the Berlin Wall. Once you stepped over that, the atmosphere was heavy, really grim. And it was bloody scruffy and depressing. The colour scheme was faded blue and khaki mostly. And a lot of the music was terrible, they were playing for nothing.

From that second year on, though, they were organised. They had four stages built from scaffolding and good public address systems, plus medical stations under canvas.

A film of some of the kids in there would do more than all the other propaganda against drugs. It was a pitiful sight – young people on really bad acid trips, smack withdrawals. They had about 15 beds ready for just this problem and there were volunteer doctors on duty.

Yet only yards away, dealers had pinned up notices on a tree, advertising drugs. 'Green acid – third tent on left behind Stage B.' Another said, 'Red Leb – blue tent left of Stage C.' That was Red Lebanese, a type of cannabis.

It was all stuff like that, openly flouting the bloody law but very useful for us. We could go along and clock everyone there. We knew who was doing what and could arrange for members of the drugs squad, who were not living undercover like us, to bust them later.

So that was the picture. A great mass of drab hippies and junkies who chanted about love and peace but had a lot of hate in their heart. They hated war – but thank God for army surplus or they would all be naked. They hated the system as well, but they used it and carried on drawing their social security to buy drugs and food.

In that order.

They were anti pretty much everything that didn't fit in with their way of life. So that year I packed my own tent and gear and headed for Windsor with my mate Dave.

Any time we were going into a scene, assuming our complete undercover role, we made sure we were properly prepared – briefed on likely characters, their activities, as much background as possible. We couldn't just drive up, lock the car and become a hippy. We had to get right into the scene, into hippy mood, mannerisms, language, looks – get relaxed. Best thing to do was start off by hitch-hiking.

It took us seven hours to reach Windsor from Oxford, about 40 miles. Hardly surprising, the way we looked. Mind you, we had a couple of beers on the way. There was plenty of time, we were a couple of days early. We wanted to get there and see if there was anything we could do to help our fellow drug users. Know what I mean?

When we reached the Great Park, we dumped the bags and I pulled out a Frisbee. We chucked it around for an hour while we eyed up everything and everyone in sight. This was the way. We weren't hippies, we were fuzz and needed to acclimatise.

By the time we wandered over to the stages and organisers' tents, plenty of people had seen us about. A bit of chat and bang, we were right in, both elected on to the festival committee.

There was just time to pitch our tent before the first meeting and pretty soon we knew just about everything that was going to happen. Call it luck, timing, experience, probably a combination.

The committee met every day, sometimes twice. Afterwards we had another meeting to attend – at our rendezvous with the top brass in a pink house in the Great Park.

Shows you how Jekyll and Hyde we were. One minute we were up to our armpits in hippies, dropouts, dirty plates and scruffy living quarters. The next we were having coffee and biscuits with the Assistant Chief Constable.

At these mid-morning chats, we told them all the plans. Sometimes it was just insignificant bits and pieces, but we were able to warn them about some very ugly talk regarding the fuzz.

Like one group who planned a nice little greeting for any motorcycle cops going through after dark. They were going to stretch some wire between two trees, about head high. So we kept the bikes out.

I suggested to the committee that I should work on the festival newspaper and they agreed. This would be an additional source of info, but on top of that it gave me the opportunity to go all over the site dropping in on every group and tent as I helped distribute the paper. Ideal.

We produced two pink photocopied pages every day, called the Windsor Free Press. I had the added kick of circulating all their anti-fuzz rantings and ravings. For instance, the first edition went on about police intrusion and ended up saying: *We must keep the police off the site. Together we can do this.*

Then again, the paper did some good. It helped control the prices for drinks, hot dogs and hamburgers on the vans and stalls. These were doing a roaring business and would have charged at least twice as much without the controls and the warnings on prices in the paper.

You could really get ripped off at these festivals. The amount of duff drugs being moved was fantastic. We found cement powder being sold as heroin, and all sorts of tablets being passed for amphets. You see, the kids were buying from any old pusher, people they didn't know. Especially the young kids, not really on the drugs scene, just trying to get with it.

Now we wouldn't do anything to stop that, it's the perfect deterrent. If these youngsters found they were wasting their money, perhaps they would finish with drugs altogether.

And the paper would describe the pushers who were selling the bum gear and detail the pills and stuff on offer. They regularly warned-off everyone about bad acid, because if there's too much concentration of LSD or the tabs have not been made properly, they produce really bad trips.

Do you know what some bright bastard was selling as acid tabs? Spaghetti! He cut off little pieces of pasta and sold them at 40p each. There were even volunteers in the medical tent, who weren't doctors, handing out downers – anti-depressants – if you went in claiming you were coming down off speed or some other pep-pills. We decided to bust some of these imposters.

We went in to test it out. They supplied us with downers and one of them, who was certainly a total impostor, wanted to keep Dave in and give him an injection. "I assure you, it will cure your drug problems," he said.

Dave Snell didn't have a drugs problem. But he overdid it a bit with the acting and this fella was really keen on showing him to a bed. But there was no way Dave was going to get himself injected and we beat it.

We discussed getting this guy busted, plus anyone else in there doctoring without a licence. But the nurses and real doctors, on the other hand, were doing a very good job. They might have believed in drugs – certainly many doctors believe in soft drugs like cannabis – but at Windsor the medics were very necessary. In the end, we decided to leave them alone, even the phoneys.

Dave was also on the committee, and got himself involved with the food tent, one big communal cook-up every day. The festival-goers gave them various tins and vegetables and, as you can imagine, it came out as slop.

Now there had been a few scraps with local soldiers who came onto the site from Windsor barracks in their civvies to have a look and listen to the music. They kept getting picked on as the fuzz. But they got their own back in the cook pot.

One wise bugger decanted some Omo detergent powder into

soup packets. He emptied the stuff in and two minutes later the pot was bubbling away like mad. I thought that was an absolute scream! They were carrying the foam away by the armful.

Dave used to keep back a few bits of meat for us and make sure our grub wasn't too bad. But we only ate lunch from the food tent because on the second night some lunatic bastard made his donation. He slipped some acid into the pot, and a few dozen kids had a mild trip. They thought it was great, but we wouldn't trust the supper meals after that. We either went hungry or sneaked off for fish and chips or Chinese takeaway.

All the time we were picking up useful stuff for later, information we could pass on to various drugs squads. I used to creep into my tent, get under the blankets and write up some notes with a flashlight. Later I would mail them to myself at home.

One night I was in the tent and right outside was a scene going strong, one little raver trying to keep four fellas happy. It went on half the night. I said to Dave, "If we're going to get any sleep, we'll have to get this lot busted."

There were lots of young girls at Windsor. The really young ones, say 13 or 14, we would earmark for the women police and have them pulled out.

There are three attractions at festivals – music, sex and drugs. And most of these youngsters were there for the last two. Any number of them were selling sex for their food, or a few smokes or tablets.

There were couples having it off all over the place. I don't mean inside the tents, I mean out in the open.

One night, Dave and I were watching a fella selling cannabis. Making his rounds, very quietly. He came to a girl kipping out in the open, all on her own and inside a brown sleeping bag. There was hardly anyone else around.

He woke this girl and there's a short chat, say 45 seconds. Next thing we see is him unzipping his trousers and her unzipping the sleeping bag. And wallop!

They snuggled up in the bag and got on with it. Ten minutes later he gave her a single reefer and carried on making his rounds. We had that guy busted, and one of the lads told him what we'd seen. He didn't know the chick, he hadn't bothered to ask her name.

"Man, I wouldn't recognise her if she walked up now, no idea what she looks like. So what." Amazing. But the way-out sex was something we would all have to get used to. It meant absolutely nothing to them.

I saw a couple at one festival enjoying themselves standing up. They were held upright by the pressure of the mob all round them who had pressed forward to see a really good group on stage. He dropped his slacks and the girl wrapped her legs round his hips. Cheers all round – for the music and this couple.

Another time, five or six couples tried to achieve a simultaneous orgasm. They were on the ground, out in the open, and they were calling out to each other, "Hang on, slow it down." Then "Hurry up, it's not going to last much longer."

Bloody sordid really, but at the time it was quite funny. The experiment was a total failure. There was a great cry of "Too late," and then loads of laughter. But I expect they had another try sometime.

I chatted up one chick. She was gorgeous. Went around with just a pair of pants on, selling bead necklaces. I bought four, then discovered she was spaced out. Courtesy of LSD, I expect.

Not many of the bands got paid at Windsor. They were mostly amateurs and glad of the chance to play before a big audience. Some of the music was quite good, a lot of it lousy and some of it non-existent – the bands just didn't show up.

On the Sunday afternoon that second year, there was a big gap in the organised entertainment and the hippies decided on an excursion to Windsor polo ground, something which had not been discussed by the committee. The uniform boys got wind of it only when the mob were well on their way.

This led to a confrontation. Suddenly there's a great crowd pushing across the ground and old Martyn is well up the front. Actually, I was enjoying myself. It was a bit of light relief looking at the expressions on the old fellas sitting there waiting for the polo to begin as Hippy United arrived.

Have you noticed on the television news or big sports programmes that whenever there's a crowd rushing across a pitch some bloody copper will bring off a great rugby tackle? And you can bet your life he will be a Welshman.

There I was, belting over the polo ground, waving my arms about, laughing like a madman and really enjoying myself, and some big Taffy wing-forward takes my legs.

I swore at the bastard and gave him a thump. But I was on the ground and it wasn't much of a thump. I got lifted for assaulting a police officer, anyway.

Straight in the van and down to Windsor nick, and this uniformed wing-forward was very pleased with himself. I thought to myself, "You can have your moment of fun, boyo, but wait till you find out it was a copper who banged you on the nose."

Really and truly the joke was on me. They took my possessions and whopped me in the cells. But Taffy had to get back to the festival as there were all sorts of small outbreaks of trouble down there.

I don't mind going in the cells. I have had some good breaks in there, but I'm not too keen on staying overnight. You don't show that you're fuzz until you have to – and the last chance is when you're warned you're going to be charged. But Taffy doesn't return and I spend the night in there.

Taffy has four or five on his plate next morning and turns up fairly early to get all his charges ready for court. He takes me upstairs first. "You're going to be charged with assaulting…"

"What's the matter, can't you take a joke?"

"... in the execution of his duty. I'll give you bloody joke, boy."

"Yeah, well the joke's over, my old mate. I'm DS [drugs squad], the fuzz, same as you. And I've got another day or two's work on that festival and a meeting with the ACC [Assistant Chief Constable] in about two hours. So, get me out of here."

While he's struggling for breath I give four numbers for him to check me out on in case there's nobody upstairs in his own CID or drugs squad office who knows me personally.

I went out half-an-hour later as if I had been bailed, and straight back to my tent.

"Was she nice?" says Dave, still curled up in his sleeping bag.

"I was inside, and I noticed you didn't come near to check on that state of affairs."

"You were lucky, Pritch, it was hell out here."

"Yeah? Seven in one of those bloody cells is no fun either. I'm going straight to the civil liberties crowd about that."

"No, I'm serious. There was a running fight all night with the fuzz. The music was awful and it bloody well rained. At least you were in the dry."

I almost clobbered him. But not quite.

Chapter Nine

Pigs and Pop Festivals

Edward Laxton: My memories of the Free Festivals at Windsor are different to Martyn Pritchard's. The first was a complete fiasco. No one expected the local council, Home Office, police or anyone else to sanction the festival, not at Windsor, and least of all the hippy organisers. Virtually no one turned up, apart from several hastily formed teams of policemen and about a dozen of us journalists.

When the go ahead in 1972 was announced, Thames Valley Police recognised they were unprepared. To avoid disaster, they mounted a high-profile presence at the local railway station. Faced with the risk of being stopped and searched, the moderate crowds that travelled from London were soon using their return tickets.

The second year there was more organisation on both sides. Rough and ready stages were built from scaffolding, a PA system-of-sorts installed, franchises sold to food stallholders, pre-publicity was launched and the larger crowds duly arrived.

The police – uniform branch, ordinary CID officers and the drugs squad – believed they were ready, but still they could not cope. They were out-thought, outwitted and outnumbered. The mild-mannered, day-dreaming hippies were infiltrated by a group of hard-headed anarchists who took over events for their own purposes.

Spot the Pig

Martyn Pritchard: I told you before how the crowds at pop festivals often play a game called 'Spot the Pig'. We figured the game was more like 'Piggie in the Middle' for us. Believe me, it's easy to pick out the fuzz – if you know what to look for. They're the people watching the sex. The rest are into the music or smoking, and screwing in public was nothing new to them.

One evening at Windsor during the 1973 festival, I was sitting at a right angle to the stage. A couple came down to the front, stripped off and got cracking just a dozen yards from me. It was the first time I had seen anything quite like it, but certainly not the last.

They got a few cheers at first, then no one took any notice. I was fascinated but after a couple of minutes I looked across the crowd. There were just half a dozen pairs of eyes still glued to this public performance.

Their faces wore amazed expressions or big wide grins. They were all coppers, including a girl from our own squad. We had discussed all the dangers of being sussed out several times, at conferences and briefings. But it still happens, the coppers can't resist clocking the sex.

I nearly got done myself once, and no one was playing 'Spot the Pig'. One of my drugs squad mates, Jonah, was with me in this group and a couple of chicks came up. Then one of them starts screaming – "He's the fuzz. That bastard nicked me."

She recognised me all right. I busted her up at Banbury about three months earlier. But I've been staying at a commune with some of the kids in this group.

So, they all think they know me well. It's a very dodgy moment. "She's spaced out, silly cow." I have to turn it into a joke.

Eventually, the girl was apologising. Then her mate lugs her away and we've escaped. That was a bit too close.

For masses of the kids who go, these music festivals are one big smoke up or acid trip. It's like a junkies' convention, the music is just something in the background.

And each time, there is a big drugs squad operation – there has to be. No one squad from just a single force can handle it. We would have about 70 blokes and probably half-a-dozen female officers, drawn from 10 or a dozen forces, at really big festivals.

So, they become a convention for us as well. We all meet up again and on one night you can bet your life we have our own party. But it's booze not hash.

In many ways, the music festivals are very good for the drugs squad. It's good business, that's for sure, and good experience. The lads from different parts of the country recognise their own customers. They see who's getting together and pick up some intelligence. All useful stuff for when they get home.

Naturally, we swap information. Just by drinking together and talking, you pick up a lot of tips. Maybe someone in South Wales has just found a new stash-place in a car. Or someone says watch these freaky hairdos – they can put the pot up there. You know, that sort of thing.

The Thames Valley force learned a lot through pop. We had the Windsor and Watchfield Free Festivals on our patch, and then the annual one at Reading. And as we were one of the first drugs squads in the country, we were always called in elsewhere – Woburn Abbey, the Isle of Wight, Stonehenge, all the big shows.

Reading was great. We developed some terrific techniques there for search and arrest, and it was mostly based on common sense.

Hundreds of kids flocked to the site on the banks of the Thames. It's all wired off and very well organised. But some of our biggest problems come from our own side. Some senior uniformed officers would rather the site became a complete no-go area for police operations, I am sure of that.

Would you believe we were ordered not to go in there one time? Uniform branch were so pleased with their control and the lack of aggro, they thought busting anyone in there would create more bother than was worthwhile.

Balls to that. They were cutting out all the challenge and excitement. And if that goes, the job isn't worth doing. That's why we wanted to stay undercover, away from this attitude of peace at a price.

Another time at Reading, we were told "no more arrests" on the last day. All the cells and detention places for miles around were full with our customers. But we found out this instruction had only been given to the drugs squad – not straight CID or the uniform boys.

That meant our success rate was putting some noses out of joint and creating problems. But the senior uniform men gave us enough headaches all year round, so now we decided to give them some. And we knocked off a few more folks.

It's fairly obvious that life is somewhat easier if you make as many busts as possible before anyone even gets there. And Reading was where our new techniques were put to the test. Masses of hippies arrived there by rail, on special trains from London, Southampton, Bristol, Birmingham, all over. It's a Bank Holiday show lasting all weekend. Even for the first year, 1971, they got around 30,000 fans.

That year the station supervision was given to Mick Strutt. As you know, he was boss of the Oxford drugs squad and this was a bit of a kick up the arse. Mick took quite a few kicks, but it never worried him. Because with three blokes he handled the station job very successfully.

In Reading itself, there was a forensic laboratory set up at the university to test samples, magistrates standing by to keep the courts going till 10pm for four days, and documentation centres at council offices to do the paperwork for the courts.

There were cells laid on at police stations and army barracks for miles around, coaches to transport prisoners, special radio wavelengths, the lot.

Normally, it takes anything from three weeks upwards to get a sample back from the lab. That means bailing the body and bail means criminal record checks and addresses and so on, to make sure the prisoner is safe to release pending the charge. You can only charge someone with illegal possession of dangerous drugs when you know, and can prove, exactly what they had on them.

All this takes a lot of time. And the boys and girls are going to miss a lot of pop, and a lot of freedom, while we go through it all – unless, of course, they put their hands up, admit the possession and tell us what the stuff is they are carrying. And saving time becomes more important as the number of busts builds up.

All this was the basis of Mick's operation. He had recced the railway station and knew exactly what he was doing.

He found the railway police had an office he could use. It was on the platform where the London trains arrived. You went through a big green door, up 28 steps, across a landing and into this office through another door.

So, Mick gets a blackboard, with big yellow chalk letters saying, 'PLEASE KEEP MOVING. EXIT FOR POP FESTIVAL'. And he puts it next to the green door, at the bottom of the steps.

He's got two blokes at the top of the stairs, hidden behind the office door, and himself and one other at the bottom, shepherding the hippies through. When he has 40 or so, he closes the lower door and shouts, "Stop. Drugs squad. This is a bust."

The boys then show at the top and the bottom. There's just about one hippy per stair, standing there and wondering what the hell was going on.

"Welcome to Reading, my friends. Have you anything to declare?" says Mick.

Naturally, there's a load of laughter at that crack and a fair amount of juicy replies.

"Let me explain your problem," says Mick.

He's very lordly, doesn't look a bit like drugs squad. Hands folded across his stomach, neat grey suit, face very ruddy, going bald. He looks like a bloody railway official himself.

"It is entirely up to you how much time you spend with us and how much you spend enjoying the music and the sunshine by the river.

"I am quite sure many of you know how long it will take to

search you individually, and my men are very experienced, so they will find it, whatever you are carrying.

"And you know all about analysis and samples and paperwork. We are entirely in your hands. Produce the stuff, tell us what it is and we can provide a speedy passage through the courts.

"Everything is laid on to expedite your passage to the festival." That's what he said.

It was more like a lecture, and he delivered it several times that day to different groups of music fans. Absolute knockout and it did the trick. It was amazing how many of them fell for it.

They gave themselves up, pulled their gear out and told us exactly what it was. For all we could tell at a glance, it might have been headache pills, tablets for hayfever or just a ground-up white powder. But if they said "Amphets" or "cartwheels" or "jolly beans", that made life easier.

We would hold them, put a note to the lab, "Test for so and so", giving as near as possible the actual ingredients of the drugs, to make their test quicker and get the sample straight back.

If only a couple on the stairs stepped forward and coughed to having drugs, Mick would start searching everybody else. And sure enough, more would volunteer. When they had shown us where their drugs were, we had to let everyone else go back to the platform and on their way without a search.

So, Mick Strutt's plan was a success. But because another train was soon due in, he had to let the remainder go and take a chance on them being clean.

All our boys heard on the radio about the arrest figures down at the station and pretty soon about 20 dropped what they were doing and joined the action. Each time a train arrived, Mick insisted on delivering his lecture.

"Stop. Drugs squad. Have you anything to declare?"

We were all in stitches. The kids were in court, pleading guilty, fined and on their way to the festival that afternoon or evening.

Now this could only work one year. But at the next festival the railway authorities helped us out quite innocently.

There had been some commotion in the House of Lords about the powers of police, and allegations about officers bullying and stopping youngsters and searching them without proper suspicion. Well, I mean, what constitutes proper suspicion?

But Mick came up with another idea and naturally, after so much success, he got the railway detail again. Well, this year the railway bosses decided that to get the crowds off the platforms they'd open an old passenger tunnel under the tracks, which leads off towards the festival site. There were two exits at the end of it, left and right.

Mick has had a look round again and sees the potential the tunnel provides. He has a rough-and-ready cardboard notice made, saying, "PIGS HERE. GO LEFT WITH THE GOODIES. RIGHT IF YOU'RE CLEAN".

On festival day, one of our lads is in the tunnel. He suddenly holds up this banner, then pulls it down quick behind him.

Further along, another drugs squad man has a charcoal message scrawled across the front of his T-shirt. He keeps opening his jacket to show it, just like a flasher.

TURN RIGHT IF YOU'RE CLEAN. COCK-UP THEIR SYSTEM'.

We reckoned anyone who turns left falls within the realm of proper suspicion. So, we have another field day. Loads of them have the gear and we put the same proposition as before, save time on the search, produce the stuff, tell us what it is and we can get you on your way.

We made sure the platforms were kept clear, so nobody could turn around and warn the next trainload.

But the next day, on the Saturday, some clever bugger had printed a couple of thousand leaflets warning everyone about our tunnel trickery and was handing them out on Paddington Station in London. Our flow of customers dwindled.

We heard about this and phoned Paddington nick and asked them to investigate. I mean, the least they could do was to get the guy with the leaflets back to their place and discuss whether he was obstructing the course of justice.

They lift him and ring us back. He's got about three copper coins on him and no return ticket. And, apparently, he has travelled up to London from Reading.

Being that short of money and without a return ticket means he can be lifted on vagrancy. So, they ship him back to us on the train and we start getting busy again.

Just to rub it in, old Mick instructs a couple of boys to get rid of these leaflets. "Hand them out to the customers, after they come through the tunnel."

We had to hand it to the crafty bugger. The third year he gets the station role once again. And he comes up with yet another idea. This time it's plain common sense and no trickery.

Mick gets half a dozen drugs squad lads and asks uniform to make sure that whoever they appoint to platform duty is big and bloody tall. At the briefing he tells these uniform lads to stand about 10ft from the edge of the platform and nearly opposite the carriage doors as the trains pull up.

The rest of us are told to stand on the platform edge and as the first bodies get off, move backwards or sideways with them. We must watch the doors and clock the hippies as they leave the train.

Sure enough, boys and girls are clambering off these very crowded special trains and one of the first things they see are these massive bobbies. No one could miss them. What happens then? They pat their pockets, check their handbags, feel for their gear. It's an automatic reaction. They check to make sure their drugs are safe – safe from the police.

Anyone would do it. This is also one of the biggest giveaways for customs officers at the airport when holidaymakers come home with more than their duty-frees. And as they pat their pockets, we pick them up. It isn't even necessary to give them the option and save time on the search. They have revealed their hiding places with these simple gestures, exposed by their guilty feelings on seeing those uniforms.

So, the drugs squad made it a hat-trick of successes at Reading. And we didn't have one complaint – not even about the tricks we used at the station or any stopping and searching.

Technically, I suppose these methods must fall outside the rules. But they didn't stipulate that you couldn't operate like this, and very often what is expedient is OK – at least the first time.

As I've said already, some of our biggest problems came from inside the force, from the guvnors, part expedience and part fear of upsetting the mandarins.

The year the festival site was put virtually out of bounds for busts really got up our noses. We had knocked off a couple of hundred bodies, some of them with no previous, and that would make them think twice about drugs in future.

As far as we were concerned, they were all potential customers, on or off the site. And when there's a group of you, especially a bunch of drugs squad lads, you can get very bolshie about orders. So, we nicked a few more.

I had been inside the wire that year and noticed a team of lairy bastards who really reckoned themselves, doing a heap of acid. One of the other lads had bought a sample from them and now we had just the excuse we needed to go in and bust them.

There were seven or eight of them in one big group, all fellas except for one girl, lying and sitting on the grass. The music was going strong and in ones and twos, about a dozen of us got near this mob, pretty well surrounding them.

It's the afternoon and the festival is going to end in a couple of hours. If we had just walked in there and made a grab, there would have been a fight. A helluva fight. The fans would have hauled us off and the prisoners could have disappeared so easily in that mass of bodies.

But we knew the band on stage were about to end their gig, so we sat there. When they got into their final number, we slipped handcuffs on ourselves and held the other end of the bracelets open and ready.

Big noise. The gig is over. A chick stands up absolutely naked and starts dancing. The crowd are on their feet cheering her and the band. We move in fast and snap the cuffs. "Wherever you go, I go, baby," I tell my bloke.

We have them up and moving before anybody notices. We might get a kicking but we're not going to lose any bodies. They're all cuffed to us, but they start pushing as we force our way through the crowd.

"These are the bastards who've been doing the duff acid." That's me shouting. "All this duff acid, we're going to sort them out."

And the crowd is on our side. They are helping us, opening up like the Red Sea and giving us a shove towards the gates. Some aim the odd swipe at these buggers.

We get them out without too much fuss. We've shown the uniform big-wigs how to do the job on-site, without causing too much aggro. An inspector by the gate pipes up, "You're not supposed to do that." And he literally runs away as we call for vehicles to take in this lot. Surprise, surprise. I bust the girl and she gives a name.

"I suppose your old man is the bloke in the Cabinet?"

"That's right, he is."

I have just nicked a Government minister's daughter for drugs possession. I couldn't give a bugger who she is. I've got her and she has coughed the gear.

But the bells start ringing and the boys in blue are in a sweat. We process her like anyone else, her mother collects her and later pays her fine.

That little lady was mixing with some very unpleasant people. There was a lot of duff acid at Reading that year, not necessarily down to this team. In fact, one kid died as a result. He was on a bad trip, dived into the river and drowned. Apparently, he thought he was a fish.

Girls caused us a few extra problems. One was the body search. The rule is – women search women. But the proportion of women police officers, drugs squad or uniform, to the number of females going to these music festivals was low.

There is no transgression of the search rule. The only exception is guns – if you think you might get shot, rules fly out the window.

Loads of fellas will give the stuff to their girls until they are in a safe spot. And the gear doesn't go in their handbags. It goes inside their bra or pants.

The girls are just as embarrassed at being approached about a body search as many of us blokes would be doing it. You often have to wait ages for a woman officer to arrive.

But we hit on a great idea – using the new pocket radios. You could put a finger over one button and make it go, 'bleep bleep bleep', like something out of Doctor Who. If we fancied a young woman was hiding some gear, and it becomes instinctive after watching a few hundred reactions to questioning and so on, we would produce the radio.

"This is our latest drugs-detection device. Do you mind if we check you over? We won't touch you."

Nine times out of 10 they just shook their head.

You concealed the thing in your hand and just moved it toward them, about waist high. And you made the radio bleep.

"Right. You are either carrying stuff or you've got traces."

That gave you a let-out if they subsequently proved clean. But this little trick produced a lot of results. The women often reached inside their clothes and came out with the goodies.

Saved time. Saved sending for a female officer, which was often impossible.

I reckon about one in five of those kids at festivals was carrying dope, pills or acid, and some had smack or coke. And that meant there were plenty of pushers doing business. And it was even worse at the free events.

The magistrates at Reading handed out some very heavy fines and gaoled a few as well, the ones with form.

We were pleased about that. We put in a lot of thought and lots of planning to cover those events. Sure, some of the smart ones found ways to beat our system. But just think what it would have been like if we had turned our backs and let the whole bloody lot get on with it. Some of the people we warned off drugs might well have killed themselves.

Chapter Ten

The Flying Pigs

Edward Laxton: In 1974, when the third year of the Free Festival was announced, the good people of Windsor set up an action committee to try to stop it going ahead. They had support from all sides, especially from Thames Valley Police.

For their part, the festival had quietly gathered lots of support as well. The accent again was on a free event, and the committee promised stronger and more professional organisation. They reckoned right was on their side… a free society… power to the people.

The drugs squad infiltrated their set-up with plenty of time to spare and thought they knew exactly what to expect. But no one could have guessed how popular the festival movement had become and how many more people would show up at Windsor that year.

A complete surprise – around 4000 were living there on site before the first note of music was played. We were heading into August Bank Holiday and thousands more turned up every day. The scene was set for a complete fiasco and a three-day running battle.

A mammoth, wide-ranging, seven-month police inquiry came afterwards. The Thames Valley chief constable David Holdsworth reported: "There were 255 allegations against the police. I recorded 13 as substantiated."

Police were ordered to clear the site the day after the festival ended, but hundreds of people refused to budge. They wanted to stay and they wanted to fight. I was asked to give evidence to the official inquiry and could confirm that the behaviour of the mob was disgraceful – stamping, spitting, kicking, biting and scratching.

The following year, as you can read later, a compromise was reached. But really, the police were able to get their own back.

Pigs Can't Fly

Martyn Pritchard: Everyone got it wrong at Windsor in 1974. We had over 500 busts in four days. The police operation must have cost a fortune. We had nearly 800 coppers there in the end – on the day we cleared everyone away.

Sid Rawle was one of the chief organisers as usual. By now he had given up the role of the Reverend Father F***, but he had plenty of other roles. Leader of the London squatters movement and a peace campaigner, he became known as King of the Hippies.

He worked pre-festival with a guy named Ubi Dwyer. I popped into his commune in Notting Hill, London, and stayed for a couple of days. Naturally, I volunteered my services again to work on the newspaper. I told everyone Dave Snell would be with me on the committee and he'd be happy to stay with the food tent again.

So, we arrived at Windsor a couple of days early and pitched our tent fairly close to the perimeter, in a nice little spot by some trees. How was I to know the trees would soon become a communal toilet?

There was trouble over sanitation and Ubi got the blame. So, he went into Windsor and spent some festival funds on 18 brand new garden spades. He called for volunteers to dig a pit and then Ubi, positively and very publicly, carried out the ceremony of opening the toilet...

We had more or less the same liaison set-up going as before, and the pink house away over in the park was again our rendezvous with the uniform bosses. The festival paper was soon in business again. The committee reported overhearing a couple of uniform bobbies talking about cutting a few guy ropes when they were making their rounds.

So out came the paper with a warning, adding: "This is an offence and together we can make a citizen's arrest." Oh boy! This mob trying to make a citizen's arrest of a couple of coppers, that would be very smart... But that mirrored the tone of the 1974 festival. There was aggro between the two sides right from the start.

Don't get me wrong. I don't excuse some of my colleagues for what happened that year. Occasionally, they went over the top but there was a total breakdown in law and order and policemen can't stand back and watch it all happen.

Aggro between the festival-goers and the fuzz was nothing new. We should have been able to take the heat out of the situation, but we didn't. Looking back, it was bound to happen, the overall operation in Windsor was a disaster.

There was even aggro with the hot dog men. All the hamburger and ice cream vans and stalls were ordered to pay a £20-a-day franchise to the festival committee that year. The committee banged on about the freedom of Windsor Great Park, but the rules changed for some when they decided.

One bloke only had a tenner when he arrived and promised to pay the other half after he made some sales. Trade wasn't too good I guess, because he decided to hang on to his money. And that was a big mistake.

Some of the committee went along and told him to cough up or they would burn his stall. He still refused and tried to close down and drive off. Now those guys may play the hippy, but they can get very heavy when they want to and they were as good as their word. They set light to his van.

Police helped to put the flames out, but it was badly damaged. There was no further trouble over franchise payments. But after that little bit of bother there weren't a lot of hot dog sellers looking to do business, either.

At every committee meeting the fuzz was top of the agenda. If they had known about us they would have lynched Dave and me.

They got really paranoid about the police helicopter, which was hired to fly over the festival and spot the trouble. They all thought it was videoing them and getting a load of faces on file. And if there's any hint of secret operations or building up dossiers, they all go bananas.

The helicopter has got to go, that's for sure, man," says one guy. We're at a very full committee meeting. All the groups are represented – the White Panthers, Henry Higgins commune, Hare Krishna, everyone. It's unanimous. The helicopter has to go. But how? It's hilarious really, but there's a lot of discussion about two of the suggestions.

"Listen, I did a vacation job at Brocks, the firework people. I can get back there and pick up a lot of that gear."

This is a young chap, about 19, with a stutter. Everyone is so surprised at what he is saying, they all shut up.

"I believe we could make a rocket, one really big rocket, and shoot the f***ing helicopter right down. Even if we miss, it will scare the pigs so much they will withdraw that f***ing machine."

I wanted to laugh so badly. This is a right potty suggestion but the way he says it, everyone hanging on his words, it's crazy. Even crazier when they tell him to go ahead and build his bloody rocket.

Then some goon suggests kites.

"We could make a couple of really big kites and use wire. Instead of flying them from string, we'll use wire and rip the chopper's blades."

Oh great. Now we've got the anti-aircraft commune.

We passed on all the news at the pink house conflabs. No laughs there – I mean these kids were ugly, they were already stoning uniform patrols and any of our vehicles in the park.

That day's issue of the paper carried a big notice in a panel. THEY SAY PIGS CAN'T FLY. WATCH THE HELICOPTER TOMORROW!

Of course, nothing happened. It rarely does with that crowd.

Great talkers but not much action.

One of the things that threw a spanner in the works in '74 was the sudden removal of Ubi Dwyer. He was a bit mad, but he was also one of the chief organisers and people did listen to him. Anyway, soon after the toilet ceremony on the Saturday, he got busted and that upset everyone. He deserved to get done, he was a bloody menace. He performed gloriously inside the nick, breaking up a couple of police cells and repeating his toilet ceremony there as well.

By Sunday, things were getting ridiculous. There were drugs everywhere, the public open toilet stank to high heaven and there were bonfires all over the place, scorching the ground. The kids were hacking down timber from live trees for fuel. There were three stages and the noise got louder, the language over the speakers got stronger, and trouble spread beyond the site.

On the Monday, a public holiday, police chiefs decided the festival must end. Now it was originally planned to run for five days. Then the organisers decided to keep it going while the crowds were still interested – a couple of weeks even, if necessary.

When we reported this at the pink house our bosses went up the wall and decided to clear the park. It was a bad operation and our advice was ignored. I heard one of our top brass say there were only a thousand kids on that site.

We told him, "There's at least four thousand."

"The helicopter has counted the tents, there are 380."

"They're not all in tents, sir."

"Where are the other three thousand then?"

"In the open, under blankets, in sleeping bags, in the woods, under bits of polythene, in their cars, under their cars."

He listened but nothing would change his mind.

Coppers were called in from everywhere. On one shift in Oxford, which was meant to cover the entire city, all that was left was a sergeant running the desk and the front office, a young woman answering the switchboard, a uniform super and two bobbies. That's all. No Panda cars, no CID. A young woman and four coppers for eight hours through the night.

Yeah, we had a lot of blokes at Windsor, but there was no planning. I know what I am saying looks like being wise after the event, but we warned all the top brass well beforehand.

"If we're going in, hive them off in groups and clear them area by area," we said.

"If we have the manpower, there will be no trouble," said the assistant chief.

"Knock out that PA system first, sir, and dismantle those stages."

"Those hippies will have to go first."

And that was it. Honestly, we were banging our heads against a wall. We'd seen the mood of those kids as their hate really built up for the fuzz. Provoke a confrontation and they would go up like fireworks.

And they did. Our lads went in, a great line-up of uniforms like Colonel Custer's cavalry descended on the encampment.

"Wake up. Pack up. Clear off." That was their message.

It was eight o'clock in the morning and the kids were taken completely by surprise. Then the uniforms stood off for three hours. This was supposed to give the festival folk until 11 o'clock to disperse.

Dave and I are summoned to a hasty committee meeting. Guess what? They all want to stand and fight. We keep quiet. "Stand our ground," they say. "Rally round the stages. Get the press and television cameras down here."

Exactly as we had forecast the previous evening. And already there are complaints of harassment and damage to property, and various guys have taken police officers' numbers and are going to make official complaints.

Dave and I have our own conference as we pack our gear and drop the tent. We are not going to blow our cover, there's plenty to work on in the next few weeks from info we have picked up. We will rally round the stage, see what we can do.

Then comes a suggestion and it spreads round the site like fury. "Everyone strip off. We're all going to march naked through Windsor up to the castle and petition the Queen."

And some of the kids are already tearing off their clothes ready for the great trek.

"There's plenty of things I will do, Dave, for the greater good of mankind and this bloody police force."

"I know what you're gonna say, Pritch, but it could be funny…"

"Bollocks."

"Exactly."

"One thing I am not going to do is strip off and parade bare-arsed through Windsor."

"Come on, mate, you've got to agree, it would be a great laugh."

Dave Snell was right, it would have been funny. But it was all hippy-talk again, nothing came of the suggestion. Instead, everyone got stuck into the fight. Everyone, that is, apart from the Hare Krishna mob. They kept ringing their bells and chanting, and, quite honestly, I think three hours of listening to that lot drove some of our uniform fellas wild.

The battle was raging all round us. Dave and I knew our target was the public address system. The hippies clambered up the stage and stamped on the fingers of any copper trying to climb the scaffolding behind them. They were yelling messages down the mike, rallying everyone together until we got right under the staging and poured sand from fire buckets into the amplifiers.

Meanwhile, the place was going crazy. There were tents and sleeping bags going up in the air and full tins of beans and vegetables being hurled at coppers. Girls were spitting and getting their dresses torn. There were punch-ups all over the place.

The festival crowds were fighting dirty, no question about that, spitting and kicking and using bits of wood as clubs. There were blokes biting and girls scratching.

Our lads had to protect themselves and they had to do their job. But although there was plenty of provocation, I reckon some went over the mark with their arrests. If two coppers have a bloke bent double, with both arms way up behind his back, he's not in a position to create any more grief.

But they were running people off to waiting vans, and at the edge of the site there was an iron rail about a foot high. These bodies were bashing their shins and stumbling as they were virtually dragged the last few yards to the vehicles.

Plenty of fights got too far out of hand, as well. I didn't like it at all and, for my money, the real blame lay with the lack of police planning. Once again it was a bad operation, bad on both sides.

Dave and l were in a fix, but my fate was soon decided. Possibly the youngest copper I have ever seen grabbed me by the shoulder and said, "Come on, you." I shrugged a bit hard and elbowed him off. That was all.

"Right, you're under arrest."

"What for?"

"Assaulting a police officer."

Second year running. I'm getting a bad name, all 10 and a half stone of me, including the hair.

I was so annoyed at the way things were going on the site, and at this silly sod doing me for assault, I belted him. Thought it would teach him a bloody good lesson.

"There you are, now you've got something to bust me for."

As soon as we got down to the nick, I owned up and told this young copper his fortune.

"Tell a bloke to move on before you start manhandling. And if he struggles a bit, that's no cause for booking him on assault. Why aggravate the situation? If we turn him against us, a bloke might see a copper getting a kicking one night and do nothing about it. There's no way he is going to help out. He is anti-us forever."

Then I got back outside and started work again.

There were two big acid pushers on that site who took a fresh delivery the night before, and I wanted them busted before they could get away in the confusion. Not merely for the sake of getting them, but because we hoped to find some addresses that might give us contacts.

Plenty of drugs squad lads were still there in the park and we found one of these acid men. The other had gone off to hospital with his chick. When we got them both down to the nick they were clean, all their stuff had gone. But I had a look through their possessions while they were being questioned and pulled a couple of interesting names and phone numbers out of a book or diary.

There were bodies everywhere, so many kids got busted. We were using the documentation centres, where coppers were doing the charge and court paperwork, for detention as well. The cells were overflowing in several nicks for miles around.

Mick Strutt was in a drill hall with a young bobby, a uniform woman and about 30 clients. He was dead scared of losing prisoners – if one had walked, the bloody lot might have followed. So, Mick sends the woman to one of the police mobile canteens with orders to bring back coffee and doughnuts or anything she could get for the kids.

They were all grateful, none of them had eaten anything decent for days. Then Mick asked if anyone could play the piano, and a couple of guys had guitars, so he started them all off on a bloody great sing-song. Very cool, it took the heat out of the situation. And quite calmly he booked them all, one by one, while the rest were singing their socks off.

It was all done and dusted. The council workmen were on the site clearing up – it took an army of them 10 days – and the stations and the town were empty. Dave and I were dying for a drink. All through the weekend we went without, except for a couple of pints brought outside to us in a pub car park by one of the CID lads.

None of the pubs in Windsor would serve you or let you through the door, not if you looked like us.

We heard that some of the lads were up at the sergeants' mess in Windermere Barracks at Windsor, where a lot of the drugs squad who weren't undercover had been staying for the past five days. So, we headed up there.

I must admit we did look scruffy. And we didn't know you're not supposed to walk across the square in a barracks. We were nearly halfway across when this sergeant major started bawling and shouting and despatched two big guardsmen to escort us outside. They were regimental policemen or something and they didn't take a blind bit of notice when we explained we had a lot in common.

We had to phone up from outside and get one of the lads to come out and escort us to the mess so we could have a drink.

And the aggro wasn't over yet. There was an internal force inquiry to come, plus a seven-month Home Office investigation, interviews and statements and all that on top of the work that came from Windsor.

By now I was getting fed up with these Free Festivals the living in a tent, sleeping on the ground, eating rotten grub and getting busted for assault. They were a pain in more ways than one.

Chapter Eleven

Getting Stuffed

Edward Laxton: Around the same period of the Free Festivals, the early 1970s, Thames Valley Police were coming to terms with the outbreaks of violence that sometimes accompanied trade union disputes at the local British Leyland car production plants.

These disputes and stoppages were becoming a regular feature of life in Oxford and neighbouring Cowley, and for me, too. The Conservative Government's introduction of the three-day week piled on the pressure. Police needed to gather good intelligence to know what they were up against.

Three detectives from headquarters at Kidlington were sent on a course to learn the art of video filming, secretly as well as publicly. The force quietly established a bona fide, small film company, and militant outsiders who stirred-up trouble at the car plants, on marches and at mass meetings were quietly filmed and identified. The trade union intelligence file was building.

That film unit was employed at Windsor in 1974. I saw them quietly at work, and their evidence helped to prove the case against 242 complaints from members of the audience. It was also useful to prove the case against allowing a repeat performance at Windsor in 1975.

A senior detective at Slough police station began working on a secret intelligence investigation well before the end of 1974. He had a team of six, frequently boosted by members of the drugs squad for special tasks. And it was he who came up with the acronym for Operation STUFF... Stop The Unlawful Free Festivals.

They infiltrated the festival organisers, they had the names and pictures of all the committee members, including Detective Sergeant David Snell. They had aliases, various addresses and more besides. All the committee had form, previous convictions for possession or supplying drugs, a few had committed assaults or robberies, too.

All bar two were on Social Security, only one had a proper rent book, none had a mortgage and many of them lived in squats. The dossier being gathered by the officers on Operation STUFF was also building nicely.

The master stroke by the opposition was not to go for an all-out ban, but to suggest an alternative site, one that was ideal for a music festival, especially a free music festival.

Watchfield is a village on the Oxfordshire-Wiltshire border, with white-washed, thatched cottages and 2000 residents alongside the relatively quiet A420, Oxford to Swindon road. A deserted, former military site – with the accent on deserted – and the Free Festival-goers were directed there for three days, over August Bank Holiday in 1975.

Miles from anywhere, the only similarity between Watchfield and Windsor is the initial letter W – they never went back for 1976...

Operation STUFF

Martyn Pritchard: I don't know who was more determined that a people's Free Festival should go ahead the following year – the hippies or the new Labour Government's Home Secretary, Roy Jenkins.

After the Windsor punch-up, the barrage of questions in the House of Commons and the mammoth inquiry into the police operation, everything pointed to the necessity for some really firm organisation. That became the theme for 1975.

Everyone was getting themselves well-prepared – the town and the residents of Windsor, the hippies and especially ourselves. The

Chief Constable was obviously taking no chances in the light of the previous year's debacle so he gave the go-ahead for Operation STUFF.

A more or less permanent group of half-a-dozen detectives working out of Slough got cracking, and from time to time one or two more like me went over on loan. We had to infiltrate the other side and see what the bastards were getting up to.

A full report was needed, secret or otherwise, to prove to the mandarins at the Home Office and specifically the Home Secretary himself, that hangers-on around genuine festival organisers were criminals planning several ways to flout the law.

The free shows were now being used to demonstrate people power and freedom for kids to do their own thing. They aimed to organise 10,000 people for a direct confrontation with the police. It was mob rule and anarchy, all set to pop music.

Lots of these people believed they were becoming untouchable, and by early 1975 they weren't far wrong. For my money, Operation STUFF was a great success. When the background reports on this anarchy movement were read by the top-brass – the decision-makers – the other side was well and truly stuffed.

Organisation on our side certainly put paid to Ubi Dwyer, the real leader. His antics at Windsor had landed him in court and his case was repeatedly adjourned. Ubi was quite happy until he suddenly woke up to the fact that he would be inside during next year's festival. If it came off.

Well, Ubi went to gaol and the festival did come off, but not at Windsor. The residents won a High Court injunction to prevent it being held in the Great Park again.

Now civil servants and politicians don't like being crossed, even if they're wrong. They usually get their own back somehow. It was obvious some Very Important People were all for a Free Festival going ahead. The Chief Constable was against it, and privately he must have spelled it all out.

I don't know whether they simply ignored him or worked towards a compromise. No one could entirely ignore the revelations of the Operation STUFF report and they all had to take notice of the High Court, you cannot flout an injunction.

So, they looked around for an alternative site and came up with Watchfield. For us on the ground, when that was announced, we were knocked out. This former RAF base between Oxford and Swindon was just a few hundred yards inside our police boundary. The chief was furious – everyone was furious – he thought the Outer Hebrides would have been too near. But the following year, he had the last laugh, we all did really.

Well, I told you this mob were becoming untouchable. That year at Watchfield proved it. The site was definitely a no-go area and although I went in to live and work undercover again, it was all low-key. The air station had a definite perimeter, with fencing, and any police action would occur on the outside.

Everything was laid on for the festival-goers: water, toilets, even a telephone. They had the run of all the buildings, living in the old huts and hangars and using the control tower as their headquarters. That would have been ideal for the police because it overlooked the entire ground. But no, not bloody likely.

One of our lads on drugs squad, John Purnell, used the old trick and quietly joined the festival committee, volunteering for switchboard duty in the tower. Only one phone but he could pick up a mine of information answering it. Marvellous.

But he was ordered out when the guvnors heard. That was aggro, incitement, they said, and it wasn't allowed. The festival organisers were supposed to pay for these services when all the money was collected. How daft – when they went home there were still plenty of debts that would never be settled.

We didn't see why we should rough it again. I worked Watchfield with Graham Jones and we hired a van for that long weekend on the site, with the tent pitched alongside. No aggro but we were thinking ahead, looking to the future, this lot were our regular customers.

Plenty of drugs squad there and other coppers living undercover as well. We had three lads with us from another force, operating totally differently. Their hair was just below the ears because their chief would not tolerate it any longer. And they could wear jeans outside, but at work it was collars and ties.

They kept tidying up our little camp and we kept messing it up again. One of these blokes even packed some shoe cleaning kit for the weekend! They had to go, and my drugs squad mate Graham and I were on our own again.

We saw some amazing sights. Watchfield really was a total no-go area. The Release organisation had their tent and outside was a van with a line-up of pictures of drugs squad officers taken at Windsor the previous year. A notice read: *These are all DS. Have you seen them here?*

This really got up our nose. I mean Release was a legal advice outfit, particularly in the area of drugs, and got a Government grant. The wife of Roy Jenkins, the Home Secretary who gave the big OK for Watchfield, was on the management board. And here were some people connected with Release not so much giving advice on drugs problems as providing info about the drugs squad.

I suppose they did a lot of good work and were an outfit the kids could turn to, but we had one very bad deal from them. They were running a medical tent with a sort of casualty department, and one night we picked up a young woman in a really bad way.

She crashed into our little area in the middle of a diabolical trip. Well, we settled her down and I waded across the site to get someone from Release to help. It was the Saturday night and the festival was roaring. I brought this guy back and he started talking to the girl, and calming her down. He had some experience in that direction. Then suddenly, he gets all excited.

"You're not on acid?" he asks her.

"No, I had some psilo."

"Where, where did you get it?"

Then she goes all vague and he keeps pressing her about her source. This girl is on the old magic mushrooms, the chemical psilocybin. South Americans have been tripping out on that stuff for hundreds of years and I heard stories about hippies who were successfully cultivating these fabulous fungi in the Welsh mountains.

Finally, she gives out a name and directions to a tent. "Hey, man, that's great," he says to me. "See ya."

"What about the chick?"

"Listen, I'm off to score some of that psilo."

"But what about this chick? She's in a bad way."

"She'll be OK. Listen, I haven't had any of that stuff for a couple of years. If that's about, it will bomb out fast."

"Aren't you going to take her with you."

"Keep an eye on her." Then he winks. "With a bit of luck I'll be right alongside if I can score from her source." And he goes off at a run, leaving us to call an ambulance.

That was one representative of Release. And the next day, another acted as a judge in a giant joint-rolling competition. The fella who won rolled one 18ins long, and they all passed it round on the stage.

There was a police video of this, shot secretly, and I have seen it at headquarters. But no one was allowed to do anything at the time – and here was a straightforward drugs possession offence right in front of our eyes. And there was a fella there we called the Rizla Man. You need cigarette papers to roll joints, right?

Well, this geezer had a 4ft high top hat with R-I-Z-L-A written up the side and he was loaded with fag papers. He was also weighed down with dope, and he went around at Watchfield with his hat on openly selling his gear. But we weren't allowed to touch him. He went free.

If he had stepped off the site, we would have nicked him, or anyone else for that matter. But when he went outside, he was clean, completely sold out.

But what would happen when they came back in? Obviously, if they went off for fresh supplies they would be returning loaded, and that was when they risked getting busted. So, we worked on that angle.

There was a screwball at Watchfield who went round naked most of the time with a beautiful black woman called Angela. He was a magistrate's son and was knocking out speed powder fast and furious. And we bought some.

He must have sold plenty through those four days, three thousand quids' worth. One day he told us he was off to pick up more, so my colleague Graham and I raced off to find our contact man, who was hanging around for us to feed information. We wanted to get the speed merchant followed and busted with his new load on board. But no contact – couldn't find anyone anywhere.

Naturally, you can't wander off the site and walk up to a copper and tell him to get his book out, but you can get yourself busted and talk to them while you're being dragged off. That's what we tried.

I spotted a police car, so I went up and hammered on the roof and started swearing at a couple of uniform inspectors inside. No reaction. I twisted their wing mirror off, and they drove away without a word. See what I mean, untouchable. I couldn't get busted and I was trying hard.

So off went this magistrate's son for more speed. This stuff gives you terrific energy. You want to race around or dance all night, you can do without food and sleep. Mixed with booze it's even stronger, and the effects last longer. But it has a very bad come-down, leaves you with a wicked hangover and can be very addictive.

MBK, the chemical in it, wasn't too difficult to come by because it either goes into drugs or is used for hardening floor tiles. Matey was getting his supplies from an illicit lab somewhere in London.

He was supplying a lot of bands at Watchfield and he told us business had never been so good. He was also pushing home-grown cannabis. A mate of his worked for the Forestry Commission and was quietly raising plants in woodland glades. Very nice.

All we could do was trace his address by the registration number of his Transit van and, without him realising it, confirm that by mentioning North London during general conversation with him.

We stuck in a report and got him busted later. When he saw us at court he thought better of fighting. He changed his plea to guilty for supplying drugs at the festival, and he copped a fine. But if we had done him down there at Watchfield with all his gear on board, I am sure he would have gone inside.

The same thing happened with the Henry Higgins commune. They were a weird lot who went to all the festivals. They all called themselves Henry Higgins, even the girls. It's the only name you can get out of them.

They were doing acid again that year, and a lot of it was bad acid, providing some very nasty trips. We pressed for this lot to get done for their own protection. Initially, this was OK'd and we set up a raid on their campsite.

I'm not kidding, we even got them videoed, on-site, while they were dealing. The copper handling the camera was obviously putting himself at considerable risk. Then half-an-hour before the raid, one of the guvnors clamps down and instructs us to leave them alone. See who you can identify and bust them later, he says. At that time, we could have arrested say eight or 10. But we could only get a positive ID on two fellas.

This pair both had vehicles and drew their social security on site. Their turn came a couple of weeks later, and they put their hands up and pleaded guilty. But we'd had to miss another golden opportunity.

That was the time I had a big problem with my sister's wedding, when my mum washed all my hippy gear. In fact, clothes were more noticeable by their absence that year. The weather was pretty good, and the freedom kick went to everyone's head. Hundreds of festival-goers stripped off and loads of the girls were topless.

And us? For undercover read uncover. Three of our drugs squad girls decided to go bare-breasted.

The camera operators were using a van that they moved quietly around the site, parked up and filmed from inside.

They got some great shots of an ice cream seller. He had one of those vans with chimes, and they filmed him working like stink for 20 minutes. People were flocking to his counter, but not one of them was buying ice cream. He was scoring cannabis and pills.

We arranged a surprise as he left the site. Now I owed Vince Castle, one of our lads, a trick after he had a joke at my expense on another job. Just for laughs, of course, Vince was a great bloke.

I briefed Vince, who comes from Gloucester, to get in with the ice cream man, and stressed how important it was for him to maintain his cover. Act up, go a bit heavy and impress the fella, I said. Then get at the suppliers behind him.

Then I briefed the team who were going to do the bust, uniform lads from my own force who didn't know Vince. They were in a special operations group, working plain-clothes that weekend, and I told them Vince was a bad bastard who had taken a couple of coppers with him on previous arrests.

"You may have to drop him, he's a bit of an animal," I warned.

They dropped him all right. As soon as Vince began his act, he got two big coppers on top of him and realised he was in for a hammering.

He couldn't care less about his cover then.

When they realised he was on our side, there were big apologies all round. Vince sussed I was calling the play in two minutes flat. So that made us even.

That was about the only laugh we had at Watchfield. It was one long disappointment, especially if you were DS. We were working against drugs full-time, yet we were forced to stand back and watch all these people knocking them out right, left and centre – and getting away with it.

Sure, we knocked a few off later but only a handful. And even that was spoiled.

We wanted to show these bloody junkies life was not so free and easy. We arranged a series of off-site busts, say 14 days after Watchfield, all at the same time. All over the country, kids who had given us two fingers were going to get busted and the press coverage would show them and their mates that the fuzz was still very much in business.

The next week, many of us were putting our heads on the block again, moving back into drugs scenes no less wicked than Watchfield. I would soon be focusing on a pub in Reading.

A 32-year-old Jamaican, known as 'The Count', was a brash, almost comic character. He was suspected of being a drugs pusher. The Count held court in The Star public house in the centre of Reading, a seedy hang-out, in the 1970s.

Soon after Watchfield, police traced one tiny acid tablet. A 16-year-old girl had swallowed it, gone on a trip and subsequently died – attributed to the LSD. She had lived in Preston, but the tab came from The Star, 200 miles away. Her boyfriend, who was in the army, had bought it. The Count didn't sell that acid, but when the decision was taken to clean up the nightly drugs scene in that pub, which was more and more in the open, he was an obvious target.

I went into that scene and had little trouble befriending him. But the Count took me into a frightening confrontation with four other dealers. The operation ended in a dangerous near-fiasco and at the end I copped a lot of credit, but I also took some bloody big risks.

Chapter Twelve

A Ton of Caribbean Grass

Edward Laxton: Many years after the original edition of this book was published, I was in Bermuda. Another exotic drugs story was under way and I made the connection. I remembered Martyn Pritchard telling me he had been offered a ton of grass – "any time, reasonable price, no problem" – cargoed into London's Heathrow Airport from the West Indies.

He told the CDIU (Central Drugs Intelligence Unit) and let it lie. The CDIU no longer exists but was an intelligence-gathering unit sanctioned by the Home Office in those far off days. He told me about this offer as well.

As the Mirror's district reporter in the Thames Valley, I was interested because Heathrow was very much part of my territory. I heard the same story a time or two, about the "ton of grass" flown in bulk from the Caribbean. It was never more than a story – until 1982. Seven years had gone by since Martyn's report reached the CDIU, but the offer held good.

Annually, the Miss World contest was big business, a big TV attraction, local title-holders elected in various countries with the final in London each November. In 1982 Miss Bermuda was busted with drugs in her luggage, not for her personal use, because this was a large consignment. The following year at trial, the unfortunate beauty queen was sent to Holloway Prison for 15 months.

Back in 1979, Miss Bermuda came to London and won the Miss World title, so the drugs story three years later was a bit tasty. There had always been a whiff of smuggling attaching itself to the Miss World jamboree. I went to Bermuda to gather some background to write up post-trial, timing my trip to coincide with a visit from a couple of drugs officers with Customs based at Heathrow.

On neutral and friendly ground, I wanted to pick their brains. Meanwhile, Customs and Excise, at a higher level, decided on a quid-pro-quo gambit. While we were in Hamilton, the island's capital, they told me C and E had written officially to warn British Airways of 'very firm action' if they didn't put their house in order – that is to say, stop carrying one ton of grass at a time into London Airports, which their guys could never find.

Under an ancient piracy-cum-smuggling act of 1361, they actually threatened to 'impound any vessel found to be carrying contraband'. The vessel in question was £41,000,000-worth of BA airliner, from their TriStar fleet, flying passengers and cargo either from the Bahamas or Barbados, via Bermuda, to London.

If the story broke under my byline from Bermuda, Customs figured it might save them some embarrassment, because it would not look as if they had leaked it to me in London. But I was certain BA would lie through their corporate hat and flatly deny the story that Customs had sent them this warning. And no amount of supporting memos could make newspaper lawyers brave enough to let the paper run the story in the face of an official denial.

Conveniently, I knew the BA chief press officer, Ted Duggan – we had worked together at a Fleet Street news agency. I phoned and hit him with the story and within half-an-hour, as I anticipated, Duggan put out a comprehensive, 100 per cent denial. And that really annoyed Customs, especially the senior officers in London.

At my request, Customs provided the initials in the top, left-hand corner of the letter sent to BA – no wording, just the date and initials – of the secretary and her boss dictating the letter. They also gave me similar details on BA's reply, the letter in response to their warning. Both letters were more than a month old, but no action had followed.

I gave Ted Duggan the initials on both letters when I phoned him again. He called me back in Bermuda, asking to retract their original denial and replace it with 'no comment'. Get stuffed! I demanded two new statements: 1) not for publication, admitting receipt of the Customs warning letter – that was for our lawyer – and 2) for publication, something along the lines of... 'We cannot comment while our investigations are under way.'

Otherwise, we would publish our story along with BA's original denial. The high-level ramifications of the follow-up stories needed no explaining, to Ted Duggan or the BA management.

All of this happened over a period of about two hours, with the full connivance of Dan Ferrari, my news editor, and the end result was a very juicy splash.

And another splash the next day, with every other newspaper carrying the story now, when Customs decided to cash-in and release all the correspondence in full. A week later BA announced the sacking of 108 ground staff in the Bahamas, Barbados, Bermuda and London.

On the Daily Mirror, we had the original story about the threatened seizure of the £41 million TriStar to ourselves. The Daily Express's Heathrow reporter was out in Bermuda with me and he also wrote it, but their lawyers were chicken-hearted – until our first edition hit the street.

But seven years had gone by since Martyn Pritchard put in the original report of: 'a ton of Caribbean grass for sale' as you will read here now.

A Knife at My Throat

Martyn Pritchard: Never volunteer. Very sound advice that, and we aren't just talking about not putting your hand up. If the boss asks, "Have you got much happening?" and you reply, "Not a lot..." that's still volunteering.

Muggins got caught by that simple question early in 1975, and I was lucky to see the year out. Halfway through that particular job,

I was in a car miles away from my usual territory, with a bloody great West Indian fella I had only just met. He was holding a knife at my throat, while three of his friends looked on.

One of his mates had taken me along and made the introductions. He had offered me a ton of grass. No kidding, one ton of grass, the actual leaves from the plant, flown in from somewhere in the Caribbean, delivered to anywhere I wanted. Now, if that was true, it was a trail worth following.

And it all started with my admission that I wasn't very busy, which was true but not very intelligent. "We've got bother in Reading," said Detective Inspector Dick Lee, who was now the guvnor of our drugs squad. "Most of the drugs action over there seems to revolve around a character called The Count. We have got to bust his operation and you're going to join him."

So, I was pulled off most other duties and told to concentrate on Reading. Graham Barnard was running the drugs squad over there with two fellas and a woman, and he briefed me – the Count was supposed to be dealing in speed, acid and a lot of grass.

Now some pushers stay well in the background while others, like the Count, seem to revel in the limelight. He had been mentioned by just about everyone on the local scene. He was supposed to be a painter and decorator, but he was too busy doing other things, like drugs.

He must have thought he was immune from the law because getting alongside this fella was too easy. The pub he used in Reading was The Star, so I went in to clock him. I couldn't show out too strong because I'd been on a couple of raids there.

The Count was really flash and stood out a mile. He was straight into the rum and coke, large ones, and straight into the dealing, too. Nothing concealed. Fellas were walking up like bees round a honeypot. A few quiet words, out came the money and the Count slipped them a deal from a pocket.

All I planned that night at The Star was a little soft observation.

I was moving around the bar, nodding and chatting. Junkie joints are just like other pubs for picking up conversations with anyone else on their tod. In fact, you would be more obvious if you kept to yourself.

It was like one big happy family in the pub, a really grotty place in those days. Just like a big cave, with tattered pop posters peeling away from the walls, very few customers over 30, beer slopped all over the bar and floor, but good music on the machine. It was the in-place for youngsters in the town.

I had all my gear on, including the Lennon glasses, to stop anyone recognising me. Luckily the busts I was on in there, about a year earlier, happened very fast. And although my hair was the same length, I wore more formal clothes on the raids.

Anyway, I stopped by the Count and started chatting. The opportunity was too great to ignore.

"You're the man I want to see," I told him.

"Yeah, why me?"

"I'm Joe, I'm told you're a good connection."

"Why come to me, man?"

"Oh, well, er Dave Little – you know Dave? He's scored in here and he told me you're the man."

"Where's Dave now?"

"He's just gone out of town, but he's coming back soon. You know him."

"OK, man, it's cool. What do you want?"

"Just a couple of trips if you've got them."

And that's all I needed. We didn't deal right then but carried on talking. And he was so flash, so bloody cocky, he wouldn't admit not knowing anybody.

I didn't even have to mention the non-existent Dave again. Just before closing time the Count said, "Two pounds," held my wrist and slipped two acid tabs into my hand. "Phone me if you want some more," he said and gave me his number.

I paid him, finished my lager, nodded to a couple of guys going out the door who didn't know me from Adam, and concluded a very successful evening's work.

Two days later I phoned and went round to see the Count. He lived in the Caversham area of Reading with a cracking white chick named Sue, who had dropped out of Reading University. She lived up to everything the local drugs squad had said about her – lovely, long blonde hair, intelligent – really nice. God knows what she was doing living with a pusher.

She led me into this spotless pad, very tastefully furnished, good lighting, very expensive stereo and a cocktail cabinet. They might have been Mr and Mrs Suburbia. It seemed weird to start talking about drugs in such nice surroundings but I was quickly brought back to reality. He threw me his bag and said, "Roll me a joint, man?"

I rolled him a nice, loose joint while he watched carefully. "You do much?" he asked.

"Enough, man."

"Yeah, how much? Tell me all." He was smoking the joint now and that loosens the tongue.

"You tell me, how much you want? I can probably do it."

"No, no, man." And he roared with laughter. "I don't buy, I got plenty. I figured you wanted to deal from me."

The Count had swallowed one of the oldest drugs squad ploys. Now he couldn't accuse me of setting him up by asking him to supply me. And my apparently naive offer to supply him had lowered his guard.

"What's your scene then, man?" he asked.

I gave him the chat. The first bit was true. "I work for a very big organisation not far from here. They're always interested in a deal, they're into drugs in a big way, any kind of drugs."

I reckon that accurately described Thames Valley Police drugs squad.

"Money is never a problem, as long as we're talking sensible prices," I told him. "I don't know too much, I mainly set up hash for the firm.

"And they're very strict with us, we're not supposed to use anything. Because once we've been busted, even on a little possession, that's it – we're out. They won't touch us if we're known to the fuzz.

"They're heavy, man. On the other hand, they look after everyone in the firm. This is strictly between you and me, and you only deal with me, OK?"

The Count was impressed. "Sounds interesting. Come and see me again day after tomorrow. We might be able to trade."

In those days I had a dark blue Volkswagen Fastback and I'd taken the precaution of putting a block on its number at the vehicle registration bureau computer. Anyone checking it would get the reply, "Owner subject of drugs intelligence". That could have meant anything.

The computer had also been programmed to warn our police headquarters if any check was made.

All this was just as well, because he was going to get a good look at my motor.

The Count didn't drive, he went everywhere by taxi. He told me when I went back to his flat again that I would have to drive him to meet his people if we were going to deal anything big. We'd heard he was dealing in Moroccan cannabis resin and some hash oil – high value merchandise – so he probably had a number of sources.

"On the other hand, Joe," he went on a bit furtively, "you and me can do a straight deal and make some extra bread if your people are interested in grass."

Now grass, as I've said, is chopped up bits of marijuana plants. It's a weaker, lighter smoke and cheaper because the growers don't have to go through any complicated production process. It's also more difficult to smuggle because of its bulk, but it's a great favourite with the Caribbean community, there and here.

"My people are interested in everything if it's the right price," I said.

'How about a ton of grass?"

Now that's a lot, and I was genuinely surprised. "The amount is no problem, but how do you get it in?"

"No sweat, man. Delivered here by air, straight from the islands."

And now he was all smiles and proud again. He could see I was impressed with his offer. "I don't know about grass, I'll put it to them. What's the price?" I asked.

"This is where you and me can make some bread, Joe. I can deal to you at £75,000 and they don't cut it until I place the order. Wholesale here, it's about £200,000 maximum. If you offer it to your people at half that price... you read me?" That would leave me a cool twenty-five grand.

"Yeah, I read you, Count. That's great. Where do we pick it up, here?"

"No man, we will deliver wherever you say. I have a lot of brothers back home and one of them works for an airline. The freight bit is no problem."

"OK, I'll talk to my people. But what about the resin? We've been doing a lot lately."

He explained roughly how much he could do straightaway and asked me to have the money ready by the next Monday – £3000. I was to pick him up at the flat and take him to Bristol. No more details were discussed and I left.

The Count was obviously confident the grass supply would be no trouble. I thought a few people in high places should know there were dealers talking about flying in grass a ton at a time. I am sure with the right contacts it wasn't difficult, so I put in a report for the CDIU (Central Drugs Intelligence Unit).

To be honest, I expected to get a call and a request to come up with more information, but I never heard another thing. No one in

London was interested but Customs and Excise never had a set-up like ours.

I had to keep close to the local problems and a meeting was called in Reading to discuss an operation for the Monday. Graham Barnard, the local guvnor, Tim Todd from Oxford and Bob Buckley from Windsor were going to help me.

To set up something like this you have to work out two plans. One is how you, posing as the dealer, personally handle the people offering the drugs. The other is the side they don't see – tailing, surveillance and the signals that let your colleagues know when to move in.

We came up with a very good operation – which somehow went horribly wrong.

We decided I would say to the Count, "The money is in another car. It will follow us to Bristol and we'll leave it parked up while you take me to see the drugs." My pose would be that I always dealt like this. I didn't intend to get ripped off by anyone.

"If I am satisfied with the drugs, we return to the money car, bring it back and make the exchange."

Tim Todd and Bob Buckley would be with the money in Bob's green Volvo, which had a police radio. A surveillance team from Reading and Bristol would follow Bob's car until he stopped, then tail me, keeping out of the way until we returned to the Volvo for the exchange and I gave the signal for the arrest.

This seemed ideal because it would involve me going back to the Volvo apparently to say, "Wait here" and later on "OK, everything's cool." If the plan was changed at all, a message could be passed over Bob's radio.

Now we had a plan. But we still needed money. It is possible to get cash officially from the police, but it's not easy, believe me. And it takes too long. Not only is there too much paperwork, but other people get nervous even though the bread is only out on loan. They also want to be part of the operation.

So what do you do? You use your own money.

We were dead keen to bust this team, but we needed enough notes to make the Count's contacts think we'd got £3000. There was nowhere near enough time to acquire that amount officially, even if it were possible. So, we didn't even ask, we got some bread together ourselves.

It was a great laugh going round the banks that Monday morning. I had a lot of cash in my account because the previous week I had sold my house in Abingdon. Thanks to rising property prices, I'd made about £2000 profit.

Bob had about £200, which he drew, and Tim took out £80 – nearly all his cash. "I want it all in one pound used notes and you can have it all back tomorrow, love," he told the cashier, who must have thought he was mad. But it wasn't so funny for me – I was putting in by far the biggest share.

I needed that money for another house, but at the time I was waiting for the lawyers, the surveyors and all the red tape. I handed the cash to Tim and Bob, who had a big joke telling me what they would do with it if things went wrong!

That morning, we parked the Volvo about a mile from the Count's pad and I went on, picked him up and explained everything to him. He didn't particularly like the arrangements, but I told him, "This is the way I always deal, that way I don't have to trust anybody."

And I went on, "I haven't exposed you. The others who drove down with the bread this morning are waiting, they don't know where you live. If you don't like the arrangement, OK. No sweat, we'll call it off. But the bread stays with them until I see the drugs. Then you can decide how we deal."

Once he saw the money inside the briefcase back at the Volvo, in tens, fivers and ones, the Count was hooked. Even though it was short, it looked the right amount.

We set off for Bristol straightaway and pulled into a lay-by on a road into the city to drop the Volvo. Everything was going to plan, and even I hadn't spotted the surveillance vehicles.

As we moved off from the lay-by I saw the first of five cars allotted to tail us, switching positions according to police practice. Whether I was in my own car or got into another, their drivers had been told to follow.

Now the fun begins. The Count directs me quite a way until we hit the docks area and pull up at a small terraced house. There are three West Indian guys inside. One asks for the car key and goes outside to search it. Another searches me, taking everything out of my pockets and running his hands all over my body. I'm protesting like mad but at least I'm not wired up.

They're satisfied at last, and we pile into a red Hillman Hunter outside, leaving my car behind. The wheelman drives like a maniac, not only fast and mostly on the wrong side of the road but hurtling round corners and doubling back on himself.

We lose the surveillance team very sharpish, although this Stirling Moss does make one mistake. He goes, left, left and left again and pretty soon, we overtake one of the tailing cars. We have driven in a complete circle!

But I'm not too worried about surveillance. I'm thinking the dangerous time will come when we arrive back at the Volvo. Little do I know. I tell them, very sarcastically, "I admire your security." No one says a word and the Count holds up his hand. So, I stay silent.

We arrive at another house, still down in the docks, and the Hunter roars away. Inside we go through another search.

"Right, man, we go this way," says the guy named Ricky. And we head through the kitchen door, up the garden, over the wall and into the house which fronts on to the parallel street. They are all back-to-back buildings, ideal for this purpose.

When we get outside again, there's another car waiting and we roar off again, this time to a pub about a mile away.

"Go inside and drink lager. You'll be OK," says Ricky.

"Listen, man, this ain't the way to deal. All this shit, what the hell is this all about? That maniac at the wheel, we're lucky to be alive," I tell him.

"Cool it, man. You're OK," says the Count. "Just do as Ricky asks. We'll deal real soon."

And they drive off leaving me on the pavement. So, I go in the pub and I am the only white man in there. But no one takes a blind bit of notice, so I figure I am expected and I order a pint of lager, as instructed. It's a grotty pub, graffiti written and carved on every wall, hasn't been swept for a week. Most of the customers are junkies. Ever since we got into that area, I've seen nothing but dirt and depression. What a hole.

Naturally, by now there's no sign of my tail. They have found the house where the Hunter dropped me and are sitting outside. They don't know I've gone out the back way. And I can't make a phone call in that pub.

My new chums are obviously a very heavy team and well organised. This situation is ideal for them. While I'm holed up in this pub with a lot of volunteer 'minders', they can tour the area to make absolutely sure they haven't been followed.

Just as I'm ordering another half of lager, two great big West Indians come in, nod at me and hold the door open. When I get outside, another car, a huge black Vauxhall, is waiting and the two fellas get into the back seat with me in the middle. There is no Count and no Ricky, but a new driver and a fourth man in the front. They're all wearing sunglasses

We drive right down to the river and pull up by a rubbish tip. The front-seat passenger, who's got a nasty scar by his right eye that looks pretty recent, goes to the boot and comes back with a canvas bag.

He throws it straight into my lap and inside there's about 50 lbs of Packy Black resin, more than I expected. But as I pick up the first slab to smell it, all four of the guys pull knives and the bloke on my right puts his blade right up against my throat.

"We think you iz de pig." They are the first words any of these bastards has spoken to me and I'll never forget them. I can feel the blade on my skin. I can't see whether it's the sharp side, I can just feel the edge of the metal.

"Bollocks. Forget we ever met," I say, not moving my neck. But when I lift a hand to take this knife away from my throat, another arm restrains me. Where the bloody hell are my tails now?

"Are you de pig, man?" says my mate with the knife. The other three are holding their blades up in the air where I can see them very clearly. It's ridiculous, they're trying to frighten me – and they're not doing a bad job, in that respect – but there's no way I am going to admit being DS, not with those things waving around.

"What is all this shit?" I have to bulldoze my way out of the situation. I don't know what will happen otherwise.

"This is no way to deal. Let's call the whole thing off." But I can't dislodge the knife.

"Just prove to us, man, you ain't de pig." My mate is getting boring.

Then they all started. "We don't like this set-up. Why hide the bread? Why don't you trust the Count?"

And then it gets even uglier. The knife slides from the side of my throat round to the front.

"Pig, they ain't so certain but I am. I know you iz de pig," says my man again. "And if you iz, I'm going to stick you, man. You got that?"

I can do without all this. So, I get ugly. "Listen, friend, my firm are very, very heavy."

I give him a piece of news right then that is very, very accurate. "If anything happens to me, they'll get annoyed and you'll wish you'd never been born. And they will definitely make sure you don't do any more business."

Well, his friends finally persuaded him to put the blade away. But when I got a look at the time, I estimated I'd been trapped there with the knife at my throat, and the other three blades waving around, for 25 minutes.

What happened then was the saddest part of the entire operation, especially after the ordeal I had been through.

First, we drove back to the house where I left my own car, and found the Count and the Hunter waiting. The surveillance team were there, too. When they realised I must have gone out the back of the second house, they had moved to watch my Fastback, and were very pleased when the Hunter turned up there again, even though I wasn't in it. At least they had picked up a trail of sorts again.

Now they see me arriving and, what's more important, I see them. What a relief! As I get out of the back seat, I tug at my beard, the signal that I've seen the drugs.

The bloke with the scar grabs the bag with the dope, opens the boot of the Hunter and chucks it inside. Then he gets into my car with me and the Count, so we can go off and get the money. All the others pile in the Hunter and sit there waiting for us to return and do the deal.

Now is the moment we have all been waiting for. While we are going to meet Tim and Bob in the Volvo and get the three grand, the surveillance team will bust the Hunter and everyone in it. Then when we get back, we bust the Count and scarface. That's the theory!

It takes us 10 minutes to reach the Volvo, and nobody says a bloody word. Scarface comes with me to see the briefcase, nods, and I say to Bob, "Follow us."

We go back to my car. As the West Indian's getting in, I say, "Oh, I forgot to tell them they've got to take the dope back because I'm dropping the Count off in Reading."

And I dash back across the road to the lay-by and tell the boys,

"The stuff is in the Hunter but warn everybody, they've got knives." Then I rush back to my car.

Another 10-minute drive and when I turn the corner, I expect to see cars all over the road, a load of guys flat against the wall, hands on head, and a lot of coppers frisking them and turning out the car.

Nothing! Absolutely sod all, that's what I can see.

A quiet, peaceful road. The red Hunter is still there with a lot of smiling West Indian guys inside, facing us with the engine running. I pull past and stop on the same side and the Volvo goes by me and stops.

Then, as I start to get out, it happens. Eight cars roar up and coppers start tumbling out. One motor, which has been following Bob in the Volvo, pulls right up alongside the Hunter, facing the opposite way, and the copper who is driving, flashes his warrant card and says, "Crime squad. Pull over."

Of course, the Hunter guns away from us like mad. Not only is the crime squad car facing the wrong way, it's blocking the road for anyone else who could have followed.

I couldn't believe it. Twenty coppers had sat there doing nothing for 20 minutes and now police response cars are skidding and bouncing off the kerbs, trying to get after the Hunter.

I don't have time for much thought, though. I'm still playing a part and I have to react as if I'm a big dealer trying to evade arrest.

I spot Bob driving off fast, and the Count, scarface and I run like mad as a couple of police teams make for us. Well, Scarface got away, but the Count and I got lifted. We were the only ones. Two of the cars chased the Hunter but it had gone. And even though the Bristol surveillance team knew who was in the Hunter and the Vauxhall, we had lost our evidence.

If there's no drugs, there are no dealers to arrest. In a court of law you need forensic proof that what you saw was a controlled drug. On our way to Bristol police station for questioning after we were busted, the Count said to me, "Sorry, man."

That was all, but it gave me an idea that we might not have lost everything. Maybe my fake bid to avoid arrest had fooled him.

"Stay cool, man, they've got nothing on us," I told him as we got out of the car and were separated. My 'questioning' was going to be a police de-briefing session. The Count was in for some heavy interrogation while we debated his future.

He didn't take my advice. The coppers who quizzed him told me the Count coughed the lot. He told them why we had come to Bristol, how much drugs were involved, the money, my name, details of my firm, everything.

Well, you need more than a voluntary statement to bust a bloke properly, and without doing him for attempting to supply me — which would involve me showing out — the Count was clean.

Tim and Bob came into Bristol nick on foot, separately. We had a lot to say about the jerk who buggered up our operation and we would dearly have liked to talk to him.

"At least my money's safe," I said.

"We were going to talk to you about money, Mart," said Tim Todd. "We thought you might like to pay a third share of what it will cost us to repair the Volvo."

"What are you talking about?"

"Tim locked us both out of the car," Bob explained. "We had to get back in and look after you and your precious money," Tim added.

"So, he broke the back window and climbed in," said Bob.

Great. A fine way to look after me — locked out of their car in a lay-by miles away while some big ugly bastard was threatening to stick me.

And when I told them my tale of the 25 minutes with a knife at my throat, Tim Todd says to me, "You're getting ever so serious, Martyn. I bet all you were worried about was us doing your money if you got knifed."

"Balls," I said.

And the three of us went on a very lively binge in Bristol, just to forget about that bloody knife and the entire operation.

Chapter Thirteen

Well Connected

Edward Laxton: The Count had many connections. From such unromantic meeting places as the rubbish tip near Bristol docks, the trail led Martyn Pritchard to a commune with the sweet-sounding title Let-It-Be.

According to the lyrics of The Beatles song, *When I find myself in times of trouble, Mother Mary comes to me, whispering words of wisdom, let it be, let it be…*

But the members of this commune, the hippies who lived in a rambling, seven-bedroomed house on the Bath Road in Reading, did not listen to those words of wisdom.

One of their number was a guy known as Joe. He smuggled cannabis resin and hash oil to England from Morocco, by road through Spain and France. That trail was littered with the victims of double-cross, clever police work, customs experience and good information.

Joe found himself in times of trouble when his ferry docked at Algeciras, next door to Gibraltar. The Spanish customs found the illegal cargo in his van and he was whisked off to prison. And Spanish cells were reputed to be among the least hospitable in the world.

When the members of the commune heard of Joe's plight they decided they could not let it be. They organised a 'bust fund' to get him out of prison, at least on bail, and arrange a defence lawyer.

But they needed £10,000, and they knew only one way to raise that kind of money – more drugs, more smuggling. So, they organised another trip to Morocco, to the royal estates of King Hassan, which were leased to Arab peasant farmers growing cannabis plants. At that time, in terms of money earned, Moroccan cannabis ranked as their country's third largest export.

The man who organised the trip was a burly Australian called Mike, who was coming off the ferry when Joe was busted.

He and fellow Let-It-Be members made another trip and successfully smuggled home 100lbs of cannabis resin, worth over £10,000 wholesale in London – five or six times more than they paid for it.

To do that, Mike helped buy and refit a Volkswagen Kombi van, with beds and a cooker in the back and shelves, which they hollowed out to hide the slabs of cannabis. Their route home, avoiding Spain, took them via Tangiers to Marseilles and then Dover.

More smuggling runs were planned – until the members of Let-It-Be strengthened their connection with the Count. He introduced another drugs dealer known as Joe, but who was actually Detective Constable Martyn Pritchard.

THE COUNT AND THE KING

Martyn Pritchard: As I had hoped, all was not lost on that Bristol operation. After we discussed the situation, the local coppers bailed the Count at one in the morning and told him I was being detained. Actually, I was half-drunk and well on my way home with a kindly mate driving my car.

I waited a couple of days. Then I phoned the Count, told him I had just got out and asked, "What went wrong? Did the others get busted?"

"Sorry, man, I just don't know what happened. That's a heavy team in Bristol. I ain't called them and they ain't called me. I would have heard if they were in trouble."

The Count was on police bail for further questioning, if necessary. I told him I was in the same boat and when we met up I showed him some fake bail papers from Bristol nick. But the Count didn't need a lot of convincing.

"I think we'd better cool it for a while. In any case, I'm not dealing with that mob again. They're ugly," I told him on the phone.

"Yeah, Joe, I know. There's plenty other places. Stay cool and keep in touch. Don't make it too long."

This seemed amazing. It sounded very much as though he wanted to carry on with the deal, and believed the tale. He didn't suspect me and, according to what he had said, he had not spoken to matey-boy with the knife, who might have put him in the picture about his suspicions.

Unless… unless the Count was setting me up. I didn't think he had the bottle to try that, but I wasn't going to take any chances. And I was definitely not getting into the back of any more cars on my own with that West Indian bodyguard again.

A few days slipped by and the Count was still dealing in The Star, according to guys on the scene. When I phoned him again he was so pleased to hear from me that he invited me straight round.

"Everything's cool, Joe. You still wanna deal, man?" That's how he greeted me.

"Yeah, man. I just got back to Reading. I ain't picked up my car yet from Bristol. The pigs have been looking all this time for traces, but they won't find any."

"Great, man. I hear them pigs were on to that team, they were tailing them everywhere. We were lucky."

So, the Count had swallowed the story we fed him in the cells at Bristol. To rub it in, I gave him a bollocking for involving me with such a risky outfit.

"I didn't know, Joe, for real. I had no idea. Have you told your people what happened?"

"No, no, not bloody likely! That could blow me out, man. The money got back OK. I told them it was a routine stop-and-search and luckily the drugs car got away as well."

"Well, if you wanna deal, I can introduce you to a guy with a connection for some really good stuff. And he really is cool, Joe."

I was knocked out. Perhaps I was better at this job than I thought! But the truth was that while DC Martyn Pritchard was also known as Joe in these circles, the Count was aka The Mug.

I started playing hard to get. I told him we should cool it for a while. But the Count was so anxious. Greed rules, OK.

Just to show good faith, I scored 15 acid tabs off him there and then. This was agreed with the bosses beforehand if the opportunity came up. A week later, I was right back in business. I returned to his flat to meet the man with the really good stuff. I'll tell you what happened.

Another phone call to the Count and he told me some of that good Moroccan had just come into the country. "I can set up the deal if you're interested, Joe, 20lbs at least."

"Whoa, man, not on the phone. I'll nip round and see you tonight. You can take it we're interested."

"That's great, see you tonight."

And when I got to the flat, the Count was full of himself. He was so eager. It was clear he wasn't as big as he made out on the drugs scene. He was too near the street, too far along the chain of command. But he had good connections.

"Listen, Joe, this is really good green Moroccan. And fresh, man, it's just been brought in."

"They give you a price, Count?"

"I told them you had three grand and they said OK. I mean, that's a good price, man."

"Only if it's the best stuff."

Actually, it was a good price. The top-grade Moroccan was knocking out at up to £275 a pound wholesale. They were prepared to take £150. He could see I was thinking, so he went on a bit.

"You interested in any more acid?"

"Yeah, but how much is that?"

"Well, Joe, we'll do the 20 weights of hash for three grand, and 250 for a thousand acid tabs."

"OK, you're on, Count. When do we deal?"

"Give us a ring in a couple of days." And I split.

I was pretty pleased with everything. We went after one punk dealer and although it all got ballsed-up in Bristol, I was still hanging on to him and he was giving me a big deal. On the street corner, those two lots of drugs would sell at around £10,000.

We held a headquarters conference and decided this wasn't a set-up. But we weren't taking any chances.

When I phoned the Count again, I was in the Oxford drugs squad office. Tim Todd had blocked all calls at the switchboard and he was on an extension. The guvnor, Dick Lee, was also listening.

"Is that you, Count?" I asked.

"Yeah… Joe?"

"Right. Is it cool your end?"

"It's cool, I'm on my own and the deal is ready, man." Then we went over all the details, the amounts involved, the bread and everything else so the others could hear the Count spelling it all out.

"When do we do it?" I asked.

"Tomorrow, Joe. Is that OK with you?"

"Make it the day after."

"OK, that's OK, man."

"Tell you what, Count, I'll be round at your place at 11, day after tomorrow."

"Will you have the bread?"

"I'll have the bread – well, at least, it will be around. It'll be in Reading, don't worry."

When we cut off, all three of us agreed he wasn't putting me on. But we still weren't taking any chances. We didn't want the National Council for Civil Liberties getting any wrong ideas, or television cameras or reporters turning up at his place to accuse us of a set-up. So, his flat went under 48-hour obs, from then until I went in to do the deal.

Don't get me wrong, we had nothing to hide. But we were after this bloke and we weren't coming out with egg on our face again. And this would give us a chance to see if there was any action at the Count's pad – if the drugs were going in and who was calling.

We had two days to organise our operation. Tim and Bob would be there again with the bread, but this time in Tim's white Marina. Another surveillance team was laid on to follow. We would all begin in Reading, and the tail would be our own mob, all drugs squad officers from Aylesbury, Oxford and Windsor.

As usual when we were going into a strange operation, we had a lot of background. Graham Barnard had given me a first-class briefing on the Reading scene. I had a string of names, I had seen pictures, I carried a load of information in my head and there was a full report back home to refresh me all the time.

One bit of intelligence dated back only a couple of months. A character named Joe had been busted in Algeciras and was still being held in a Spanish prison. He lived in Reading, in the commune called Let-It-Be, a seven-bedroomed old house on the Bath Road. He was busted with nearly a 100lbs of cannabis resin and about a litre of hash oil in a bottle in his van as he got off the ferry from Tangier, in Morocco, on his way home.

That's a lot of oil – it takes around a ton of cannabis to make five litres. The resin is about 15 per cent pure cannabis, if it's any good. But the oil is around 85 per cent pure. It's expensive, obviously very strong and usually easy to smuggle. This guy Joe had cut down the petrol tank and hidden the dope in there. But the Spanish police dipped the tank and found it as soon as he landed in Algeciras.

We knew the commune was involved in the Reading scene, but the report of that big bust in Algeciras raised our interest. We had plenty of info about the Let-It-Be mob and news of the Count moving Moroccan hash pointed to a link.

Anyway, this particular day we all arrive at Henley nick at nine for a final briefing. Nothing unusual has happened at the Count's flat in the last two days, and by the time I get there smack on 11, the obs team has moved out and our boys have had it staked out for half an hour.

The white Marina with the money – our own money drawn out again – is already parked up in the Butts multi-storey car park, in the centre of town. It's on the top floor, under observation from another high building close by, and one of our cars is on the floor below to block off anyone who tries to grab the bread and split fast.

After all, can you imagine anything more embarrassing than a team of detectives getting ripped-off and losing three thousand quid to a hairy-arsed outfit of hippy villains? We would all be directing traffic the following shift.

Apart from that, the bread van, our money vehicle, was the link for the entire operation. I was going in alone and Tim and Bob were the only contacts I had. But if I could keep letting them know our progress each time I came back to see or fetch the bread, and tell them the venue for the meet, we could get our cars staking out sites before I arrived instead of having them follow me in various cars.

We had rearranged the signals too. The main one was this – if I got out of a car or walked away from a house smoking a cigarette, the drugs were inside and they could go in on the bust.

The Count is all laughter and chat when I get inside his pad and 30 seconds later, there's a knock. Whoever it is I'm meeting has clearly been waiting outside observing my arrival. That's not unusual.

'Joe, meet John and Chris.'

We shake hands and flop down in the Count's lounge. Sue is in another room and there's some music on the stereo. Thanks to Graham's briefing I've already clocked John. He's a big Yorkshire fella, crashes out in the Let-It-Be commune, a mate of the poor, aggrieved smuggler Joe in the Spanish gaol. Suspect acid dealer. Not known a lot outside the Reading scene. Seen his picture on file.

Who's the other bloke? Chris… Chris… never mind?

John is already talking. He's obviously the dealer. "The Count says he spelled it out. You got the bread?" No niceties, we're straight into business.

"This is the stuff," he goes on, "this is what you are buying. Moroccan Deuxieme."

And he takes a lump of cannabis resin out of his pocket, breaks a bit off and hands it over the coffee table. I smell it, scratch it and sniff again. John pipes up, "You wanna have a joint and see what it's like?"

"Yeah, of course. We got time."

John rolls a joint, it gets passed round and I do my blowing trick. I have to stay right on the ball, so I'm extra careful.

The hash they are offering looks very good, that's why we are getting less for our money. Green Moroccan is reckoned to be among the best in the world. It goes in grades. There's the premiere, deuxieme, troisieme − first, second, third, and so on − and we are getting the second grade.

Chris starts talking about Morocco, about the farm at Ketama where they bought this stuff, and how he's going over on the next trip to act as quality control.

"We've only got 20 weights, but we can do more and it will be regular," he says.

Then John starts again while everyone is puffing away. "The Count tells me you're interested in acid?"

"Sure, who's got the thousand tabs today, you or the Count?"

"That's with the hash, but if you're really on, I can do you 10,000 tabs man, 10,000 a week if you want."

This scene is getting better every time I make a meet. "That could be very cool, man. The acid I've scored off the Count so far is very good."

"OK, Joe, let's deal. This is the way we're gonna do it today. We'll have the hash and money coming together at a cool house not far from here."

"No way," I tell him. "That's not how I deal. You can see the bread, but it stays hid until I see the gear. Then we put it all together and split."

"No, no, no. That's not how we're dealing…"

"OK." I interrupt him straightaway and stand up. "Let's forget all about it. You're concerned about a rip-off, so am I."

"Hang on, Joe, there's no hassle," says the Count.

"Yes, there is, we can't deal, simple as that."

"We can compromise, man," says John.

"No compromise. You have shown me a sample and I agree it's good. I can show you and Chris all the bread. When I have seen all the hash, the full 20 weights, you can come with me to fetch the bread and then we make the exchange at your cool house, not before. That's the way it is or there's definitely no deal."

We haggle for just a few moments more and then they all agree with me. They've got to agree. The four of us and Sue leave the flat, with me making sure I am not smoking, not giving the warning signal.

John tells Chris to meet him at a post office. Then he drives off in a Capri. The rest of us use my wheels to go and see the money in the car park.

I'd told the Count my own car was still in Bristol, so I'd borrowed a motor from a mate who wasn't in the job. It was immaculate and very flash, a mauve Ford Zephyr with big, wavy twin aerials, and cushions and jazzy seat covers.

I put five pounds worth of petrol in it – and landed in trouble with headquarters. When I put my expenses claim in, with a note explaining why I borrowed the car, I got queries back: "What cc is this vehicle – why no receipt – can anyone verify your mileage?" What a pain.

I'd have looked pretty silly if someone on the drugs scene had searched my clothes again and found a petrol receipt. It wasn't as if the police were paying for the hire. How could they worry about me going bent for a fiver when I had been offered all these big deals – a ton of grass, 25lbs of Black in Bristol, now 20lbs of Moroccan and 10,000 acid tabs a week – which would have netted me thousands?

Anyway, John is happy when he sees all the money stuffed in the briefcase. He studies Tim and Bob for a while, but they look as scruffy as me and we leave them.

At the post office he says, "Right, Joe, we'll all split. It's nearly half 12. Be back at the Count's flat at two. I'll phone you there soon after."

Everyone disappears and I rush back to the car park. We move the white Marina so it looks as if we're safeguarding our money. We call the rest of the team into a pub outside town, have a couple of drinks and bring everyone up to date. I tell the guvnor about the big, weekly acid offer, then take the Marina to a spot near Reading football ground and rejoin the Count.

He wants a joint again and lights up, but I say, "Not during business," and Sue makes me a cup of tea. We are all very pally and relaxed. The Count's enjoying his smoke and I'm sipping tea. Suddenly he says, "What about speed, Joe?"

"What about speed?"

"Here's a couple of tabs. I know where there's a quarter of a million more. Straight!"

I look at the speed and push both capsules deep into the pocket of my combat jacket. "How much, Count?"

"I buy at eight for a pound. I can do them at three for a pound on the street. Say you take them at five for a pound?"

"Mmmm… could be, let's talk later. We've got some dealing and celebrating to do first, man."

I'm getting some new respect for this fella. He's coming up with a lot of impressive propositions. Then the phone rings, Count answers and hands it to me.

"I need the bread nearer to where we're gonna meet," says John.

"OK. Where's the meet?"

"You have the bread at White Knights, in the Reading University area. Meet you in the car park at Bulmershe College at half past three. The gear is five minutes away, right?"

Ideal! We're going to play in my own backyard. My sister Jane went to Bulmershe and I lived most of my young life in that area, until I was 16. I just hope the cool house isn't going to be too near anyone we knew – my parents lived there a long time.

The Count and I have to re-site the bread to the spot John mentioned, so we drive off. When we see the Marina, I stop and nip across to talk to the boys.

"Move this to the White Knights. I'm meeting again at Bulmershe car park." Then I run back, knowing the team will now stake out the new meet.

At the car park John drives up in an old Morris, a converted post office van. He then dumps it and jumps in the Zephyr. The Count is in front, so John sprawls right across the back seat, looking out the window. Then he calls directions and we go all round the back streets.

"Sorry, Joe, I've got to check."

"I really don't mind. Next time we can deal real cool." But actually, I'm getting nervous because I've spotted a surveillance car in the mirror.

He hasn't. "OK, we're not being tailed, let's get there," he says.

We had six cars on that job, plus mine and the Marina, so it was hardly surprising he had not picked them up. We stop finally in Crockhamwell Road, nice street, very wide, with an infant school and ordinary suburban-type houses.

It's fairly quiet, just a few mums on their way to school to collect their kids. We go straight inside. Chris is there and another bloke, a hefty Aussie fella who draws the curtains in the front room. But there are no introductions. It's really heavy in there. Chris tosses over a leather, hand-tooled bag, obviously Arabic. Inside there's 20 slabs of cannabis in plastic wrappings.

I sniff, count the slabs and say, "OK. And the acid?"

"It's in the fridge," says the Aussie, and leads the way back through the house to the kitchen. In the fridge there's a little oval container, about the size of a bantam's egg, with the thousand trips inside.

"Wanna count them?" And the Aussie smiles.

"Right, let's get the bread," I say to John, and reach in my pocket for the cigarettes to give my mates the signal.

But, I've left my matches in the car – and I need to walk out of here smoking. So, I hand round my packet, and everyone refuses. I pat my pockets and ask: "Anyone got any strikes?" Trying to keep cool.

I can't believe it. All this fine planning and no bloody matches. Not one of these geezers has got a match! Now we are walking back through the house, and my left hand, groping desperately around, finds one solitary match at the bottom of the jacket pocket. Is it live, though? I pull it out and it's got a red head. I strike it on the frosted glass in the front door and my luck's in, it lights first time.

The cigarette is already in my mouth because I was going to make it look like I was smoking. So, I light up on the doorstep and walk out. There's two of our team, Mick and Glynnis, walking arm in arm down the road. They've clocked.

Into the Zephyr, turn left and more trouble. The Count spots Graham Barnard and Trevor House in a car. "Hey, man, that's the Reading drugs squad."

"Shit, let's call it off," I say, getting away from there fast. I am not too worried because I know they're going into the house and we're heading for Tim and Bob.

John looks out the back. "There's nothing tailing us." He is right for a change. "I'm telling you that pad was real cool, not even the people living there knew what we were doing. Maybe it's a coincidence, they could be just driving around."

The Count looks at me. "What do you think, Joe?"

I know what I think but they're both drooling about the money. "If there's nobody behind us, it's a coincidence," I say. "Got to be, they're after someone else."

We reach the white Marina and John says, "I want the bread in here. The other fella can follow us back in the car."

By now I'm spending all my time running across roads and talking at double speed. I rush out again to the Marina, "Have they bust the house yet?"

"They're just going in. I told them as soon as I saw your car, and they were off," says Tim.

"They want the bread in their car. Quick, Bob, shove all the money on the floor and just bring the briefcase. For Christ's sake don't bring any cash. They've already spotted Graham and they think it's a coincidence. But I don't want to risk that bread."

Below the line of the car window, Bob is yanking the money out of the brief case. It's going all over the floor in the back.

I return to the Zephyr and Bob gets in the back with John. Tim follows in the Marina and as we turn the corner in Crockhamwell Road, we spot the reception party.

"Jesus Christ, it's the fuzz," shouts John. "Move, Joe, let's go man."

As I start to move away, Andy Beaumont, parked down the road, sees what's happening and pulls right across in front of me. By now some of the team are hitting the house, the rest are doing us in the Zephyr and Tim in the Marina.

Brakes and tyres are squealing, cars are all over the road and mothers are clasping their kids close to them.

The only people enjoying it are the kids. To them it's like television in real life. Wallop, one of my alleged mates has crowned me with a pick-axe handle. He's aimed for my shoulder and luckily has connected.

The Count has got his hands up, John's struggling a bit, and Tim and me are having a bundle with a couple of coppers. Bob has dived back in the Marina to protect the money!

Handcuffs come out. We're sprawled across the cars for a body search, then cuffed and frogmarched back down the road to one of the drugs squad cars. Suddenly, Dick Lee comes out of the house and I get pulled out of a car and taken to another one on my own. The same thing happens to John, so it won't look too obvious.

"Where's the bloody dope?" asks the guvnor.

"In the house. Inside a Moroccan bag in the front room downstairs."

"We've got the bag, Martyn, but there's no dope."

"It's got to be there. If no one came out after I left, it's inside. I bloody saw it. The acid is in the fridge."

"Right, we've got the acid, but we can't find the other stuff. Never mind, we'll turn the place over, we'll find it."

"I hope so, guv, we don't want Bristol all over again."

"Well, it might have gone over the back wall. How many fellas were in there?"

"Two others, the bloke Chris who I met this morning, and a big Aussie."

"Yes, we have them and we found the chap who owns the house upstairs fast asleep."

"Well, stick me in the cells with the house owner. It's his place, he might know where the stuff is."

"That might save us time. We'll find it, don't worry."

"Yeah, but listen, guv, there's some speed in my pocket and the Count has just offered me 250,000. Can you take it out?" Remember, I was still handcuffed.

Half the squad move off to take us back to Reading nick, while the others prepare to take the drum apart. I am sweating now, more than I have during the entire operation.

The house owner gets processed first and I have a chance to

tell the Count, "Don't say a word, we're clean, man." I turn my pockets out next, answer a few questions like name and address, and then a uniform bloke – who has no idea I'm a copper – takes me downstairs, obeys instructions and puts me in the same cell as the owner.

"What's going on? I'm Joe, who are you?"

"Alan. I don't know a thing, John just wanted to borrow my house."

"Well, he took me there to buy some dope and…"

"Sssssshhh," he interrupts. "They bug these cells and I don't know anything. I don't want to be implicated."

A lot of the junkies think police cells are wired up, and they're not. But if the bobby on duty hears anything from outside the door, he's entitled to report it.

Anyway, I whisper to him, "They're going mad upstairs, they can't find the dope. I hope you got it stashed away?" He just shrugs and shakes his head, he really doesn't want to know, and he's scared.

About an hour later Dick Lee has me dragged out and taken upstairs for interrogation.

"You little bugger," he says to me. But he's smiling, so I know it's not all bad. "We found it in the mattress on a double bed upstairs, all 20 weights. They didn't trust you, they thought you were going to rip them off."

Then we have a debriefing. The Count is dumb this time. Some of the others are talking but John is silent, though he's denied involvement. His story is that he was out driving and just happened to call in on Alan at an unfortunate moment.

Now, will our bail trick work again? We have caught a fair-sized team, plus the hash and the acid, but John and the Count know a lot more about big acid and speed supplies. If we can let them – and me – out on the old section 38/2 police bail, perhaps we can find out a lot more.

It was a difficult, chancy decision to make, but I admired Dick

Lee for his courage and he gave the OK. I get my bail papers again and tear off to the Rainbow at Henley for a proper celebration with the boys. After they throw us out of the pub, I phone the Count.

"This is getting past a joke, Count, but I'm glad you're out."

"I'm glad for you too, Joe. I don't know what the hell's happening, man. I think it's the guys with the bread, it keeps happening after we get back to them."

"Don't be bloody daft, Count, I've worked with them loads of times. Who else is out and did they find the dope?"

"Yeah, man, they found it. John's out, he's here with me but all the guys at the house are still in, I think. How about the guys with the bread?"

"They're still in."

Then John comes on the phone. "This stinks to me, Joe. The Count has just been telling me about Bristol. I would never have dealt if I'd known. You were taking a chance."

"I know, man, but the Count said everything was cool. With a new team, I thought it would be cool too. Perhaps it's the phone, man. We'd better be careful."

Then the Count comes on again, "Give us a ring on Monday, Joe, about the speed. John is staying here with me for a while."

"No, man, we'll leave it for a week." I needed that much time to get the lab tests back on the two capsules he had given me as a sample, and we needed to review our information and question all the others who'd been arrested.

This was another incredible phone conversation. The Count still wanted to deal and John wasn't blowing me out as yet.

When Alan, the big Aussie, called Mike, and Chris came up in court on the Monday morning, a few of the hippies from Let-It-Be went into the nick and started getting stroppy. "What's happening to our friends? What are you pigs doing to them? Why can't we see them? Are they in pain?"

Trevor House, one of the local drugs squad who was on the bust and who had read all the statements made by the three accused, heard all this and asked, "Is that your van outside?"

"Yeah, what's it to you?"

He motioned to some uniform bobbies, then told the Let-It-Be crowd, "I think we will have a look at the van. You had better stay with us for a while."

And that was how we got a few more bodies in the bag. We took that Volkswagen caravanette apart with an oxyacetylene torch and found traces of drugs inside and hollowed-out shelves in the back. It was very clever – exactly 48 kilo slabs of cannabis could be hidden there, and hash oil could be stowed in a tiny compartment of the petrol tank.

Then the speed came back from the lab marked 'not a controlled drug.' It was probably part of a consignment stolen from a chemist's shop, but we pulled the Count on a charge of supplying me with the hash.

He just wouldn't believe I was drugs squad. I showed him my warrant card time and again, but it took 20 minutes to convince him. By this time, John had broken his bail and was away, hiding somewhere in Wales, or so we heard.

I had to go up to London and fetch the Aussie's car, an E-type Jaguar left parked on the street in Maida Vale. The boot was unlocked and inside I found five half-pound slabs of hash and a lot of correspondence that helped the prosecution case. There were hotel bills from Morocco, letters and instructions, and a load of general info on the hash smuggling operation they had talked about.

On the way back to Reading nick, I boiled the E-type and had to buy a new fan belt at a garage in Chiswick.

I sat down in the afternoon to read through all the correspondence I found in the car. A mechanic's report read, 'Reline front brakes,' and 'steering and suspension faulty.' Then came a list of all the work that was needed. It should never have been on the road!

We went down to Wales to find John and raided three addresses. One of them tied in with another job, which I'll describe later. Anyway, we eventually pulled him – he actually drove past our car quite accidentally.

Dick Lee, Bob Buckley and Trevor House took him along to Aberystwyth nick. We wanted to surprise John, give him a jolt. Then he might cough the acid connection as well as this job.

So, the guvnor tells him, "There's someone outside I want you to meet." The door opened and in I walked. Now I had got ordinary clothes on, not hippy gear, and I smiled. "Hello, John." We shook hands, then he connected, "Joe, you, a pig?"

"Right on."

"Hey, man, how about that." And he started clapping. "I like it, I really do. You bastard. That's fantastic! No wonder we had all the cock-ups."

In fact, he took it so well we never had a chance with the acid. He said it was a phoney offer. On the way back to Reading with him, I said to the guvnor, "There's four of us and one of him, and he's not going to get a drink for a long, long time. What about it?" So, we stopped, took the cuffs off and all had a few beers together.

John got three years. The Count, who couldn't take his eyes off me in court, he got four and so did the big Aussie, Mike.

When the guvnor went abroad to check their stories, he found the trail led from the dear old Count all the way to a real King. They were buying the hash up in the foothills of the Atlas Mountains, where the cannabis plants were being grown on the royal estates, leased out to peasant farmers from King Hassan of Morocco. And Dick Lee went on television to tell everyone about it, too.

So, our chase after one small but flashy dealer netted 10 altogether on a variety of connected charges. It was a royal progress to some of the evil rulers of the drugs world. And that trail was still warm.

Chapter Fourteen

The Biggest Bust in History – Courtesy of Martyn

Edward Laxton: According to Interpol, 'Operation Julie' was the biggest drugs investigation in the world. It centred around two laboratories: one in a sedate London suburb, the other in a tiny Welsh village. These two places made 95 per cent of Britain's LSD and more than half of the world's illegal supplies.

In 1971 and 1975, attempts had been made to bust the organisers – doctors and scientists, university-trained acid producers and suppliers. But their set-up remained sound until Operation Julie (named after one of the officers involved, Sergeant Julie Taylor) landed them in gaol.

At precisely 5am on Saturday, 26 March 1977, 800 detectives raided 83 homes in England and Wales and made 120 arrests.

A few months later at Bristol Crown Court, a judge handed out sentences totalling 120 years to 31 defendants involved in the main organisation. Fifty or more drug pushers and dealers were dealt with on less serious charges in local courts all over the country.

LSD networks in Holland, France, Denmark, Sweden and West Germany were wrecked by Operation Julie. And America's narcotics force, the DEA (Drugs Enforcement Administration), ran a parallel operation, Centac X, to shut down the US organisation whose LSD supplies came from the two British labs.

Operation Julie had halted a massive drugs network around the world, worth many millions of pounds. At one stage the operation became so unwieldy police ruled a cut-off point. Anyone involved in deals of £5000 or less would escape attention.

One of the top four conspirators who went to prison had an

estimated £1.2 million hidden away in secret numbered accounts in European banks. While police estimated another £6 million awaited other members who were gaoled at Bristol.

And two men, involved purely in the production, were suspected of stashing quantities of essential chemicals to start up again when they were released.

From 1970-73 there was just one laboratory, run by Richard Kemp, an American who had discovered how to make the purest ever LSD, and Henry Todd. The ideological belief of Kemp in the powers of acid to examine the inner mind came into conflict with the financial opportunism of Henry Todd.

The labs split. But the London team headed by Todd, made sure all their supplies went back into Wales before they went on circulation around Britain. That way, if news of the operation leaked it might expose the Welsh lab, run by Kemp and his girlfriend, Dr Christine Bott, but leave the London set-up in the clear.

All the way down the line of the supply chain in Britain were cut-off points. No one in the organisation knew every other person involved. Most of them met each other for the first time on the morning of 26th March at Swindon police station, when they were introduced by the detectives on Operation Julie.

It is impossible to estimate exactly how many LSD microdots or tabs they made altogether, but police reckoned it was more than 30 million. Within a year of their arrest, lack of availability meant LSD rose in street value from £1 to £8 a tab. And the vital information that set Operation Julie in motion, came from Martyn Pritchard.

Operation Julie

Martyn Pritchard: No one has ever really explained exactly how Operation Julie began. I am credited with picking up the information that set the ball rolling but when that happened, do you know what I was doing? Rubber heeling – investigating another police officer.

Undercover work often rolls on and on and overlaps. While you are working on one job, you pick up some information to follow up later. In 1975, when I was involved with the Let-It-Be commune in Reading and arranging the regular purchase of large consignments of Moroccan cannabis, I was offered any amount of acid.

For some time police had suspected a big factory was producing LSD here in Britain. But this acid offer in Reading came just before we bust the Let-It-Be team. They all went to prison and my cover was virtually blown when I had to give evidence at their trial. Most certainly, my face was now well-known around Reading.

The next job was entirely different. I was loaned to Wiltshire police to work undercover again because they had a uniformed sergeant apparently living with a girl who had some very strange friends.

His bosses were worried about him. A lot of drugs were available in the area where he worked and their CID were not coping too well. Wiltshire police had no drugs squad as such, so they decided someone was needed to infiltrate this ring, which they thought might have their sergeant on the fringe.

It turned out very nicely. The sergeant was as clean as a whistle, and so was his girl. That really pleased me. But the Wiltshire junkies had the freedom of the county. There was any amount of pills, cannabis and acid available around there, in Frome, Bath and Swindon, in Chippenham and Cirencester.

It was incredible. These were quiet country towns but the dealing, smoking and tripping were all out in the open. Kids even used to cut up cannabis on the bars of grotty old pubs where the elderly landlords didn't realise what was happening.

So, I moved around getting my face known in the drug-dealing haunts, joining the scene, getting back to parties, bumming lifts and kipping down whenever a bed was available. Then I had this fantastic offer in a boozer in Cirencester. I had talked to this guy before and I knew he worked at the big safari park at Longleat.

Someone else in that conversation told a lovely story. This bloke was supposed to be growing his own cannabis. He was said to be raising about 100 plants in the lions' reserve. Sounded good but I didn't believe it, not then.

But it was a fine opener for a chat and this young feller insisted it was true, and he would soon see how good a crop he had grown. "But what about acid?" he asked.

"Go on, what about it?"

"If you want, I can supply plenty, anything from one to 10,000 tabs."

We were interrupted then, but I nearly always delayed taking a first-time discussion too far. I intended to take that conversation further – at another time.

About a week later, one Friday night in the back bar of the Bear Hotel in Chippenham, I watched another guy doing small-time dealing in acid. He got rid of 100 tabs like candy floss at a fairground. No nudge-nudge, wink-wink. When he walked in, everyone knew he was the acid man.

I had my mate Andy with me that night and we moved alongside while this gent had a smoke. We called this guy Woodrow. He was a builder and lived with his folks on a big estate in Chippenham. We weren't strangers, he had been around and seen us a time or two, and we got ourselves invited to a party. We made sure he had plenty of booze and a couple more smokes. Drunk or high, that's how we wanted our Woodrow. I suspected he was the Longleat man's supplier.

The party was at a commune called The Wombles. About a dozen youngsters were staying there and a couple of French lads in the pub came along as well.

This helped us immensely. They had some unbelievable dope, very high quality, green Moroccan and really fresh. It was the 'Premiere' at £30 an ounce.

The Wombles' lot didn't speak any French and the lads only

very broken English. They wanted to sell a couple of pounds of hash, £1000 worth, a nice little bust under normal circumstances. But we were focused on the acid deals and the French lads were after some LSD to take back to Paris.

Now I got 'O' level French at school and I'm not bad at the language, and neither was Andy. We did all the translations and negotiations and changed grams and francs into ounces and sterling. Good job I got maths as well.

Man, we were popular. And all this was going on with 150 watts of Queen and Freddie Mercury blasting away with their Night at the Opera album and 20 people blowing dope like it's going out of fashion. And there's me and Andy getting a secondary high from all this cannabis smoke in the air, trying to do business. Our business and their business.

It all paid off. Old Woodrow was spaced out when we lugged him out of the party and drove home. We arranged to see him again in the morning, back at The Bear. Told him we wanted to set up a deal. We weren't looking for anything spectacular, just thought we would see where this guy led us and eventually give that scene a bit of a shaking.

We all arrived early next day and started drinking. And half-way through the first pint he drops the acid news. "My contact in Cirencester can supply all you want."

"Like how much and what's the fee?" I was just making conversation.

"From us to you it's £300 a thou. What can you do? Fifty thousand, 60, 70, 80 thousand?" My head is racing now. This is very big talk. These tabs are £1 each on the market.

"Can you do that much?"

"Sure, man, if you can do the bread."

Wow! This is the second time in a few short weeks someone has made me a big acid offer. Reading, and now here. Eighty thousand tabs!

I knew the biggest seizure of acid in this country had been just over 32,000 tabs in November 1974. But here is the real significance of what Woodrow was talking about. At that time, in November 1975, the average total of seizures across the world by all the police forces, customs officers and drugs agencies put together was 80,000 tabs a year.

That's what stuck in my mind as Woodrow and I chatted. Anywhere around the world, in New York, Los Angeles, London, that would be a lot of acid. But this is 11o'clock on a Saturday morning, back bar of The Bear in rural Chippenham, Wiltshire. Hang on, Martyn…

"Could be we can't handle that much acid, not yet anyway. I'll put it to my man." I'm stalling now.

"No sweat. Let me know. We can make a meet with my contact any time."

Andy and I compare notes later and we decide he's talking crap. No one is going to supply that much acid to an unknown buyer, even if it's available. But is it available? That's what we have to find out.

Woodrow thinks we have some very heavy connections. We mostly used that line. It helped with the self-protection because no one was going to mix it with a really heavy team, try and rip them off or use any muscle. Now it was paying off better than we could have dreamed.

I had no idea this would lead to Operation Julie or anything like it. But if this was on, it would need a lot of care. Freelancing as a copper is one thing, and we were always ready to work and chat and graft straight off the cuff. But mostly, the good undercover work is well thought out and rehearsed, at least in your own mind.

But the temptation was too great. I decided I would have to push for a bit more news. I wanted to see if this was in any way genuine or if Woodrow just had a big mouth, so I kept going.

"Is it all £300 a thou, any amount?"

'Right. Same price, every time. That's regular wholesale from us to you. What you charge your man is your business."

"Have you got lucky or something? This isn't a one-off?"

Woodrow shook his head, and then there were no more answers. He switched tracks and I let it die. A couple more guys walked in and joined us, so that was that.

It was three hours later when the pub closed. We didn't have too much to drink. I wanted to think about LSD and concentrate. Bugger the rubber heeling I was supposed to be doing.

But I couldn't split. We got into Woodrow's car and went off to his pad for a kip. There was a smoke-up later that night and we were well into Sunday morning when I started to write up a few notes. In the car, under the courtesy light, I got down some names, popped the details in an envelope and posted them home in my own name.

In that job, you decide what goes in front of the boss and when. You are supposed to write up your detective's pocket book daily, but I often went weeks at a time without even seeing mine. This way, mailing your own notes to transfer later, the details stay fresh and you stay alive.

Looking back, I am still surprised Woodrow put up the acid connection without really knowing me. My sales talk that night, and organising the French deal, must have clicked. He figured I was in touch with a big operator and obviously saw a great chunk of bread for himself.

He was only moving 100 tabs a time and I knew the language of the big pushers. Now I needed to get further into the operation. Checks on all of Woodrow's mates were made. I wanted to keep this quiet, so I used a pal in the West Midlands force to run it through the Central Drugs Intelligence Unit.

Nothing. And Woodrow was clean. Just one previous for nicking a bike.

So, there I was, on loan to investigate the background of a

uniformed sergeant and suddenly, accidentally, I was on the brink of something big. But I had to handle Woodrow carefully – I couldn't risk rushing him. I waited till the following weekend, then bought four tabs and I opened up.

"Made a call to the big guy about the acid deal. Reckons the price is right."

"What do you need, how many?"

"You mentioned 80,000 tabs. That's £24,000 – I guess that much. Money is no problem to my man, he has great contacts."

"This operation is really cool. They can supply and keep on supplying."

"We can be ready in three weeks. What about you?"

Old Woodrow flips then. This is for real, his big chance, and he almost runs out of the bar. I guess right, he's headed to a phone. But he's gone for nearly half-an-hour.

It's bad news when he comes back. His man is none too pleased with him. That's obvious but he isn't about to admit it, so I play him along. It isn't difficult, he's greedy for the money.

"We've got problems, Martyn. My man's not too sure they need any more business. I'll get back to him next week. They're really cool."

Really cool! Is he joking? We're discussing 24 grand changing hands for drugs that could fit into a reasonably sized paper bag.

While he's muttering and trying to get over his disappointment, I am idling around with some very juicy thoughts. If I put these tabs out at 50p each – that was still half the street price – it leaves a nice £16,000 profit for Martyn.

Just one transaction. Do it four times and that covers all the wages I am going to earn from the police until I retire. That's what I'm thinking. Very naughty.

But I hate acid. You will find 90%, if not more, of all drugs squad coppers put it top of the hate list. They see the results of bad trips. The intellectuals, really good brains, even doctors, they reckon acid is great. Enables one to examine one's inner mind. Balls!

Out of all the drugs – hash, coke, heroin, pills – there's nothing like acid. Now Woodrow, he knows someone who can lay on supplies in really big quantities, and regular. But he's telling me more than his supplier would like, so I'm not surprised his firm are annoyed. Concentrate, Martyn. Woodrow is leading you to the Big One.

"Let's make the meet anyway. Put me up. Let your man decide for himself," I tell Woodrow.

"Well, Martyn, he went bananas. I agreed some time ago if I found a dealer I would make the intro and let Alan make the decisions, let him make the running."

Good old Woodrow. Now I had a name too – Alan. Just in time for my report to the boss.

Dick 'Leapy' Lee was the detective inspector in charge of the Thames Valley drugs squad. Let me explain, we were all headquarters-based. Like there were units in Aylesbury and Reading and Oxford and so on, but we were not attached to a division. We were HQ units.

Dick Lee was a good guy. He won't mind me saying that the lads on the Thames Valley squad literally taught him everything he knew about drugs. He was a uniform Crown Court Officer at Reading before he came to us – balding, wearing a waistcoat and puffing a pipe. He thought LSD was old money – but he learned fast and was a great guvnor.

He used to say, "I think I will come on this raid," and we had to talk him out of it every time. No amount of disguise would have covered 'Leapy' Lee on a raid. But he was a good guy. He backed you all the way whatever you were doing. And it was 'Leapy' I had to see with my little report.

I will have to explain here what we already knew about LSD. The Central Drugs Intelligence Unit had a very fat file. They had names of people in there who would eventually be arrested on

Operation Julie and who would go to gaol for a very long time.

The CDIU also had reports coming in from police all over the world, turning up LSD supplies that pointed all the way back to Britain. Melbourne in Australia was one of the first, then Sydney and Johannesburg, Washington, all over the West Coast of America, Montreal and just about everywhere in Europe.

So, LSD is big in Britain. We know that and we know what the CDIU have – and I summarise all this for Dick Lee in his office at Kidlington, just north of Oxford. Dick keeps puffing and nodding and he knows I've got something. I keep it short and in about seven or eight minutes I hit him with the 80,000 tabs offer and slide my report across his desk.

Now I had often wondered why no one had launched an anti-LSD operation before. I didn't know it then, neither did Leapy Lee, but there had been an attempt earlier, in 1971 to be exact.

Dick Lee was only a D.I. but being at headquarters and in charge of a specialised unit, he had access to the Assistant Chief Constable Crime, Robert Henry Smith. That man knew about the 1971 LSD job. And there was only one other officer in Thames Valley with the same knowledge and he had never shown it to me.

What happened was this. A guy in London who they code-named Paul was playing around with cannabis and his contacts got mixed up with LSD. Now, Paul hated acid. I think a sister or girlfriend or someone pretty close had suffered a very bad trip.

In those days Scotland Yard's drug squad didn't have a very healthy reputation, and you may recall in the early Seventies it was broken up. Some guys were gaoled, others disciplined and there were some early retirements. So, Paul didn't feel inclined to talk to anyone from the Yard.

He had a connection to a VIP in our area, Thames Valley, and gave him some very good information. The VIP knew a very senior officer who had just retired and he fixed a meet between a member of our drugs squad and Paul.

A team was set up. Customs in London were heavily involved because smuggling was going on and the inside man was Paul. But the link was through a young detective in Thames Valley, the only man Paul would trust.

They would meet. Paul would provide information and our man would report to London. Customs had phone taps working and a few names were picked up – nothing very much, but it was a start. And even in 1971, there was enough news about to suspect a big British LSD factory was in business.

After every meeting, our man would do a separate report for the ACC, Robert Henry Smith. So, when Dick Lee went to him with my report four years later, little did we know there was all this background – which now made some sort of high-level action inevitable.

Anyway, according to Paul, he was in a flat in St John's Wood one night in the winter of '71, quite close to Lord's Cricket Ground. He doesn't know there is going to be a delivery, but a fella arrives with two bags holding about 90lbs of cannabis.

A suitcase is produced from a bedroom with a load of cash inside. The drugs and cash are shown, bags change hands and there is general conversation. Ten minutes later they're all busted, four blokes and a girl. Paul says no one was surprised at the knock on the door, that flat was supposed to be cool. Well, two police cars are waiting downstairs and off they go to the nick.

But the drivers don't touch the local nicks or go anywhere near the Yard. They all end up at a small police station somewhere in south east London, and are questioned and released, says Paul.

The delivery man is charged with possession of about half-an-ounce of cannabis and bailed. But the drugs have disappeared and so has the money, 90lbs of cannabis resin and a few thousand quid.

Next day Customs call the Thames Valley detective. They tell him to arrange an urgent meet with Paul and by way of a briefing they say, "Just ask him what happened last night." So our man does just that. He figures Customs have picked up some scrambled information on a phone tap and want Paul to fill in the details.

Paul is asked what happened and blows his top. He tells his tale and not unnaturally, says he wants out. He also says that his friends have discovered the same thing occurred, involving slightly smaller amounts of hash and cash, at another flat in West London that same night.

When our man reports what Paul said, there are no surprises with Customs. They have obviously picked up a certain amount of what took place from their phone taps. When our bloke adds the bits and pieces from Paul it all fits together. Their suspicions of some bent activity are confirmed.

But what can they do? The police involved are going to deny everything. The drugs dealers have been ripped off, but they don't want to go to prison while they're getting even with some bent coppers. And the Customs investigators are working without the Yard's knowledge.

Three weeks later that particular LSD investigation following Paul's original info was closed down, and the acid production kept going for five more years.

I went to see Paul after Operation Julie began. He swore everything he had told us was Gospel. I don't know. I wasn't there and he wasn't my contact. All I know is that certain bits and pieces fell neatly into place. Names he had supplied five years earlier were the same we were picking up on Julie, the names of people who eventually went to prison.

And when Julie was put into motion in March 1976, the bosses found out about 1971 and asked for the original files. There were none in London apparently. It was like the earlier job never existed, phone taps and surveillance never carried out, names and meeting places never recorded.

The only papers available were transcripts, held by Thames Valley police, of conversations between our man and Paul.

But our ACC Crime knew all about 1971. So, he knew Leapy Lee was on to something big when he received my first brief report about this fantastic LSD offer. The ball was rolling.

Chapter Fifteen

LSD and Acid Trips

Edward Laxton: The first recorded LSD trip occurred on the seat of a bicycle. Scientist and chemical researcher Dr Albert Hoffman was experimenting with hallucinogenics, looking for a drug to help doctors with psychotherapy.

He was cycling home for lunch from his laboratory in Basle, Switzerland, in 1942, when he tripped-out on the effects of lysergic acid diethylamide. LSD, the mind-expanding drug, has travelled far since then, perhaps too far in the wrong direction, and his company Sandoz no longer produces the drug.

It is colourless, tasteless and odourless. A trip may be exhilarating or terrifying, and can induce violence or even self-destruction. Fact and fantasy merge together. Users say they can see sounds, hear motion and taste colours while on trips, which usually last eight to 12 hours. They call LSD acid, cubes, heavenly blue, pearly gates, sugar, Big D, wedding bells, royal blue, instant Zen, the Chief, or the Hawk.

It used to be taken with a sugar cube, chewing gum, sweets, biscuits, an aspirin or vitamin tablet, even on blotting paper. Just a tiny droplet was enough for a trip. And sometimes, a second trip followed, unexpectedly, from the same dose.

But the 'Julie' acid producers discovered how to crystallise the chemicals and made microdots in eight different colours. Ten thousand would fit into a matchbox. They called them domes, dots or volcanoes. And they even discussed pouring pure LSD into Birmingham's reservoirs as an experiment and sending over a million people on a mass trip.

Military leaders in America and Russia have taken note of the possibilities of LSD in chemical warfare. In the United States, notable scientists have claimed that far more LSD has been produced by the two world powers than was ever made illegally for the drugs market.

Ergot, which is the fungal disease, found in LSD is much the same as the ergot in the fungus on stale bread, produced by diseased rye, which induced so many involuntary 'trips' among the poor in Britain in the Middle Ages. The resulting hallucinations were known as 'Saint Anthony's Fire'.

The drug's popularity raced away in the early 1960s, mainly in America where Timothy Leary, the Harvard psychologist whose aim was to "turn on the world", founded the League of Spiritual Discovery – another LSD.

America's Flower Power people, the Californian hippies, were forever grateful to Leary – and for a time, to the laboratories which were uncovered by 'Julie', which in the 1970s provided most of their supplies.

Carry on, Martyn

Martyn Pritchard: I had a flat in Kidlington, less than three minutes drive from headquarters. I left my report with 'Leapy' Lee and went home. He phoned me after lunch. "Carry on working down there, Martyn. The old man has talked to their ACC. He's agreed and nobody else is to know. Concentrate on the acid."

Great! But whatever they had decided, I was always going to keep my meet with Woodrow. I would very likely have carried on working that scene without their blessing. What's the point of freelancing if you need permission every time you blow your nose?

That Monday night really got me. Old Woodrow was good and brave, dragged me out of the pub and drove me straight to his contact. Not to Cirencester, though. The old bugger went in a completely different direction, to Frome. Told me on the way he didn't fancy getting the elbow again, so he was taking a chance on his contact being at home.

The fella had a pad above an empty shop, right in the centre of town. Woodrow rings the bell and his mate yanks up the window and throws down a key. That was his usual practice, he never opened up himself.

Well, matey's not pleased, that's very clear. What is also clear is that matey is heavy, very heavy. I reckon he's a Londoner, obviously a bit old for the hippie game, probably got some previous and very shrewd.

Woodrow blows around for half-an-hour before he mentions the acid, but Alan had already worked that out for himself. We were introduced without names being mentioned and Alan says nothing for ages.

"We can't deal, man." He says it suddenly, right out of nowhere. "We don't need favours, we're cool. Who needs the business?"

"No sweat. We've got some gear. This sounded good, but…" and I try to pass it off. At that stage I'm happy. I might get blown right out but I have a name, an address, a face, possibly a car outside that I had spotted. A little surveillance here might pay handsome dividends. Play it cool, Martyn.

So I do. Then Alan speaks again.

"Stay there," he says to Woodrow. And obviously, I've got to follow him.

We go to his pub 100 yards away. The back bar again and there's some guys playing pool. He's very agitated, drinking vodka and tonic.

"I've told that stupid bastard never, never bring anyone to my pad. Who the hell are you?"

Then he starts giving me the third degree about London. Woodrow told him I was from the Smoke and my firm was in the Midlands.

"I never name-drop. You wouldn't like it, neither would they."

I brazen it out.

"The organisation is there, it's together. We don't need the extra business. You could be the fuzz. How do I know?" he says.

"Look man, it's not my fault. I thought you knew we were coming. I thought Woodrow set it up."

He keeps on talking about the fuzz and says, "You read in the papers what happened at Reading? The pigs look like us."

"Like us?" I say, and even he laughs. But this is only a couple of months after Reading, after the big Moroccan job. And I flip when Alan says, "Listen, I will show you the story and a picture when we get back."

Back at the flat, out comes the cutting from the Mirror with the picture of 'Martyn' – back view fortunately, but my picture – and Alan's saying, "There you go. Now look out. They're right there, man."

He never suspects I'm fuzz, he just thinks I could be. He even laughs when I point to the picture caption, "Hey, man, same name, but different spelling." He thinks I spell it Martin. If only he knew.

Eventually we leave the flat with Alan, have one more drink in his local, then move on to a couple more pubs on our own. Woodrow feels bad and keeps apologising. But what hurts is the bread, or rather, the loss of bread from our deal.

He's sorry. But old Martyn isn't sorry. I'm into a new scene. I'm sure, I'm positive, things will get better. Alan will deal, no sweat.

Wrong! I was so wrong, but I didn't find that out till much later in the game.

In my short report and my briefing to Leapy Lee, I built the scene too much. All I had was three or four conversations, but the couple of hundred words I had written out were being treated with a lot of respect at my headquarters.

Add a heap of Leapy's bullshit to mine and certain senior officers were getting excited. I didn't realise all this and I was the only guy who knew how little information was available at this point.

Just to show you how little we had, when the Julie raids were made a year later, both Woodrow and Alan were clean. Maybe the guys who busted their homes didn't know where to look, but we never had enough on either man to hold them.

So, after that initial meeting, I had some work to do. I found out Alan's surname, ran it through records with my pal in Birmingham and I was right. Alan was heavy. He had form, plenty of action with the Met. In London, he had three convictions, a spell in prison and a note: 'Suspected cannabis and LSD dealer.'

Now I had something else for my boss, a big acid dealer from the Smoke.

We didn't need to watch his flat. He moved around enough and over the next few weeks I bumped into Alan frequently. Still no one in the Wiltshire police knew what I was doing. That was fairly usual, the fewer the better. Coppers are fantastic gossips.

Alan would not trust me. Any time he was around I could feel him trying to weigh me up. He said it often enough.

"You could so easily be the fuzz. No credentials, see. Give me one mutual friend in London and we'll do the deal."

And I just had to laugh. It was no good protesting. More than that, I was in no position to do any deal on thousands and thousands of acid tabs. The police won't fund that sort of caper.

"I've had the fuzz. They got very heavy with me in London. They kept trying to bust me, they knew I was doing acid," Alan told me one night.

"They kept raiding my pad. They turned up one evening and looked around, no more than five minutes. There were 100,000 acid tabs taped under the carpet. But they weren't interested in a proper search. They obviously made their minds up before they came through the door.

"This sergeant says, 'Here, cop that,' and stuck three grams of hash in my pocket. I went down for possession."

Well, I have heard similar tales. It was obvious I needed some background from the Smoke to keep Alan happy. This was creating a problem which I would have to overcome. Then one night back in Frome, Alan called me back to his pad with a chick he had just picked up in the pub. He threw me his bag of baccy.

"Roll me a joint, Martyn, while I get cosy with this one."

He started stripping the chick but I had to concentrate on hash, not flesh. Alan was trying me out. If I couldn't roll a joint, I was definitely the fuzz.

It had been done before. But I have rolled a few joints and convinced a few folks. I put in plenty of practice at home to make sure I was never caught out.

"I'll show the bastard. I'll do him a great five-skin," that's what I decided. I pulled out the tobacco, and a little purse inside with the grated cannabis and the cigarette papers. I laid one paper longways, joined three going across, then another longways on the end. A proper five-skin. On the other side of the settee Alan and the bird were getting down to business but he kept peering over the top.

I was finished well before he was, with the tobacco all laid in there and the joint rolled nice and loose. I had sprinkled on a nice helping of hash, just like the old Oxo touch in the telly ads. They always made me smile.

He was impressed with this bloody great long joint and we all three shared it, with me blowing instead of drawing, as usual. I needed my brain box going on all six cylinders with this one.

Nothing happened then. Alan told me a party was fixed for his place on Saturday, just 48 hours away, and asked me to drop this bird off. By now, the chiefs were getting official wheels turning and Leapy Lee was demanding daily phone calls to him personally, home or office.

I called in on Friday and I told Mr Lee, "I think I'm in. At long last, I'm in."

Party night arrived and Alan gave me the big chat-up, like he was sorry about not trusting me, and then, "We'll do the acid,

Martyn. Come round and we'll set it up on Monday. Tell your end it takes three weeks."

That was exactly how it happened. I was delighted. It had taken two and a half months to get that far, but now I would have to work out if there were any reasons for not doing the deal.

The party was a knockout. Everybody was high except Alan, but he was always in control. And me of course, but I was 'high' for very different reasons.

Must have been three o'clock in the morning, I was just going and the bell was ringing downstairs. I told you, Alan never opened up but this time instead of throwing the keys out, he said, "Let them in as you go, Martyn."

As I pulled back the door two guys stepped in and one looked straight at me. I certainly didn't recognise him, but his face fell in. He just stared, you know, couldn't believe his eyes. Then he bolted past me and shot up the stairs.

I felt sick. As I drove home all the way to Oxford I kept thinking, "That's done it." I had to go back on Monday to see Alan and it was like ice.

"Changed my mind, Martyn. Don't need the risk. We don't know you, man, and we don't need anybody." I realised it must have been that chance meeting at the door as I was leaving his bloody party. The late arrival had recognised me.

But I was wrong, I never saw that guy again. And one thing was for sure, he never blew me out. Alan's sour mood was just a coincidence. Of course, I didn't have a clue at that time. I spent a very dodgy few days waiting for something nasty to happen to old yours truly.

Later on, I met a chick named Marcia, a gorgeous girl from Mauritius and one of Alan's circle. She told me Alan only thought I might be fuzz, that was at first, and later on he didn't make the connection.

Yeah, that was later. I had to stay around that scene without knowing the score and I had to move right in there with all the pressure in the world bearing down on my brain from HQ. Our Assistant Chief Constable had reported my LSD set-up to the Home Office. There were supposed to be other leads and Robert Henry Smith proudly wrote, "We have an officer inside, infiltrating this organisation."

Not any more he wasn't, as from that Monday. I phoned Leapy immediately. I felt him stand up at the other end of the phone, take out his pipe then walk round his desk while I explained and apologised. I told him I was coming straight back for talks. But it was too late.

There is an outfit called ACPO, the Association of Chief Police Officers. And lysergic acid diethylamide was near the top of the agenda for their next meeting on Wednesday. And it was all down to my original report.

Leapy Lee explained all this in his office as soon as I arrived. I knew there was a meeting, but I didn't know it was so high-powered. I had no idea until then that they were going for something as big as Operation Julie.

I am in great shape for this job, I thought. Very, very unpopular on the acid scene and not smelling too rosy with the guvnor at headquarters either. I admitted a bit of bullshit in there and Leapy agreed he had done his share upstairs. And very likely, Mr Smith had gone in a bit heavy.

I knew my return ticket to Wiltshire was booked, even though I didn't know for sure whether my number was known. I also badly needed a pad in London to build up a real junkie character. If I could become a familiar face to dealers in the Smoke and in Wiltshire and do a bit of name-dropping, I might get really warm on that scene.

"Right," says Leapy after I explain all this, "you and Andy [Beaumont] must come along to Wednesday's meeting in Swindon. Let them hear you.

"I'm going down with the old man in his Rover," says Leapy the next day. "You make your own way down there. And wear a suit. And wash your hair. They think you are police officers."

When we got to Swindon nick, we had trouble getting inside. With all that brass around no one was taking chances. We showed our warrant cards five times before they let us into the pre-conference room. That was a great day. The one and only time I got to eat in the officers' mess. All this brass and a couple of detective constables.

After coffee, the meeting starts. There are about a dozen ACCs there from different forces, the heads of drugs squads, the Home Office, forensic scientists from Aldermaston, and Derek Godfrey, head of CDIU (Central Drugs Intelligence Unit).

Everyone gets introduced, names and official titles. "And that's Pritchard and Beaumont," says our ACC, very nice touch from Robert Henry Smith, showing he is with us all the way. Andy and I are both wearing the Thames Valley drugs squad tie, with a cannabis leaf. So is the ACC.

He starts the spiel. How the operation is needed, a proper operation, and how Thames Valley and Wiltshire cannot finance it alone. And he points out the spread into other force areas, across the borders into Gloucestershire and Avon and Somerset, where I had been going.

Then forensic science come in with graphs showing four big acid runs a year. Coming on to the streets, the busts and seizures. That is very impressive.

The two Welsh forces chip in. I knew there was an end in Aberystwyth. By pure coincidence, I was there in 1975 when that came up, but I'll tell you about that later.

Then we hear from CDIU. No mention of that 1971 operation, none at all. We knew from their files that two of the principal suspects on the LSD thing were a scientist, Richard Kemp, and his common law wife, Dr Christine Bott. They lived near Aberystwyth.

Then we hear the Yard had a go at these two the previous year following some information from Montreal. The Mounties bust an American with some 'coke' and he offered information, in exchange for a deal. Derek Godfrey, the CDIU man, tells the meeting he flew to Canada to interview this guy. He opened up on the American scene so much he had to live under protective custody from the DEA.

Surprise, surprise! This all makes me feel a lot more comfortable. We hear how impossible it is to keep surveillance on the Welsh scene. How the Yard blew it when they tried to track down a picture of this pair and the news got back to them.

I'm feeling a bit happier but I still don't know whether I'm on solid ground in Wiltshire, or whether my cover blew as I left that party. Yet if we failed, we wouldn't be the first.

Now it's my turn to speak to the meeting. I am very impressed with these guys. They are all in their mid-fifties with two long-haired herberts talking about undercover work, how we need a London pad, money to set ourselves up, everything.

They know nothing about the drugs scene. But they listen and they ask some very constructive questions. Only Leapy Lee and Andy know what a dead duck I'm holding. Well, not dead but badly wounded.

After lunch they go into what's needed – manpower, equipment, vehicles. The Wiltshire man offers Devizes as HQ. They have a fairly new building with an incident room set up in their driving school, and it's roughly halfway between London and Wales. And that's where, hopefully, it will all begin.

A report will go before a full meeting of ACPO the following week, but we are told to go ahead, get whatever we need and set ourselves up. They have a lot more information than I suspected and more ends to work on than mine alone.

Then they tell us we have three months to crack the job. That was February 1976. I had already been at it since October and I finally left Devizes in October 1977. The trials finished in March 1978, two years after Operation Julie was mounted.

The full meeting of ACPO endorsed the action and put four assistant chiefs in overall command. Leapy Lee would be second-in-command and Detective Superintendent Dennis Greenslade from the Regional Crime Squad would run the entire unit.

There were 26 detectives, the greatest bunch of blokes and women I ever worked with, drawn from 10 different forces. But no one from the Yard, they still didn't know what was happening. That was a relief. I had to work in London and their drugs squad still had a lot of ground to make up after the fiasco a few years earlier.

Dennis Greenslade, the boss, wasn't from the drugs squad. But that was useful, he didn't get in our way. And knitting everything together at Devizes was essential.

We spent the first two weeks doing surveillance training and getting everyone briefed. It was very exciting. This was going to be the crack at LSD, the big crack that many of us on the drugs squad had dreamed about.

Well, 1975 had been pretty busy for me. I missed leave, loads of weekends and days off had disappeared. I was grateful to get Christmas clear, but I knew then that 1976 was going to be twice as hectic.

Three other Thames Valley detectives were on the Julie squad. The 26 of us spread out. An HQ outfit was based at Devizes, two working undercover in Wales, Andy and me working undercover in London and Wiltshire, and the rest doing surveillance all over the place and making inquiries home and abroad.

I was given a £2000 allowance to set myself up in London, get a pad and pay three months' advance rent. I moved in some hi-fi gear, posters and all the rest of the back-drop, a few old copies of International Times, my guitar naturally, some of our own records and books and some we bought. And then I had to get out on the town, put the face about.

I set up a bank account in my phoney name and a business as a painter and decorator. I had a driving licence, tax forms, bank card, the whole bit.

Just in case anyone had contacts at the Yard and could check us out with the Criminal Records Office, I had a file inserted at Bristol, complete with pictures, fingerprints, some extra details and records of two previous convictions.

I was supposed to buy my own wheels, but they changed their minds and gave me an old police car. They also gave me promotion to detective sergeant.

The car was a Ford Cortina, re-sprayed yellow, with 90,000 miles on the clock. Naturally, the aerials and light were removed, and the radios and everything else taken out. It was re-registered in my name – 'Martin Poole'.

They did a very good job at the police garage. At least, that's what I thought until I opened the bonnet. Stamped on the metal in one corner was 'FORD POLICE PACK' – the car had been supplied with certain extra bits and pieces. So out came the hammer and chisel.

In the early days, we had a lot of beat-up gear on that job – old radios, worn-out cars. But things got better, very much better.

Someone organised an introduction to the Home Office police research laboratory in Hertfordshire. Our operation was ideal to try out some of their new toys. But even then, things went wrong.

They loaned us a van with remote-control video tape cameras, movie cameras and some sound equipment. The idea was to park it near a house you wanted to watch, leave it empty and control everything from another vehicle a mile away. Marvellous.

I had a look at it one day and the excise licence in the wind-screen showed 'No Fee'. So it's got to be a ministry vehicle. Then I ran a check on the index number through the vehicle registration bureau.

Anyone with the right know-how can do that. Back came the answer: 'Registered owners – Home Office Police Research Laboratory'. Charming. All the money spent on perfecting that vehicle and it could be blown out with a 2p phone call. This had a direction-finding aerial, built like a luggage roof-rack for a family saloon car, for tailing a vehicle carrying a hidden transmitting signal.

Unfortunately, before it could be used, one of my colleagues had an accident on a mountain road in Wales and overturned. The aerial was in lots of little pieces and it had been worth three times as much as the car.

But some of the other gear was great. Like portable scramblers you could fit to a public phone box and make sure no one listened in on your calls. We also had high-powered listening devices, so sensitive, you could hear the beating of a little bird's wings 25 yards away.

Lastly, of course, there were the phone taps. I think Customs organised those – much easier for them as it involved smuggling. For us, it needed authorisation from the Home Secretary himself.

The LSD producers guessed we'd been listening when we busted their factories and started interrogating them. It dawned on all of them. "You bastards tapped the phones."

When 'tinkle bell' taps gave us some really good information, we would have six or seven cars doing a tail through London, changing places, relieving each other. It sounds very James Bondish, I know. But that's exactly how it was.

For many months the 26 drugs squad detectives on Operation Julie thought they were chasing only one lab, and one network of suppliers and distributors – a single acid organisation that spread out across the world from a cottage in the hills of west Wales.

In the beginning, there was indeed only one organisation, the 'Cambridge Connection', dating back to 1970. Richard Kemp, a brilliant chemist, was studying nuclear magnetic resonance at the university to get his PhD degree. With him was Dr Christine Bott, his common-law wife, who had recently qualified as a medical practitioner.

Kemp, who was then in his late twenties, had already produced LSD for an American organisation in a Paris back-street laboratory, and for a mobile "suitcase operation" that operated elsewhere around Europe.

Also living in Cambridge at that time was David Solomon, an American author of several books on drugs who was then in his mid-forties. A mutual acquaintance introduced Solomon and Kemp. The fourth member of the team, Henry Barclay Todd, was working as a hospital porter in the city. He was interested in drugs – and also in Kim Solomon, the author's daughter.

Kemp, Bott, Solomon and Todd, the 'Cambridge Connection', formed the core of the original acid organisation, from 1970 until 1973. Then came the ideological and financial rupture between Kemp and Todd, and the laboratories started production independently of each other.

Chapter Sixteen

The Acid Organisers

Edward Laxton: The Welsh Acid Operation... involved Kemp and Bott, who lived together in Tregaron, near Aberystwyth, making acid tabs mostly for export. Solomon, sometime importer of chemicals, sometime exporter to America, and Dr Mark Tcharney, who replaced Todd in the distribution set-up, and for a while in the affections of Solomon's daughter Kim, were also there.

There were two more leading figures, one an American who later escaped arrest because he was holidaying in Majorca and then disappeared. He was part business brain, part overseas dealer. The other was an Israeli who called himself Zheni or Zahi, with homes in Golders Green, London and Amsterdam. This man, a big international acid dealer, was never traced.

Todd parted company from Kemp in 1973, receiving a 'golden handshake' of £7000. The motivations of Kemp, the ideologist who made 99.7% pure LSD, set him at loggerheads with Todd, the 'bread head' whose principal interest was money – the cash drug users were prepared to pay for their acid trips – and the lifestyle this could provide for him.

By 1976, when the Julie detectives discovered the second lab in the capital, it was bigger and busier than the one in Wales.

The London Operation... was a breakaway and had three principals, all aged around 30 and working from their laboratory in Seymour Road, Hampton Wick, just behind a vicarage in a quiet suburban street.

Henry Barclay Todd – who had taken some minor members of the original Welsh organisation with him and recruited others

– was the financial controller, chemical importer and tablet-maker. Andy Munro was the chemist, and Brian Cuthbertson was the general assistant in charge of the distribution network.

For the most part, their export supplies went to Holland. The acid for home consumption was sent to Wales first, and then along a number of channels.

The Export Set-Up... Richard Burden, who ran a London restaurant, The Last Resort, collected large consignments of acid tabs – from 50 to 80,000 at a time – from stash points in Berkshire and Hampshire woodlands.

These were literally holes in the ground. He delivered them to a man – still unknown to the police – whom he called 'Vince' or 'Dave'. They met by arrangement in Amsterdam bars. The tabs were then dispatched all over Europe.

In 1976 alone, Interpol recorded 24 different seizures of LSD in Belgium, Denmark, Germany, Switzerland, Holland, Spain and France, all traceable back to Amsterdam and from there directly to that one lab in London.

When Burden collected the cash, £300 per thousand, the rate was worked out according to that day's Financial Times into dollars, guilders, francs or marks, whatever was being paid over.

He deducted £15 per thousand for himself. When he got back, he met schoolteacher Martin Annable in a London pub and paid him sums that varied from £14,000 to £23,000. From Annable, the money went back to the principals at Seymour Road.

The dealers had codenames that they used between each other. Cut-off points were specifically planned to thwart the police.

UK Supplies... Nigel Fielding was the man who stashed the acid tabs in the woods for export. He owned a health-food store in Reading and used the same method to store his supplies for the home market.

From him, the drugs went to Russ Spenceley in Wales and his neighbour Alston Hughes, a bricklayer who acquired a liking for champagne. And from Wales the acid went to main dealers and sub-dealers, who in turn had their own underlings.

It went back to Anthony Dalton in London; in the Midlands to ice cream seller John Preece, who hid his supplies behind his front-door chimes; and to a cottage in Hankerton, Wiltshire, where Martyn Pritchard infiltrated the network and actually lived with acid dealers Stewart Lockhead and Bill McDonnell.

As the tabs went down the line of supply, the price rose. The rule is: the nearer the street, the bigger the risk. But the Operation Julie detectives slowly and carefully worked through the network back from the street, where the tabs retailed at about a pound each, to the labs from which they had been dispatched in lots of 50,000 or more.

The investigation lasted 13 months. Thirteen is unlucky for some, but as Martyn Pritchard says, where Operation Julie was concerned, luck played a very big part indeed.

Luck Plays a Part

Martyn Pritchard: When you get lucky, you tend to think it's one particular incident in isolation. Looking back on Julie, though, I realise I had a string of lucky breaks. Some of them were coincidental; the rest were just pure good fortune. Lucky old Martyn rides again.

Remember, it was now a dodgy scene for us down in Wiltshire. We needed to raise a cover identity in London while inquiries were being made all over the place by other detectives in the squad, and by now there was a definite location in Wales for them to work on.

Richard Kemp and Christine Bott, the chemist and the doctor, lived near Aberystwyth and were already strong suspects on the LSD files. I knew nothing about them until I went down there on a cannabis raid late in 1975, in connection with a big job at Reading.

Now this raid went horribly – and hysterically – wrong. We were busting a cottage where a fella named Alston Hughes lived. His nickname was 'Smiles', partly because he was usually smiling but mostly because he had very big white teeth.

Smiles' pad was in the sticks about 10 miles from Aberystwyth. Just before the raid, a senior officer wanted to get a message to us. A call was put through to the village bobby's home. He had already left to join us at the briefing, but innocently told his wife where he would be going eventually – the pad we were going to bust.

So, the bobby's wife goes round there on her bike, knocks on the door and when Smiles appears asks for her husband. "Well, he'll be here soon. Just give him a message that I want him," she tells the very surprised and grateful villain.

Naturally, when we roar in there about an hour later, the pad is very, very clean.

But at the inquest on this unsuccessful raid back at Aberystwyth nick, we get talking and hear about this local man, Kemp. He is a suspected acid producer; his record with the Central Drugs Intelligence Unit (CDIU) is very interesting. He is supposed to be a brilliant chemist and has just been involved in a fatal accident. His Land Rover had knocked down a vicar's wife. That's the info on him.

Why not give the vehicle the once-over there and then? It's outside in the police garage. We'll see if we can find any traces. We find something, all right. Detective Constable Trevor House discovers eight torn scraps of paper in the back with the words 'hydrazine hydrate' written on them. It's one of the ingredients you need to make LSD.

That's exactly how it happened, luck and coincidence. I guess Kemp's home at Tregaron would have come in for a check eventually. But that sort of clue is like gold for the detectives involved. From the off they know they are not swatting flies.

If the raid on Smiles's place had worked, we might never have searched the Land Rover. There would have been too much other work to do with prisoners and exhibits.

So, when Operation Julie got going, Kemp and his girlfriend, who did locum work for a nearby GP and was mad keen on breeding goats, were well in the frame.

That was the Welsh end. The lads were keeping observation on the Kemp and Bott place, following their car, identifying callers, checking registration numbers of visitors' motors. And listening. Honestly, the amount of info we picked up on the phone taps was amazing. Even though they often spoke in a sort of coded language, we soon got to understand them.

At my end we had a few names – mostly nicknames and Christian names. But these were all tiddlers, small-time pushers, and I needed to move back a few stages and get at the big boys.

Although the operation was under way, and I had been promoted to detective sergeant, nothing I had done really amounted to a row of beans.

Now Andy and I badly needed a permanent base in London. But to landlords we both looked like no-fixed-abode, care-of-Hyde-Park, turn-up, drop-out layabouts. We couldn't find a pad anywhere. It seems our disguise was just too good.

There were plenty of communes in Notting Hill and Shepherd's Bush, and we had no difficulty finding a bed. We had our gear, sleeping bags and such, but we had to have a permanent base, get a phone – no mobiles back then – accept visitors, the whole bit. We did the papers and the agents, and eventually one of them showed up. We paid £25 a week for a dump in Burlington Court, Chiswick.

When I tell this address to Alan back in Frome, the suspect I'm trying to get close to, we discover our pad is one and the same flat where he lived three years earlier. It's a knock-out, he cannot believe it. He is not alone, we can't either.

"Hey, what about that uuugh-green paint in the bathroom. You do that?"

"'No, man. That was in there when I took that pad." And he thinks we're really cool.

Old Alan starts laughing and suddenly remembers a hundred things about that place. Of all the coincidences! Two million homes in London, at least, and we dropped into his old pad.

We were in. I mean really in. There was no mention of acid, I never put a deal to him again. But the locals looked on him as a top man. He was heavy, ex-Smoke, so they took a lead from Alan. Now we were big buddies. Another stroke of luck!

And when we were in the Smoke, we could drop his name. Alan was well-known and now he was sure of us, he would provide back-up if anyone checked us out.

An added bonus was having the lovely Marcia from Mauritius on our side. Some other gent, not Alan, had left her four months pregnant, but we were buddies. She was commuting, like us, between London and Wiltshire and she was a handy introduction anywhere because, once seen, Marcia was never forgotten. Believe me, she was a gleaming knockout.

Marcia lived round the corner from us in London. She had tried to commit suicide and a social worker was handling her case in Cambridge, her old home. She took Andy and me up there one weekend.

Guess what? The social worker had a few cannabis plants in a big old greenhouse. And tucked away at one end was a thing she called her Henry plant. She was trying to grow 'H', bloody opium poppies. She is out of that business now, back in teaching. But her card was well marked locally, we made sure of that.

We were now playing both ends against the middle, London and Wiltshire, where the drugs scene was even bigger than we thought. Old Alan was doing so well, he taught his three-year-old boy how to weigh out his dope and wrap it in special packets. He was too busy to do it himself.

About this time, three things happened. We decided to shift from London and find a pad in Wiltshire. Now that we had our cover, we needed to be on that scene more permanently.

Then Andy split. He had to go on a course and got taken off Julie. I couldn't introduce a new face and, in any case, I prefer to work as a loner. Of course, we didn't always go around as a pair, that gets obvious. But now I was on my own.

Third, a pair of names kept cropping up – Lockhead and McDonnell. They seemed to be the source of most, if not all, the acid in the Wiltshire area.

I switched now, right out of London, gave up the dump in Chiswick and moved into the scene in Bath. I met a couple of guys straightaway who knew me from being around, and one of them had a pad. He had moved in with his girlfriend and his own place was empty, so I took it for three quid a week.

There was plenty of acid on the rounds in Bath and I started buying a few tabs here and there, mostly in pubs, once in a coffee bar and once on the street. It all went back for analysis, and apart from the colour, it was all the same, exact ampoule markings and quality. Interesting.

Next, we had to find Lockhead and McDonnell. I am not claiming credit for that. It was down to someone else on the team and I never asked him how.

At one of the weekly conferences in Devizes, he gave their address: Chapel Lane, Hankerton. Smack in between Chippenham and Cirencester. And I was told to move in as best I could.

Luck was with us again. Lockhead had a previous conviction for drugs and there was a picture on his criminal file. I drove into the village at dawn next day, found the cottage and sat in a hedge, trying to decide what to do.

One thing was certain: observation was impossible. There was no way you could keep 'obs' on their drum without them coming out to see if you would like a cup of tea. For a start, Hankerton was very small and their stone cottage was right on the edge of the village with just a chicken farm some way beyond.

I drove off and returned that night to pad around the place, clock a few faces. We couldn't do any other checks like the postman or milkman because this operation was so secret. If an inquiry might show out to the opposition, you didn't make it. Simple as that.

The cottage was no hippy home, for sure. A small green in front and an old chapel to one side. The garden was cultivated and some kiddy toys lay on the lawn. Three cars stood outside.

The furniture was a mixture, some pinewood and beaten-up sofas, but the place was well lit. That was handy. I stood about 10ft back from the window, so no one inside would see me, with all that electricity burning.

I could identify most of the people inside: Bill McDonnell from descriptions, Stew Lockhead from his photo, a woman who was probably someone's wife, and a couple of guys I didn't know, but who fitted in with the general picture. I went around to the back. The garden was fairly neat and tidy.

A hosepipe ran right up to the end of it. And behind a thick hedge was the Hankerton hash crop. This lot had their home-grown cannabis well established. The plants looked very healthy.

I had to try to infiltrate this set-up. This must be the source of all the acid I had seen being moved around there, the source behind the offer made to me months earlier – Old Woodrow and his 80,000 tabs. So here was a big scene.

Next day I went back to Devizes and looked through the files again, reading everything we had about these two, especially Lockheed, who had a conviction six years earlier. We had some names of his known associates, and we could throw everything together.

You see, a Criminal Records Office file is not just a record of criminal convictions, sentences, personal details like address and date of birth. Attached are notes of contacts, aliases, known associates. All of this is very useful if he or she comes into focus.

Getting that far had been methodical and routine detective work. Now came the lucky break. One of Lockheed's associates from 1970 had long since moved from Wiltshire to Brighton, and he was doing drugs all along the South Coast, as far as Bournemouth. We will call this bloke Mick.

One of our Julie team, a copper from Hampshire, knew him well. He had never busted him but had come close to it. He also knew a lot about his recent activities.

It seemed that Mick was our best bet, so I went down to Brighton with this Hampshire copper to stake out his address and identify him. I knew the scene down there pretty well and quite a few of the heads. I had worked there a year or so earlier, on loan from my own force.

I got myself an introduction to Mick when I followed him to a pub one night and found three or four guys I knew inside. It took me five weeks, backwards and forwards from Bath and Devizes to Brighton, but I eventually made a good contact with him. He thought I was quite a big dealer.

He knew I was into acid and I talked about my connections in Frome and Bath, about Woodrow and Alan and various other people he knew. I let on that I was trying to locate the big supplier and told him I had plenty of bread and would give him a fee just for the introduction.

And one day, after a few ales in his favourite pub, we got talking about Hankerton and he offered to take me up there and meet his old mate Lockhead. And that's how I got in. It took a long time and a lot of effort, but it was worth it. Mind you, I hadn't pinned all my hopes on Mick. I was working on some other possibilities as well, but he was completely fooled.

He took me over there exactly five weeks and four days after I first found the cottage and this spadework proved worthwhile. I sat there with Lockhead and McDonnell for about two hours that first evening, casually mentioning about a dozen names who were all known. I left the acid deal for another time.

When Mick collected £150, he thought it had come from a big

drugs dealer. He would faint if he knew the true source… police funds.

There was definitely going to be another time at Hankerton. I made sure of that. Turns out Stew Lockhead had bought the old chapel house next door and was about to convert it, but he was having trouble with the plans. If you recall, I was an apprentice engineer. So, I knew about plans.

"No sweat, man, I'll do the plans for you."

"Listen, are you sure? I mean, that would be great."

"No problem. Just tell me what you want to do with the place."

"I had a builder look it over and talked to him. He thought I was crazy but I'm sure it's a good idea."

Basically, he wanted to put in a false floor and make an upstairs, but the builder reckoned it would cost too much to be worthwhile. He couldn't understand that money was no problem for Lockhead.

I arranged to go back the next day to look over the chapel. He wanted to turn the vestry into a kitchen and knock in some windows. He had very good ideas and we started work on the plans straightaway.

To return the favour, guess what?

"Mick tell you I was interested in acid?"

"He mentioned it."

"Can you do it?"

"What do you need, Mart?"

"If it's good, I have a connection. At the right price."

"It's good, don't worry about that. Only one price man, 320 a thou.'

The upshot of all this comes within a few days. I am invited to stay at his cottage while we sort out the plans and measure up for timber and concrete lintels and all the other materials. And while I am there he agrees to supply me. So, this is clearly another client for tinker bell, and we get his phone tapped.

Bugger me! In one of the first conversations we taped, Lockhead mentioned 'Smiles'. And when I saw the transcript at a conference in Devizes... BOING!

It's yet another stroke of luck. There could not be two drug pushers with a name like that. It was Alston 'Smiles' Hughes, the fella we missed down in Wales because of the bobby's wife.

This was a great turn-up. We were sure he was on the acid scene, but we never had any evidence. He joined the telephone tappers' club as well. On the debit side, we mistakenly linked Smiles Hughes with Kemp and Bott. After all, they were near neighbours in Wales and in the same business. But they didn't know each other.

This was exactly why Henry Todd's London lab sent their supplies back to Wales, to be dispersed again from there. It was designed to fool us, and it succeeded for quite a while. But Hankerton was a terrific break for us. The information I gathered, the surveillance work, the discovery of their contacts and the phone taps – all gradually built up a picture of the supply network. We still had to acquire the evidence but at least we knew where to look. So, for the time being I had to concentrate on Lockhead and McDonnell.

Lockhead was a nasty bastard, really. Very cocky, a bloody big know-all, and I had to keep swallowing every statement he made on any subject. I couldn't afford to upset him. Even when he was nicked and met me again under very different circumstances, he couldn't admit I'd fooled him.

He said, "I knew you were fuzz, I could tell." Rubbish, but his wife Cathy was nice. I felt sorry for her.

As far as I could see, Lockhead lived on his drug dealings. He certainly didn't work. It was his cockiness that gave so much away though. He couldn't help boasting, and through him we penetrated the London set-up. By then, in 1976, it was much bigger and busier than the Welsh operation.

Lockheed took advantage of McDonnell, who was the money-man in that pairing. He was supposed to be a car dealer, but

BUSTED

Lockhead had the contacts and McDonnell put the money up for their big LSD purchases. Then they shared the profits as it was sold off in bulk lots.

McDonnell was about 25, quite a bit younger than the other fella, and he was fat and stuttered. He had to do a lot of fetching, carrying and driving around with the acid. But they both lived well: the best and biggest steaks, lots of booze and expensive presents for each other. Money was never a hang-up.

When we finished the plans, I started to help them on the building work in the old chapel. One day Stew tells me the acid has joined the inflation scene. He gives away a lot more too.

"If you're going to score, Mart, make it soon."

"Why, is it getting short?"

"No, man, it's getting dearer, 360 a thou."

"Three hundred and sixty quid! That's strong. I'll get it elsewhere."

"It won't be any cheaper, Mart."

"I reckon it will."

"I'm telling you it won't. Our people have cornered the market. They control supplies and prices."

There are just the two of us in the old chapel at the time, taking up some old floorboards. But I'm concentrating on what Stew is saying. And boy, am I interested.

"Are they heavy, then?" I ask.

"No, they're not heavy, they don't need to be. But they've got everything buttoned up, believe me."

"How can you be so sure?"

"I make a phone call, see, get through to this chick and give her the word. Then I get a call back, from a different person, telling me where it is, how much is there, where to leave the money or whether it will be collected. It's cool, Mart, very, very cool. The stuff gets delivered. We literally pick it up from a hole in the ground.

"When we pick it up, the tabs are all in Typhoo tea packets.

That's how they move it around the country, in packets of tea and dog biscuits and cornflakes. I'm telling you, man, they have this acid all sewn up."

"OK," I tell Stew, "let me have 500."

The very next day, another conference was scheduled at Devizes. When I repeated this conversation, everyone laughed and I got a new name, the Typhoo Terror.

But I had the last laugh. Because after the bust, various people started telling the story, and that is exactly how they transported their acid – in packets and boxes of groceries, which looked perfectly normal in the back of a car.

At the same conference I asked for permission to buy the 500 tabs, for £160. That was OK'd, but it took three days to get official clearance, and it went to assistant chief constable level at least. I had to make out a form stating they were for 'test purposes'.

They weren't, of course. They were just to keep me in at Hankerton. I was supposed to get a receipt from Lockhead. You know, like everyone does on the drugs scene! I just scrawled any old signature on the form – in fact, if anyone could have deciphered it, they would have read the name 'Harold Wilson.'

When I gave Stew the money he told me he would be picking up more supplies soon. Shortly after that, the phone taps gave us what we wanted. You see, not only are the conversations taped, but the tapping device tells us the numbers dialled on outgoing calls. Then a special set of reversing directories tell us who lives there.

The London lab had a very sophisticated operation. There were so many cut-off points that very few people in the chain knew anyone else involved beyond their immediate link. Acid was left in stashes in all sorts of deserted spots. Money was sometimes deposited in the same place, sometimes in a different stash. Or it might be picked up by the official collector.

Occasionally, they risked a straight exchange at a motorway service station for example, or did a very fast swap in a car park behind a pub. I once talked to Stew about the risks involved in this operation.

"The pigs down here aren't interested in drugs. They're just catching poachers," he said.

"How do the suppliers get all the stuff? Isn't it supposed to be illegal and completely unobtainable?"

"They can get everything here apart from one chemical, and they import that from Switzerland." Yes, it was a good set-up, and it might have gone on for years.

There was one more chunk of luck I must tell you about. Remember what I said about the 1971 drugs squad in London, the Met's operation, and about the informant Paul? Well, a decision was taken at Devizes that all the names we picked up on the phone taps should wherever possible be checked with our informants in case they could fill in any gaps.

I had been to see Paul and, as I said earlier, some of the names we were picking up on Operation Julie were the ones he had provided way back. Well, one day we picked up the name 'Leaf' on a taped conversation from a London phone.

I had heard that name on the drugs scene in Reading, but I had no idea who it was. When I fed it to Paul, it clicked.

"There was a guy named Leaf, didn't know he was involved, could be by now. Yeah, Reading, he used to have a chick named Caroline. She was an air hostess. I think they got married."

This was five years before, but it was worth a try. We contacted British Airways, hoping that they would have been Caroline's employers.

"Can you go back through records? Girl named Caroline who lived in the Reading area. Left during the last three or four years."

It took airport security one day. Only two girls fitted the bill. We cleared one. The other we found through a series of addresses. She was living just outside Reading and was married to Nigel 'Leaf' Fielding. We'd made another connection.

The various bits of the operation were being slotted together like a bloody great jigsaw puzzle. And luck was providing a lot of the important pieces.

Chapter Seventeen

Finding Mystery Man

Edward Laxton: When Operation Julie was first set up, an index was prepared for the secret Incident Room at Wiltshire police headquarters in Devizes. Locations like pubs and private addresses were filed away together with the names of individuals, nicknames, codenames and car numbers. Every possible piece of information was recorded, using the widest cross-reference system. Eventually, the index contained more than 20,000 cards.

Initially, there were few sources of information. The Central Drugs Intelligence Unit, based in London, had background files on LSD and people suspected of being involved in it, like Richard Kemp and David Solomon. They had come to the notice of the police over the years.

There was also Paul, whose tip-off in 1971 unfortunately foundered. And four years later, there was Gerald Thomas, arrested by the Canadian Mounties in Montreal, who bargained for his release by telling what he knew about drugs smuggling over there. Thomas gave information, about American smugglers and dealers and also named a number of British acid operators. He specifically named Solomon, Kemp and another man named Henry or George.

Paul had heard about this character back in 1971. And in a very fat general file on LSD, the CDIU had references to a big London dealer of the same name – Henry or George.

Who was this mystery man, so determined to hide his true identity that detectives later learned he used a different name wherever he had dealings? His aliases included John Webber, Stephen de

Warrenne, Peter Hollander, Mr Bright, Mr Dier, Mr Martin, Mr Muller, G. Blunt and JJ Ross.

In the early days of this mammoth police investigation, no one could find the slightest clue to this elusive figure. None of his common Christian names was ever connected to a surname. But Henry or George had to be traced – he had been specifically mentioned as a leading light on the acid scene in Britain.

So, Gerald Thomas, now living in protective custody in America, was pressed by his custodians, officers of the Drug Enforcement Agency, for more details. Thomas said he thought this man was the tablet manufacturer, the person in the lab who turned LSD into tiny acid tabs.

The only other thing he could recall was the fear and concern among members of the Cambridge Connection, including Kemp and Solomon, "when this guy got busted with some Californian Sunshine [LSD] in his car", in case he talked.

And that was the first and only clue they had.

The Operation Julie squad was determined to find out more about Henry or George. If he had been busted, a file must exist somewhere. A file prepared by police, with a lot more information – like a proper surname, an age, a description. Maybe even a photograph.

Who Is Henry or George?

Martyn Pritchard: It's no good sitting around waiting for your luck to happen. It was pretty obvious we needed to go looking for this Henry or George. He was supposed to be big and he wasn't going to come to us.

So where could we look? In the police force, you always make a routine check with the Criminal Records Office. You feed in a full name and date of birth, and you get a club number, a CRO number. This leads you to the full file, which has a lot more detail than merely a record of previous convictions.

But we had no full name or birth date to go on. All we had was a hint that our man was busted in possession of acid, the Californian Sunshine, and was probably living in Cambridge at the time. So, three detectives were sent from Devizes to Cambridge County police headquarters to search their records for the past 10 years.

We didn't know where he got busted, so they checked the files of seven magistrates' courts back to 1967. There was another hope – if he was living in Cambridge at the time, the local law would have been notified. Anyone who had got arrested for acid was checked out.

They spent three weeks in Cambridge and found nothing. And back at Devizes, we still couldn't get a pointer for Henry or George either. The guvnors decided to send a team back to Cambridge.

They started again, working by the book. A routine search through mounds of paper is hard graft. There are two recognised methods: CRO and the local police collator, who oversees the intelligence nerve system of any good force, where snippets of information, criminal gossip, background reports, and other kinds of invaluable leads are filed away.

In Cambridge, a third possibility came to light. A uniform sergeant was one of their collators, and he looked after drugs. When the boys first went up there, he was away on a course. Upon his return, he was only too ready to assist them.

"Did anyone show you my private file?" he asked.

"What private file?"

"I keep a more simplified record on drugs, without all the complicated cross references. The name you want might be there under LSD arrests."

And there it was: Henry Barclay Todd. They knew straightaway that this was our man because a brief detail threw up the name of Kim Solomon, the woman who was in his car when he got busted.

One of our boys at Cambridge, Detective Constable Alan Morgan, had helped to prepare the original Julie index at Devizes and he immediately remembered another Solomon – David, this chick's father. Bingo! We had a link.

This was in the days before computerisation. And we were lucky again, really lucky in finding Todd through this collator because Todd's bust hadn't been in Cambridge. It occurred near Glastonbury, in the area where I was working, but several years earlier. And it just so happened that a diligent officer there had sent a file up to Henry Barclay Todd's home town. OK, our search and the intelligence file, that's laid-down procedure. But it doesn't always happen, especially when someone is busy.

So now we got out Todd's CRO file, and bugger me, there was no photograph. Maybe the camera was out of order that day, or the negative was fogged. I don't know. These things happen.

The address was old and all the other details on his file were out of date – phone numbers disused, places he frequented closed down or under new owners. His known friends named on that file were people we were already interested in.

But at least we had a name. Now, I'm going to let you into a little secret. Just because we were in the police force, it didn't mean we needed to operate any differently from a company making legitimate business inquiries.

So, checks were made in the name of Henry Barclay Todd through banks and insurance companies, credit card outfits, hire purchase groups and building societies. We checked electricity bills, rate demands, airline bookings, driving licence, phone bills, income tax returns, health service, car registration, everything we could think of. And all we could turn up was an accommodation address in London – Cannon Street Road, E1.

Even that wasn't much good. We couldn't bowl in there and start asking questions. And there's not much point in setting up observation on an accommodation address because it's just like a box number. Anyone with the correct authorisation could go in and collect Todd's mail. We were stuck again.

Our next move was kept very quiet. It was a channel that I am sure is rarely used. I don't even know whether it was done through an official approach – more likely it was round the back door on the old-boy network. Because this fella Todd knew how to stay out of the way. We had to pull a trick.

The passport office is hardly a police file but... he was in there all right. So, we get a copy of his photograph and his passport application form. All the details written on it were the same as we had collected elsewhere, including the holding address.

But there was one tiny exception – the slip that led straight to Henry Barclay Todd. Against the query 'daytime telephone' was a number completely new to us.

It's funny how people rarely lie all the way on these forms. Subconsciously, maybe Todd was thinking as he filled it in that here was one proper link with home whenever he was travelling abroad. After all, he might have an accident or land in trouble, and maybe a next-of-kin would need to be informed.

Anyway, there it was, a phone number. Easy enough to check back through our reversing directories, or the Post Office, and get the name and address of the subscriber... a Maureen Ruddy, who was living in a flat in Fitzgeorge Avenue, close to the Olympia exhibition centre in west London.

We couldn't phone the flat, they might have been using some kind of verbal code. All we could do was watch the place to see if Todd lived there. We set up an observation in a van down the road and kept an eye on the entrance.

It turned out our man was actually staying there most nights. Maureen Ruddy was his long-time girlfriend. At last we had snared the mystery man. We knew who he was and where he was. Now we had to tie him in with the acid scene and we realised from the crafty way he behaved, and from the great care he took to cover his tracks, that that wasn't going to be easy.

I was still at Hankerton at the time, staying odd nights in the cottage and living the rest of the time in Bath. I wasn't getting any time off and I was seeing very little of home, which was only an empty flat in Oxford anyway.

At that stage, remember, we were only concerned with one lab, in Wales, and one organisation. And we daren't move in because what we didn't have enough proof.

The boys in Wales didn't know it, but they were spending a lot of time watching a lab that wasn't a lab at all. Kemp and Bott had moved home from one cottage to another. In the first, there was plenty of evidence that LSD had been manufactured in the cellar. In the second, as it turned out, there was none.

We had pieced together some of the lengthy distribution network, but we couldn't understand why there were two big gaps. First, there was no connection between the two groups in Wales – Kemp's lot, very intellectual and full of university graduates – and the others. Spenceley and Hughes were both unemployed, one a former garage hand and the other an ex-bricklayer.

The other gap was between everyone else in the operation and Henry Barclay Todd, who seemed to be entirely on his own.

Todd forced us to change the course of Operation Julie. We had solved one question – we knew who Henry was, never mind George. Now we had another poser – exactly who the hell was Henry Barclay Todd?

We held a big conference and decided to concentrate on him. We organised a massive surveillance. We had found his home so the orders went out – get an obs van cracking, start video filming, tail him, see where he goes and who he meets. His phone was tapped, too, but Henry was always very cagey on the blower. He didn't trust it, and he was dead right.

Meanwhile, I was pulled out of Hankerton, gave up my flat in Bath and moved back to the Smoke again.

The lads on the early Todd inquiries stayed in hotels, but the guvnors were worried about us becoming too conspicuous – and the money and time being spent as well. We had gone way over budget, way past the period allotted for the operation. And we were not going to get any reinforcements.

So, the Home Office borrowed a three-bedroom house from the Air Ministry, inside the RAF station at Hendon in North London. It was married quarters, and people nearby were told we were in the Air Force Special Investigation Branch, all on a detective training course.

Eventually, 18 of us were living there. A couple of our female colleagues, Glynnis and Devine, occupied a small room down-stairs, and the blokes slept wherever they could find space. We often worked 14-hour shifts, had a meal and climbed into a warm bed – just vacated by the bloke who was taking our place on observation.

There was a cupboard under the stairs, nice and warm and big enough to take an armchair and a sleeping body. Sometimes you slept on a camp bed, at other times on the settee or the floor. And unless you were in a hell of a hurry, it took about two hours to get out in the morning, waiting for the bathroom, trying to cook breakfast, getting cleaned up.

With all those bodies, it was essential to keep fairly tidy. Another problem was the heat. Some of the team, including my namesake Fred Pritchard, moved up to London just in time for the heatwave in 1976 – for 18 consecutive days the temperature was around 28°C – so you can imagine what it was like.

But even worse was the observation vans. These were borrowed from various police forces to make sure the same motor wasn't seen parked in the same street day after day.

I have already mentioned our new vehicle, a breakdown truck containing our remote-control video cameras. You could leave it empty and operate the cameras from another vehicle a mile away. The camera lens was hidden inside the 'TOWING' sign on the cab roof.

Well, we soon realised it was a dead giveaway. A breakdown unit is a working vehicle and it can't be left parked in a street for longer than a day at a time without becoming obvious.

So, the team worked in closed vans. Some were specially built for the job, with cooker, toilet and camera installations, but others were make-do efforts with sandwiches and a bucket. And that summer, the temperature inside them soared into the hundreds. Salt tablets and lots of liquid were always on hand and everyone inside stripped right off.

Whenever Henry drove off, we tailed him. There were sometimes six or seven cars and a motorbike following and changing places, and all in contact through car-to-car radio. Where possible there were three of us to a vehicle, one driving, one map reading and one working the radio.

Naturally, the bike was a bonus in heavy traffic. It's rider, usually Alan Buxton, could stay really close with less likelihood of being spotted. We used a light green Triumph, and Alan had a special helmet with a mike built into the visor and earphones inside the headpiece.

We used very common cars like a Maxi, a Marina, an Avenger, a couple of Fords – and a well-tuned Dolomite Sprint in case we had to hurry.

Very often the phone tap told us Henry was going out, so we could get the surveillance team ready. We would follow him to meets, and on one occasion we even ended up in Geneva and got into trouble with the Swiss police.

Let's say Henry was going out in London. Our first car would be codenamed 'Eyeball', followed by car No. 2, then 3 and so on. Everything was pre-arranged. There was no outside control involved. We were a self-contained unit and 'Eyeball' would be completely in charge. Everyone else on the radio network would stay silent unless he invited them to answer. It would go like this.

Observation team outside his flat near Olympia reports: "Suspect is getting into his car, moving towards Kensington High Street. Eyeball take over."

"Eyeball. I have him. All-cars move off."

Then the radio operator in the Eyeball car, beside the driver, would give a running commentary. Don't forget, none of us was a London copper, so we needed landmarks as well as street names. The other cars would stream out like a convoy, with car No. 2 always keeping Eyeball in sight so he's ready to take over.

"Eyeball. Suspect proceeding towards central London. We are passing Olympia on left. Traffic light. Straight over lights…

"Eyeball. Suspect now passing Odeon cinema on right. Halting at traffic lights here. Suspect indicating right turn. This is Earl's Court road. Turning right now…

"Eyeball. Traffic getting heavy. Close up. Bike move in to assist. Report position."

"Bike. I have Eyeball and suspect in sight."

"Eyeball. Big church on left now, suspect going straight over lights. Earl's Court Tube station on right. Slight jam now at lights. Suspect indicating right. Car No. 2 report position."

"Car 2. We can see you. We are at lights, in same hold-up, centre lane, four or five cars back."

"Eyeball. Car 2 take over."

"Eyeball. We have turned right into Brompton Road, heading west. Speed increasing, 35 now, just passing big Esso garage on right."

Everyone else can tell from the change in voice that car No. 2 has taken over control. He is 'Eyeball' now. Everyone moves up in order and the original lead car drops right back to last, if that's possible.

In light traffic and with lots of cars, the convoy might stretch out for a mile. But in heavy traffic, you might all be there within a space of 200 yards.

If the suspect makes a turn on a busy major road, there's no need to switch. But if he turns into minor roads, you usually change over to avoid suspicion. And the bike is always there in reserve, for he can beat traffic and stay on the nearside, the blind side, so the suspect rarely sees him. Then when the difficult moment passes, the bike drops back again.

On motorways it's different. There is always one car ahead of the target motor and he gets off at the first exit and sits or cruises on the roundabout, waiting for any movement. If the suspect goes straight on, he rejoins the convoy and the cars move up and down on the tail all the time. Another car overtakes and he gets off at the next exit, and the process carries on.

If the suspect thinks he's being tailed, he usually turns off, drives round the roundabout and goes back on the motorway, travelling on in the same direction. That way, anyone following him and doing the same thing stands out like a sore thumb.

But if a car is already on the roundabout and then joins the motorway, the suspect is hardly likely to spot it. And the lads waiting will study a map or an AA book as if they are checking a route.

Our surveillance technique was getting plenty of practice and we became really good. That's how he eventually led us to Seymour Road at Hampton Wick, way out of town near the River Thames. More on that in a moment.

Things do go wrong though, and if there was the slightest hint Henry had become suspicious, we broke off. It wasn't vital to succeed with every tail.

Sometimes the reason was funny, like the day we were outside a pub, miles from Henry's flat. When we were in the cars, we used the wavelength allotted to Hendon police driving school, which they didn't use very often.

Police calls occasionally blurt out of a radio or television just by accident, especially when a copper presses the speak button and opens up. A few words come out, then the radio settles onto the correct wavelength.

Well, we were sitting in a car outside this pub when we hear the obs van report, "Suspect leaving his flat, heading towards car. Prepare to move."

Next thing, a couple of big blokes come out of the pub, look around, see us, and walk straight over. They are Flying Squad. They flash a card and say, "Your call just came over the jukebox!" It was a freak radiowave, nothing you can do about those.

Another aborted car surveillance had its funny side – in the end – but at the time it unnerved us, we thought everything had been buggered-up. The phone tap told us Henry was buying chemicals from BDH, the British Drug Houses company.

We followed him. On the way back to Seymour Road he went down a couple of back streets with us fairly close behind. I was Eyeball, doing the commentary on the radio, and Fred Pritchard was driving. Suddenly, Todd stopped at some green traffic lights. When they turned red, he roared away through them.

"Eyeball. Abort, abort surveillance. Return to Hendon for debriefing."

I was sure he had spotted our car. It was a terrible moment, it seemed all our work was ruined, but later that evening our obs van clocked him back in Seymour Road unloading his chemicals. We soon realised everything was OK.

After he was nicked, I put this incident to Todd. He remembered that day and laughed like a drain.

"I got lost," he said. "I was trying to work out the quickest way back to Hampton Wick. Did I go through the red lights? Well, why didn't you nick me?"

When Todd went on foot, so did we. When he shopped, we shopped as well. And if he ate in a restaurant, we often had some-one in there, checking on his friends, grabbing the odd snapshot, trying to overhear conversation.

It was a sweaty job for us and that had nothing to do with the weather. Tailing is always a challenge, you're always on tenter-hooks. The success or failure of the entire operation could rest on you putting one foot wrong, alerting a careful fella like Henry Todd and losing the lot.

It's not only the villains who suffer from paranoia, so do we. You think everything's gone wrong, you've been blown out, just because the target looks you straight in the face and winks. Henry did that to one of the lads on his tail. It was only a simple gesture but too much was read into it. Again, we thought Henry had sussed us out. And again, we were wrong.

When I was following him on foot, he often headed for Harrods food hall. I got really anxious about going in there, because I always had to buy the same thing, garlic sausage. That's all I could afford. Everything else was so expensive, but I thought it might look suspicious, going in and coming out empty-handed every time.

You see, money was tight. We were only given three months for the operation at first, and now it was running on and the cost was mounting. The acid dealers weren't the only people making a fortune. So were we on a minor scale – at least, when compared to our normal pay.

Our car allowances sometimes came to more than our basic wages. There were also detective allowances, out-of-pocket expens-es, subsistence of £3.70 a day, and overtime. But overtime was no great money-spinner. We were told that if we charged it all, the operation would be closed down. We used to work 70 or 80 hours a week, but the maximum overtime we entered was 15 hours.

And the expenses had to be kept down too, even garlic sausage was a luxury.

From our massive surveillance of Henry, we had built up a picture. He stays with his girl, drives a light blue Volvo, eats in top restaurants like Wheeler's and the Savoy Grill, buys food for home at Harrods – but doesn't appear to have a job.

He plays rugby for a junior side at London Scottish, likes a few drinks, meets up with friends – but not with anybody we know or suspect is on the acid scene.

We have to be patient, but we badly needed to know more about the house at Seymour Road, Hampton Wick. A nice road, nice house, not far from Hampton Court Palace, London Airport and Twickenham rugby ground. It didn't fit into the drugs scene at all.

But anywhere Henry visited and stayed for any length of time, even a few hours, rated a check by an observation team. They would look at his possible contacts, photograph them, buzz along to the local town hall and check the voters' list, ratepayers' list, generally see who they were and what they did.

We found Seymour Road was owned by a JJ Ross, who bought it in 1974 for £24,000. The obs teams clocked cars arriving there and ran a check through the vehicle registration bureau.

You phone in, someone taps out a message that feeds straight into the big bureau computer down in Swansea, and the answer comes back in 30 seconds. You just provide the number, and the computer gives back the owner, plus make and colour of car. So, you have a double-check.

We noticed that the driver of one car pulling up there let himself into the house by key. So, he belonged. Vehicle registration gave us a name, Brian Cuthbertson, a different address, but more checks give us a CRO file. He has previous for drugs.

Another guy arrived on foot and had a key. We followed him back to an address not far away, did a rates' check, and his name was Andrew Munro. Guess what? CRO revealed he'd got previous for drugs as well.

Central index at Devizes had a lot more on Mr Munro. Our friend Gerald Thomas in Montreal talked of a chemist called Andy, a member of the Cambridge Connection. This guy Andy was sent out to Canada by Kemp to buy acid tabs on the street to analyse the contents.

It was discovered that there was only 100 micrograms of LSD

in the tabs instead of the 200 micrograms specified by Kemp. Who had cut the dose in half? The tablet-maker, old Henry or George. That's what had led to the split in 1973. Kemp wanted to provide a great trip for anyone who bought his acid. Henry Todd argued they could put half the acid in, make twice as many tabs and twice as much profit.

Finding that Todd, Andy Munro and Brian Cuthbertson all had keys to Seymour Road, and all with previous for drugs, had a great effect on our team. More pieces were slotting into place, if not yet fitting completely together.

The house was put under constant observation and now all three were followed. Wherever they went, whoever they met, we ran more checks. The index at Devizes was getting very fat.

Andy Munro often used buses and Underground Tube trains, so we had to tail him on foot. You need three or more people to do it properly and make it difficult for the subject to spot you. Say there's three, you have one on the tail, behind or alongside, wherever was best and convenient; another somewhere behind; and the third on the other side of the road.

We had pocket radios to talk to each other, but switching the tail is usually done by hand signals, instinct and experience. On public transport, you have to merge in with all the other passengers, so the way-out hippy gear is no good. Thanks to phone taps, we often had advance warning of where our suspects were going, and tried to dress accordingly.

We would have one in the Tube carriage with Munro, and perhaps a bloke and a girl in the carriage in front and another fella in the one behind. When we got on the train, someone would have to stay on the platform until the last moment, in case Munro stepped off just before the doors closed. Anyone jumping off with him would stand out like a sore thumb. Munro never twigged our tail, nor did the others when we followed them on foot.

Back at Seymour Road things were beginning to look interesting.

Not easy to nose round the house, two inches of gravel drive and path surrounded it. The boys had noticed lights coming on inside when they were sure everyone was out. Then they would go off – although there was no sign of anyone in the rooms.

So, the boys started checking these lighting-up times, and found they were the same every night. That meant time clocks were operating the switches. Why go to all that bother unless you wanted to make it look as though the house was quite normal, as though someone was living there most of the time, which they weren't? What were they trying to hide?

Then the obs team checked all three guys into the house, and one of them had obviously got supplies. They stayed locked in there for three days, and when they reappeared, it was very clear as they walked down the road that Munro was tripping. We recognised all the signs, Andy was well spaced-out. He was ashen-faced, absolutely miles away, freaky. His eyes were drawn and he looked terrible.

Perhaps they've all been enjoying a great trip together, that's what some suspected. The rest, including me, decided we had found another lab, with Todd, Munro and Cuthbertson making acid tabs.

But even if it was a lab, how did it fit in with the Welsh scene? We still had lots of loose ends to tie up.

We started by discovering that Cuthbertson knew Leaf – the guy living in Reading and married to the airline girl – when they were at Reading University together.

We had already tied in Leaf with Spenceley and Hughes, the non-academics in Wales, and then Dalton, a big dealer in London. And Dalton was tied to the guys I lived with in the cottage at Hankerton.

There was more. We had a bloke called Burden – who ran a restaurant in London and had form for drugs – down as a suspect running the acid to Holland.

And Leaf was talking a funny language on the phone to a guy

who was arranging LSD drops. It turned out to be a sort of code, and after a few recordings, and keeping watch on houses and doing a bit more tailing, we broke that code.

On one end of the phone was a schoolteacher called Annable, who had to be one of the cut-off points. These links made life a bit easier. Instead of keeping observation outside these people's houses for goodness knows how long, the phone taps told us roughly when to keep watch and what ought to happen.

Apart from the phone calls, we recorded meetings with cameras. When Spenceley drove up to Leaf Fielding's cottage at Binfield Heath, near Reading, I photographed him getting out of his Range Rover, going inside, and leaving an hour and a half later.

Pictures like that would help us later on and make it impossible for them to deny knowing each other. We also used cameras when they went abroad. Once we heard Henry Todd book a flight to Geneva, so we sent two lads along as well. Henry was followed to the airport and our blokes Graham Barnard and Ray Shipway were waiting in Switzerland for him.

They needed some help from the Swiss police but were under orders not to say what it was all about. Very tricky, and they got quite a bit of aggro before they got any assistance.

Pictures have a big effect on prisoners. After the arrest, you start slapping down photos and telling them, "That's you arriving back from Paris, on Flight No. 123," and give them the exact date. It shakes them, and they realise you have been watching everything. And man, they talk.

But what did all this new info mean? Was there another lab at Seymour Road?

Well, I will never forget the day in Devizes, at yet another Julie conference, when that was first suggested. Remember, the operation is now about eight or nine months old. We have plenty of information, photographs, taped conversations by suspects, our own observations and reports. But so far, we had not taken a single statement. And suddenly, everyone is faced with a complete revamp of our inquiries.

Are the London lot bringing in chemicals and taking them all to Wales for manufacture? Is it the other way round? Are there two labs? And could there now be two organisations?

Our camp was split down the middle, and one or two battles at the top started. A London lab meant more inquiries and more work. That meant more time and more money. The bosses decided – find out, that was the order.

But how? Getting at that house when it was empty was so difficult. So, we went to the town hall and the planning department. Scientists had told us LSD would probably be manufactured in a basement, and the lab had to make the acid before they put it into the tabs. Well, we found out that the house in Seymour Road had a basement, with plenty of room to do everything.

When we were sure the house was empty, some of the boys went up to it, shone lamps through the basement windows and looked in through the periscope mirrors held upside down. The basement was bare.

So, we held more conferences at Devizes, and our camp was still split. In fact, Dick Lee, my boss from Oxford and by now an acting Chief Inspector, came out with a famous remark, "No way is there a lab at Seymour Road."

There bloody well was – but not in the basement – and it finally proved to be doing a lot more acid than the one in Wales. When Dick Lee retired, after Julie, we made a presentation to him, a plaque which read:

NO WAY ITALASR

That was a great laugh at the farewell party, but it wasn't so funny at the time, for those of us who believed in the Seymour Road lab but couldn't prove it...

The final proof came only two days before the big bust. I was out all night working and had just got into bed on Wednesday, 23

March, when the phone went and the obs team at Seymour Road reported a lot of activity plus the arrival of a hired van.

"Someone bring the bike. We need a strong team," they said. Everybody whether in bed, just going to bed, or planning other duties for the day, piled out. And guess who was left with the motorbike? Right first time.

Alan Buxton, the regular bloke, wasn't there. He was fantastic on the machine. He could do wheelies and thought nothing of belting it through traffic. I hadn't been near a motorbike for 10 years.

I stalled at practically every traffic light, and I nearly went over the handlebars. The lads in two of the cars following me were in hysterics, but I managed to get it down to Hampton Wick. Luckily, Buckie had been contacted and took over from there.

Anyway, Todd, Munro and Cuthbertson were moving things out and loading the van. When they moved off, we went too. When they headed out on the M4 motorway, we thought, "Was everyone else right, are they taking the gear down to Wales?"

But they turned off at Reading and went straight to the town rubbish tip. As we watched through binoculars, they started to unload stacks of laboratory glassware, cardboard boxes and plastic containers.

We were right. Dead right. There was a lab at Seymour Road. But what was happening now? Were they packing up and shoving off? Did they know we were on to them?

They piled everything together on the massive tip and set light to it. They were destroying our evidence and we were in a frenzy. But we couldn't do anything.

"They won't like that," I said.

"Does anyone like it?" said somebody in the car.

"No, I mean the tip men, the blokes who work here. They had a fire here two or three years ago and it burned for a week. Caused a lot of trouble."

And just as I was explaining this, the foreman came rushing

over and gave this team a bollocking. Next thing, a bulldozer came over, scooped up some mud and rubbish and put the fire out.

Our evidence was safe. And as soon as the hired van drove off, we got stuck into all this muck and rubbish and started recovering everything that might have the slightest trace of LSD.

By the way, I must tell you, that on the way to Reading, Buckie on the bike ran out of petrol. He missed the turn-off and was half-way to Bristol when he got the message. On the way back, he was going so fast he blew the bike up!

Back at headquarters in Devizes, everything was hotting up. They thought, like us, that the Seymour Road team was getting ready to split.

In fact, the trips to the dump happened quite regularly. After every production run they got rid of most of the stuff in the lab, so it wasn't just sitting there for us to find. They kept some of the more expensive machinery hidden away, but all the glassware went. They had plenty of money. They could afford it.

But we only found that out later, much later.

Next day, the Thursday, the same thing happened, only this time the van took the gear to a tip at nearby Kingston.

Something else important had happened that day. Only we didn't know at the time. When we were chatting to Todd in the cells after the bust, he told us that when he switched on the ignition in his car that morning, his radio, which he'd left turned on over-night, came straight on. And he heard our message.

"Suspect has got in his car and is just moving off towards railway station." Yes, it was another of those freak radio signals.

Todd told us, "You would never have got me. As soon as I heard that, I was off. I made up my mind immediately, I was going home for my passport and away.

"Then I drove round the corner, and right outside the railway station there was a police Panda car and a sergeant talking to the driver. And I relaxed, I thought it was this other bloke you were talking about on the radio, not me."

That was Henry or George, Mr Barclay Todd. His luck ran out after seven years. He had made a fortune, working about once every three months, in the lab. He put a lot of money away in foreign deposit boxes, so much money that he went to the Bahamas once just for the weekend.

But he enjoyed a much longer holiday, as a guest of Her Majesty. Operation Julie broke many records. On D-Day – 26 March 1977 – the simultaneous raids by 800 officers proved to be the biggest combined operation in British police history.

When it came to committing the 31 principal defendants for trial, the court was handed over 3000 typed pages of evidence – a near average of 100 for each prisoner.

In London, the raids went according to plan and police found the laboratory at the house in Seymour Road. But in Wales, the detectives were in for a shock.

They already knew that LSD had been produced in the basement of 'Plas Llysin' an old mansion house. The building was empty most of the time; Kemp and Bott lived in a cottage nearby.

When police checked the basement halfway through Operation Julie, it was spotless. The lab had been dismantled, but scrapings from the walls proved LSD had been produced there. Unknown to police, all the lab equipment was hidden down the well at Kemp's home.

The evidence began to point to another drug-making centre being set up about an hour's drive away, near Lampeter, at the home of Dr Mark Tcharney. Police believed this was the new Welsh lab, so it was put under surveillance.

At 5am on D-Day, the place was busted – and it was clean. There was no current Welsh lab. In fact, there had been no production run in Wales for some months. We had no idea.

Chapter Eighteen

Danger From the Second Trip

Edward Laxton: Seventy-five years ago, pharmaceutical researchers were looking at LSD, aiming to produce a medical aid for psychiatrists to help them fathom the workings of the human brain. The acid trips, similar to the hallucinogenic effects of magic mushrooms, were not the intended result. But worse still were the surprising, the unexpected and unscheduled secondary trips.

Regular acid users often ensured they had a 'minder' in case the expected trip went awry and perhaps induced them to think they could fly. They might be anywhere when a second trip occurred, even in a car and behind a steering wheel.

When the Beatles launched their song Lucy in the Sky with Diamonds – with its obvious capital letters in the title – it was adopted as an anthem by the acid freaks. It was said to be among a number of pop ballads, written under the influence of LSD, and by now established as the fashionable drug-of-choice.

When the BBC realised this link, the Beatles' classic was banned from being broadcast for a long time, on radio and television. The bad trips gave acid a bad name and were the reason drugs squad detectives badly wanted LSD, a cheap and readily available drug, off the streets and out of circulation altogether.

The Last Trip

Martyn Pritchard: I suppose it was bound to happen. I was starting to feel a bit empty when the day of the big bust arrived, the climax to well over a year's hard and fascinating work. But from then on, a way of life which had become almost second nature, was going to change drastically.

No more hiding, chasing, watching or waiting. When we got this mob inside we could become policemen again, and start putting the case together for the court. And I knew that after five and a half years, my days on the drug squad were numbered. A lot of people were heading for their last trip, in more ways than one.

The entire team must have averaged about a dozen hours sleep each, that week. A plan for the big bust had been drawn up at Devizes well in advance, and when we saw all this activity at Seymour Road, the lab breaking up and so on, we thought we had to go in fast, couldn't risk any of that lot disappearing.

Everything else was timed for five o'clock in the morning on Saturday. However, at seven on the Friday evening, a team went over the vicarage wall at the back of the house in Seymour Road and straight through the French windows. Another hit the side door with the universal key, a trusty sledgehammer.

There were about eight locks, but they belted away so hard and often the wall must have shifted, because the interior door fell in first. Inside were Todd, Munro and Cuthbertson. Still a load of gear inside too – rotary evaporators, a vacuum oven, a special fridge, scales, magnetic stirrers and lab equipment.

The first thing our team did was rip the phone right off the wall. That meant anyone ringing in would get 'unobtainable' and think it was just out-of-order. Then the prisoners were taken to Swindon nick, soon to be joined by lots of the others.

Eight hundred detectives were involved. Every group had a drugs squad officer who would know what to look for on the raids. We made well over 100 arrests on that first day and carried on knocking people off right through the weekend. The overall plan worked a treat. Even though a few did slip the net, that was bound to happen.

Detectives from the Julie squad travelled all over England, Wales and Scotland. They conducted police station briefings at three o'clock that morning. These were rather strange – detective constables were telling chief inspectors what to expect, what was needed, what it was all about. For the Julie detectives were the undisputed officers in charge wherever their bust took place, irrespective of rank.

I did the briefing at Reading. There was a farewell party for someone going on at the nick that night, and as everyone realised we were onto something big, those detailed for the bust drank a lot slower than at most farewells.

Dick Lee led that team. He phoned me at Reading at 8.30 that evening. All he said was, "We've got one lab." We still didn't know the acid organisation had split up and we had a lot to learn over the next few days. But it was great knowing that stage one had gone so well.

Like everyone else conducting the briefings, I was able to stand up at three in the morning and start addressing 40 coppers in the big new briefing room at Reading with the words, "Gentlemen, I can tell you that early last evening we took out one of the biggest LSD laboratories in the world, and all of you here are involved in cracking parts of their organisation."

Our job was to hit three houses in the south of Reading, a health food shop in town owned by Nigel 'Leaf' Fielding, as well as his cottage at Binfield Heath. I was leading the cottage bust, and I knew it was going to be very dull.

Every place due to be raided had been under obs since six the previous morning. Leaf and his wife, Caroline, had left in the evening and were already reported arriving at the Spenceley place down in Wales. They were obviously staying for the weekend, so they would get busted down there.

Nine or 10 to a police team – drivers, exhibits officers who would be handed everything suspicious we found, plus dog handlers, searchers, questioners, and uniform police to secure the house after we left with our prisoners. We were organised up to the hilt.

We went into the cottage spot on five. It was empty, as we had expected, but we found a few papers and a piece of cannabis.

I was really drained when I got back to Reading, but I debriefed everybody and checked over the exhibits before they were taken down to Swindon. Then I drove down there myself in my Spitfire.

Swindon again. I was back where it all began 13 months before, with that high-level conference and lunch in the officers' mess. Quite honestly, I could have cried now it was over. It all seemed unreal. We were usually on a high after a bust.

Loads of people rushing around, all with pre-assigned duties. The police station had been cleared, apart from uniform coppers doing the normal town duties, and you couldn't get in without a warrant card and a special Julie pass. Every possibility had been catered for, even three uniform officers to deal with any complaints from our prisoners.

The Assistant Chief Constables from all the combined forces started arriving, pleased and relieved it was over. But I couldn't come to terms with what I saw, all this bustle and bedlam. Where was our tight-knit, long-haired team of weirdos, my mates – car mates, roommates, washing-up mates, observation mates? All this palaver at Swindon nick, this no longer felt like Operation Julie.

But deep down I knew it was and the awful anti-climax was really getting to me. So was the tiredness. I knew we weren't going to question any prisoners that day.

Down in the cells the truth really hit home when I saw all those names against their cell numbers. Henry Barclay Todd, his brother David, Lockhead and McDonnell, Munro and Cuthbertson, Kemp and Bott, Spenceley and Hughes and Fielding, who was my particular interest now.

Dick Lee had very carefully sized up the opposition and had tried to line up all the detectives on the Julie squad to interrogate them. He matched each of us against the individual he thought we would get on with, comparing our personalities and backgrounds.

It was all aimed at getting the most out of our questioning.

We knew very well we had a lot to find out, an awful lot. If we could get them talking, we could piece together their entire operation, from purchasing the chemicals abroad, turning out the acid, producing the tablets in Wales and London, and, finally, to selling them all over the world.

But that wasn't due to start until tomorrow, the Sunday. Now I had to get the initial paperwork done in Swindon and then snatch some sleep upstairs in a room in the single men's quarters. When I came to it, though, I found I just couldn't tear myself away from those cells.

I went down again and looked at all those names. Then I went along the corridors and peered at each prisoner through the Judas holes in the cell doors. For so long these people had been targets. We'd watched their movements in secrecy and became part of their lives, but they never realised we were there. Suddenly, they were real people. And I felt sorry for them.

In an odd sort of way, it was like seeing Muhammad Ali lose his heavyweight title. These people had been top of the tree and we knocked them off, in more ways than one. Our guvnor Dick Lee was a court officer for a long time, so this huge case was going to reach court in prime condition.

We had all been given a report on the backgrounds of the people we were going to interrogate and were prepared thoroughly. I knew where Leaf was born and went to school; what he studied at university; where he was married; how many guests were at the wedding; where his wife worked; who was on her stewardess's course; where she usually flew to; how his shop was doing – absolutely everything.

If I had been ordered to write a report on his life, I think I could have filled another book. According to my notes, it was 15.05 on that Saturday when I stepped into the cell to confront Leaf. He was sitting there hugging his knees, his hands clenched. I closed the door and leaned back against it.

"Do you know why you are here?"

"I suppose it's because they found some dope at Russ's."

"That's not the main reason. You see, at the same time I was executing a search warrant at your house. So, you know what I found – cannabis. But that wasn't the drug I was looking for."

"What were you looking for then?"

"I think we both know the answer to that question."

Fielding shrugged his shoulders and stared at his feet. I didn't know how much and who else he had seen when he and his wife, Caroline, and the Spenceleys were brought into Swindon nick. But he was obviously nervous and very worried. He had every reason to be. I thought I would wind him up.

"Well, I'm not going to talk to you today, but I want you to have a good think about everything, especially three letters – LSD. OK?"

"Yes."

A lot of the lads felt exactly like me when we met for a chat that afternoon, tired and drained, keyed up but depressed. Even the married ones, who knew that now they could tell their wives everything about our operation and start living a normal home life, they felt this anti-climax too.

I slept round the clock and past it. I started Sunday very slowly. Just after 11am I went to see Caroline Fielding in her cell. We talked for a few minutes. I told her about busting her cottage and the cannabis find before I got down to it.

"OK, Caroline, this is the real reason I'm talking to you. I want to know about your involvement with Nigel and the LSD."

"Nigel doesn't use LSD and neither do I."

"We're not talking about the use of LSD, Caroline, but the trafficking of it."

"You're not serious, are you? Nigel, a drugs dealer, that's ridiculous."

She was either a very good actress or we had just given her a bad shock. I had Steve Bentley, another detective, with me, and we just sat on our chairs in the cell very quietly while Caroline fidgeted. Her eyes were going up and down, towards me and then the floor. I didn't think she was acting.

"Well, I'm sorry if it sounds ridiculous, but it just happens to be true."

"I don't believe it. Nigel couldn't keep anything like that secret from me. How do you know he's involved? Has he admitted it?"

"Now calm down, Caroline. I'm afraid, however ugly it sounds, Nigel has been dealing in hundreds of thousands of LSD tablets. I'm trying to find out if you're involved, because if you're not, we don't want to keep you here a moment longer than necessary. Now, did you know what was going on? Because, believe me, we will find out in the end if you don't answer truthfully."

I am telling you all this as it is written down in my official detective's notebook. Looking back, I remember she wasn't taking her time with the answers, as she would have done if they were lies.

"Look, the only thing I know about drugs is the cannabis you found. I don't even smoke cigarettes. I know Nigel smokes, but I can't see any harm in that. But acid, that's impossible. Are you sure you've got the right person?"

"Oh yes, we've got the right one." And I produced the pictures we took of Spenceley's Range Rover, and another of her husband and Spenceley together outside the cottage.

I told her how we had broken the laboratory in London and the one in Wales, and where her husband and Spenceley fitted into the operation.

"This really has come as a terrible shock. I just can't believe it. This is obviously very serious for Nigel," she said.

"Yes, I am afraid so, Caroline."

"You know what you've done, Mr Pritchard?" she said as I was leaving her.

"Yes, I've done my job."

"No. You've made sure that Nigel and I never have a family. By the time he gets out, it will be too late for me."

She was really bitter, but it was her husband who broke the law, not me. Anyway, Caroline was innocent and I arranged to get her released straightaway.

We left and spent the next two hours writing up our notes, having a quick lunch, and preparing ourselves. Then Steve and I went to see Leaf in his cell. I had a fat file, about 6ins thick. I held it out so that he could see the cover with his name in bold letters. I smiled and waited, then told him, "Nigel Raymond Spencer Fielding... this is your life."

A bit corny, I suppose, but I wanted him to know how much we knew about Nigel Fielding. It wasn't enough, not yet, but the folder was impressive. I told him about my chat with Caroline and said, "We want to know about you and the acid."

"Yes, I see." And there was a long, long wait. He was hugging his knees again and staring at the floor.

I decided to go in hard. "When you were busted at Russ's yesterday, 800 police officers were doing other raids, just to knock out the manufacture and distribution of LSD. The three of us here know you are involved. What we want to find out now is your specific role. I can show you a lot of photographs with you and your cottage and shop on them, and people you were meeting. And I can tell you, I have been working on this for over a year."

"Really?" And he was shocked right down to his stockinged feet.

"We are giving you an opportunity to explain in your own words how you got involved in all this." And I reminded him that all his business associates were along the corridor in other cells.

Then I said, "I want to determine Caroline's involvement, if any."

That did the trick. It usually does, especially if the little woman really is innocent. I know a lot of people reading this are going to holler 'unfair'. But you have to consider how Caroline had been enjoying the proceeds of her husband's criminal activities. And if she wasn't involved in them, she was going to walk out a free woman.

"She knows nothing about what I've been doing," said Leaf immediately.

"OK, but I've got to know."

"No, really, she doesn't know anything. I purposely kept her out of it."

Then he started to talk, but he started off with too many lies. So, after a while I interrupted. "Listen, we know you were supposed to take 100,000 tabs to Russ this weekend, but we also know that Brian and Henry were at your place on Wednesday and there was a delay.

"Now you know I'm not making that up, and that's just for starters. Here are some photographs you might like to see. And I can tell you about a lot of things you've been doing lately."

I opened the folder and showed him the snaps we had taken. Then I read him notes about the visitors I had observed at his cottage. He would have to work out for himself how we acquired the rest of the information.

Leaf Fielding was getting one shock after another that day, and he started telling some of the truth – not the whole truth, not yet. He kept quiet about how he first got involved two years earlier, and how he'd acted as courier, and stashed away literally hundreds of thousands of tabs in the woods near his home.

He was getting only £5 a thousand, but he handled up to 112,000 at a time. That amounted to £560 for one simple but highly illegal middleman deal.

That's how the questioning was going in cells all along, either side of us. The main conspirators were gradually filling in the missing bits and pieces we needed. The lesser lights in the acid set-up were farmed out to police stations for miles around and ferried in to Swindon by car and coach for questioning over the next six days.

Leapy Lee, who had assigned us to individual prisoners, took it on himself to go for the big one, the most difficult one, Henry Barclay Todd.

And Leapy had bad luck, because he was the only member of the Julie team who didn't get a cough. All the others talked to some extent, but I don't think Henry would have coughed to any of us.

Anyway, my task was to sew up the first part of the London distribution network, the first cut-off point after the acid left Seymour Road for Fielding, passed down the line to Spenceley in Wales and over the water to Holland.

Now Fielding had met Cuthbertson when they were both at Reading University and it was he who had brought my man Leaf into the organisation. Basically, Leaf operated like this.

He had a number of stash points – literally holes in the ground – in woods near his home, and one or two other places a short car ride away. This kept his house clean and meant the cut-off stages were more secure.

He would get the tabs delivered by London. Hole one was his personal stash, his 'safety deposit box' and nobody else knew where that was. In holes two, three, four, and so on he would leave consignments of tabs for collection by people down the supply chain.

There were a few personal hand-overs, but that's how it usually ran. Some of the others used open-air stash points as well.

Fielding used to package the acid into bags of dog biscuits or tea, putting the LSD right in the middle of the bag, and leave them in the holes to be collected. If someone who picked them up was stopped by police for any reason, these packages would look innocent.

We knew about Spenceley and Wales, but now the export division needed sorting out. Fielding had links with a guy named Martin Annable, another friend of his, and we also suspected a man named Richard Burden, who ran this London restaurant the

Last Resort, but we hadn't pulled him in yet.

The Last Resort, in Chelsea, was an in-place for a lot of bands. In 1974 it got busted, and a fella was lifted with a lot of acid – more than 20,000 tabs. So, from the beginning of Julie it had been watched.

Fielding was starting to open up, so we moved him to an interview room to get more comfortable, and I went into the export scene.

He didn't want to know at first, until I started to tell him what we knew about the UK organisation. He was shattered again, he didn't realise that side was so big. After all, because of the sophisticated cut-off system, he had never heard of Kemp, Bott or Solomon, and he barely knew Todd.

I showed Leaf pictures I had taken at London Airport of some of these people returning from Europe. I was never a good photographer, but I did well at Heathrow because I used to arrange for the baggage conveyor belt to break down for five minutes. This gave me time to get off plenty of shots.

This information gave Fielding even more to think about, and he wasn't the only one. Over the six days, all the Julie detectives were exchanging info between ourselves, then going back into interrogation and telling their subjects more and more about their own set-up. We even introduced a few of the prisoners to each other.

When we finished on that first Sunday night, I needed a pint badly. As Leaf was returned to his cell, with a lot on his mind, I was on my way over the road to the Wiltshire Hotel.

It was gone eight o'clock and right outside the nick I bumped into Cathy Lockhead. She probably thought I had just been bailed, but she was certainly surprised I was there at first, because she hadn't seen me for six months or more.

She threw her arms round my neck. "Oh Martyn, I'm so sorry, have they got you as well?"

I let her hang on for a few seconds and then she said, "Stew's inside, they're supposed to have lots of people inside. How did they get you?"

I took a deep breath before I answered, "Well, Cathy, I work here."

"What do you mean?"

"See that building behind you, Cathy? I work in there."

"I don't understand."

"I work there and at the moment I'm living there."

"Oh Christ, you're not a pig are you?"

"I'm a detective sergeant on the drugs squad. Sorry, Luv."

And she burst into tears and just leaned against me. I didn't feel bad, just uncomfortable. I needed that pint even more. I mean, this lady had cooked me breakfast a time or two. Her husband was the villain, not her. But everybody was getting shocks that day.

I took her back into the nick, sat her down in reception and gave her a cigarette. "Then there's no point in Stew trying to kid his way out of it," Cathy said. She just wouldn't let go of me, her hand was squeezing my arm really tight in her anxiety.

"There's no point in any of them trying to kid their way out of it, Cath, we know too much," I told her.

The copper interrogating her husband told him all about me, and when I looked in on him later in his cell, the first thing he said was, "I knew you were fuzz." Typical bighead, he couldn't admit he'd been caught with his pants down.

On the Monday, Leaf Fielding started to give, but first of all I told him, "Listen, Nigel, you might as well know that you're not a very good liar. Parts of your face redden up a bit and your Adam's apple goes up and down when you're trying it on. We know every time you're not telling the truth."

This was absolutely true, and now he would be even more nervous with his lies. He started again at the beginning and drew us maps of his stash points.

He emphasised they were all empty, but his Adam's apple was

still going strong. I'll give him this much: Fielding had bottle. He would talk but he was avoiding naming names, and I admired his loyalty.

"Tell us about Martin Annable," I said.

"I met him through Brian."

"You know he's here as well?"

"Yes, I do. OK, we had a stash point acceptable to both of us. I just put acid in there for collection."

"Where was it?"

"At Nine Mile Ride, a place called Caesar's Camp. I'll draw another map. But that's empty as well. And that's all there is, there's no more stashes."

Oh yes there were. He was a terrible liar, but we let him dig his own grave. The more he got muddled up with all these tales, the bigger his problem. Eventually, he would seek the relief of telling the truth, the whole truth and nothing but… and then he would be grateful to have me as his audience.

Steve Bentley and I went straight to the stash points, starting at Nine Mile Ride, in the woods near Crowthorne. We found them quite easily from his maps and they were empty. The same evening, we went to Fielding again and I took another tack.

"When Brian Cuthbertson and Henry Todd came to see you last Wednesday, they brought something with them."

"There was nothing for Russ."

"There was some acid though?"

"Yes, I suppose so."

"If it wasn't for Russ, who was it for?"

"Oh God, how did you know they had some acid?"

"People here are talking, Nigel, you had better start talking too." I was bluffing him a bit now, but it worked.

"Was it for Annable? You know Burden as well. Was it for him?"

Fielding nodded slowly and sadly. "There's another stash I haven't told you about."

"Where is it?"

"In the Hartley Wintney area." Bugger me, that was very close to the senior police officers' training college!

"It's not empty, is it?"

He just shook his head again.

"How much is in it?"

"Oh God, a hundred thousand. This really makes things bad for me, doesn't it?"

"No, you are surrendering them to the police. I take it they are still there?"

"Yes, I put them in early and I hadn't phoned Martin to tell them they were in. Then I got busted."

Now it poured out. He had met Burden a couple of times, but Martin Annable was Burden's contact man. The rest we worked out. Burden smuggled the tabs to Holland. Then Annable would collect the money from Burden when he got back and pass it on to Cuthbertson. The drugs went from Cuthbertson to Fielding to Burden to Holland. And the money went from Holland to Burden to Annable to Cuthbertson.

Very neat, and very confusing. If the prisoners hadn't talked at Swindon, we would have been putting a much more involved and much weaker case to the jury.

Now there were two things to do. First, get Burden pulled in. Second, get Fielding to show us the stash with all this acid. We took him across into Hampshire, to Hartley Wintney, and for 24 hours I held the world record for the seizure of acid tablets.

Next day, Leapy Lee took Cuthbertson and Todd to Pangbourne woods, not far from Reading. Todd was a bit of a conservationist and Leapy, who'd found out they had an acid stash in the woods, was threatening to tear down all the trees if they didn't cough. He even had a bulldozer standing by, and that really shook Todd. It indicated the lengths to which we were prepared to go.

Henry gave in, Leapy's men got 670,000 tabs out of the ground.

That was their warehouse, or one of them, anyway.

The acid I found was wrapped in plastic and put inside big packets of Winalot dog biscuits. Annable used to phone Fielding and say, "Do you want to go out for a drink tomorrow?" That was the code for Leaf to stash another acid consignment for Burden to pick up.

Then from time to time, Fielding would drop in on Annable at his house in London and collect his dues.

On the British supply set-up, Russ Spenceley would pay Fielding, who would then meet Cuthbertson at Kew Gardens, deduct his £5 a thousand, hand over the rest of the money and arrange the next delivery. It was a perfect business arrangement – Russ paid for his last supply when he picked up the next lot.

Russ was obviously building his business well. Fielding told us he started with 10,000 tabs, but his last lot was 112,000.

The top men, Todd and Cuthbertson, had to approve everything. No one could just slap in a big order. Just like a legitimate business, they kept control and made sure the people at the end of the network grew slowly and carefully. That was for self-protection, naturally.

By now we had arrested Burden, and I started questioning him on the Wednesday. It turned out he was at college with Russ Spenceley and was finally recruited by Cuthbertson, who told him exactly how to operate.

Burden was no trouble, he was soon talking. He confirmed all the pick-up arrangements in England and said he delivered the Amsterdam consignments to bars behind Dam Square. He gave them to an English guy whose name was Dave, but who used the code name Vincent. Martin Annable also had a code name, Paul, and he used to meet Burden in pubs around Hammersmith, in London.

Every time these two pairs met, in Amsterdam and London, they would arrange the venue for their next meet and sort out the dates. It turned out Burden was doing a bit of freelancing too, supplying a guy named Charles, a blond-haired fella he used to meet by the Serpentine, the lake in Hyde Park, or in a hotel near Harrods.

We also knew he had Australian connections. A kiddie's Teddy Bear with 2000 tabs sewn into its stomach was posted to Australia and disappeared. We know it left Britain for Aus, but then we lost the trail. And on another occasion, there were 5000 stitched into the lapels and seams of a suit worn by a guy called Robin, who was nicked still wearing the suit in Australia and got four years. We traced those tabs back to the Last Resort, but Burden would have none of it.

Let's face it. We tracked down a lot of the organisers when we busted the operation, but there's an awful lot that isn't known to this day, and there must be quite a few people on the fringe of the distribution network who got away.

We had another failure – with the money. The team's elaborate precautions, like the system of cut-off points, also extended to the way they hid their vast fortunes. Their cash was held in safety-deposit boxes and secret numbered accounts in Switzerland, France and other countries. I'm sure of that.

We got quite a bit back from those two countries, but because we didn't know the system, the names they had used and where to go looking, we were constantly being led up blind alleys.

The boss, Detective Superintendent Dennis Greenslade, told us all, "We have recovered about three quarters of a million pounds in cash. I can tell you, gentlemen, from my information that is less than 10%."

As the judge said later to one of the defence barristers, in Bristol Crown Court, "Come now, don't let us argue over a few million pounds in this case."

The prisoners gave the power of attorney to each other, in case only one or two were ever arrested. And to make sure their money stayed intact, some of them briefed outsiders with instructions about what to do in case everyone was caught.

We had the City of London Fraud Squad working on that aspect and even with all their experience, we couldn't crack the system.

But we had a pretty good idea what was going on. One deposit box we had 'frozen' in Switzerland suddenly got some attention from a known London villain, and the Swiss police tipped us off.

They wouldn't let him touch anything, and this character soon realised he could be in lumber. As soon as he got back, he came straight to Swindon with a lawyer, a doctor's certificate, which claimed he didn't have a bruise on his body, and said, "I think you gentlemen might want a word with me."

He even had an overnight bag and a couple of books ready to read in the cells. He told us quite plainly, "I am telling you nothing. I know nothing."

But we let him out that same afternoon, and my old mate Vince Castle took him on the piss. He told Vince a lot then, including how a lawyer for one leading member of the acid team had told him exactly what to do – clear out his safety-deposit box and bank account.

"Did you have to make any more calls?"

"That's all I'm telling you, my old mate. I'm out of it now, I am not interested. Before, I didn't know what was involved. Now I know – all this drugs business – I'm out, mate. Got my plane fare and 500 quid.'

Well, we had guessed as much. Some of them were making sure all the risks they ran and all the prison time they might be serving would not be in vain. The money would be there when they came out.

Strangely, we built up a hell of a rapport with some of the guys in those cells. We talked to them about drugs in general, and they were interested in hearing our view. Many of them were university-trained, brainy and intellectual, and they wanted a two-way discussion.

We told Munro about some of the experiences of acid victims.

There was the bloke who said he could feel the pain of the orange he was eating when he was actually chewing through his own hand, and the babysitter who trussed a kiddie like a chicken and popped it in the oven. When he heard all this, Munro, the brilliant chemist who had made so much acid, just cried like a child.

We even got to the stage where three of us were asked to give evidence for the defence, to testify how helpful these characters had been in our investigations. So funnily enough, after all the time I spent giving evidence for the prosecution, my last appearance in the witness box was for the defence.

Yes, my man Fielding was helpful. He was among the 30 defendants who helped us put together the story of this international acid organisation.

The last one to go down was Henry Barclay Todd – Henry or George, that man of many names – who maintained to me and every detective who went near him, "In the end, on the final day in court, it will all be between two men, me and the man in the wig."

We thought he would tell the judge something big, like the whereabouts of some more acid or money, something which would get him a lighter sentence.

But in the end, on the final day, when thanks to our work the price of an acid tab had increased from £1 to £8, Todd got 13 years. Aged 32, he had set up and headed the London organisation, and imported the essential ergotamine tartrate from Basle in Switzerland. As he turned from the dock he looked at us, the members of the Operation Julie squad, and he winked.

That's all.

Todd knew there were stacks of questions we were dying to have answered. We reckoned we had won, but Henry probably figured he hadn't lost. He would be out in the early 1980s and probably having the last laugh.

Money safe and he probably knew where an enormous consignment of LSD was waiting to be processed into millions and millions more acid tabs. He stayed silent but nearly nine months after his arrest, Richard Kemp revealed his hiding place – beneath the quarry-tiled floor of the lounge in his cottage.

Kemp, 34, founder member of the 'Cambridge Connection' and the chemist who produced the LSD, was sentenced to 13 years.

Brian Cuthbertson, 29, who helped run the supply network between the London laboratory and the wholesale pushers, and helped Todd recruit members of that organisation, got 11 years. Russ Spenceley, 28, one of the biggest dealers who was first suspected as an LSD supplier back in 1971, got 10 years.

David Solomon, 52 – authority on drugs, author of several books on the subject, importer of ergotamine tartrate from Laupheim in West Germany, elder statesman of the Cambridge Connection who provided so many American contacts vital to their organisation – 10 years.

Andy Munro, 29, also got 10 years. He was the chemist for the London lab who produced the LSD and then, with Todd acting as tablet-maker, turned it into acid tabs in different shapes and colours. This was to fool police and the 'acid heads', for some preferred blue to green or orange. But they were all the same.

Dr Christine Bott, 32, who liked to breed goats and live off the land, lovingly tending her kitchen garden and breaking off to help Kemp make the acid tablets in Wales – she was given nine years.

Alston 'Smiles' Hughes, 30, friend and assistant of Spenceley, with a liking for champagne to which he occasionally treated his neighbours in Wales in their local, and Nigel 'Leaf' Fielding, 29, the first cut-off point between the London producers and the top rung of the supply ladder – they got eight years.

Stew Lockhead, 32, and Bill McDonnell, 28, who lived at Hankerton and made me welcome in their home, they also got eight years each. The acid I was first offered, which set Operation Julie in motion, almost certainly originated from them.

Martin Annable, 29, the schoolteacher who helped create that first cut-off point in London and was also a money collector – six years. Tony Dalton, 33, a London supplier – five years. Dr Mark Tcharney, 26, the go-between and acid-carrier for Kemp in Wales and Solomon in London after the Cambridge split – three years.

The charges at Bristol Crown Court against the 14 main conspirators included conspiracy to produce, supply and possess LSD.

After the judge sent those off to gaol, he dealt with another 17 defendants facing lesser charges – and lighter sentences – including the wives and girlfriends who knew what was going on and occasionally took a telephone order or drove a car with the supplies.

Others among the 120 originally arrested were dealt with at their local courts on more minor charges, and some were released.

There are still some who were never caught and who went on to be involved, elsewhere in the world, in putting together another LSD laboratory and supply network. But there will never be anything to rival Operation Julie.

Chapter Nineteen

Celebrities on the Oxford Drugs Scene

Edward Laxton: Joshua Macmillan, the ex-Prime Minister's grandson, died from a heroin overdose in his rooms at the university in 1965.

On the last day of June in 1986, Olivia Channon was celebrating the end of her finals at a party in Christ Church College. She was 22, an heiress of the Guinness brewing family and daughter of Tory cabinet minister Paul Channon. A wild girl through her three years at Oxford, she had mixed alcohol and heroin. Fully dressed but draped across a friend's bed, she passed out and died during the night.

They had both enjoyed hard drugs.

The so-called soft drugs had a much stronger following in Oxford, but during his time at Balliol College, Macmillan was a contemporary of Howard Marks, who achieved celebrity status elsewhere and much later on.

A brilliant student and formally educated at a Welsh grammar school, Marks was awarded his degree and later returned on a post-graduate course, to achieve a PhD in nuclear physics.

During this second spell at the university he was a contemporary of former US President Bill Clinton, who was a Rhodes Scholar for almost two years, in 1968 and '69. He was at University College and has admitted to smoking weed while at the university.

We don't know whether Marks and Clinton knew each other, but Howard Marks supplied a lot of cannabis in various forms around Oxford at that time. And they were near neighbours, living in flats at Leckford Road, about half-a-mile from city centre.

It's doubtful that they met doing drugs. The ex-President, by his own admission, was a small-time user. Marks was very much a big-time smuggler and during his later lifetime, clamouring for publicity, so it is doubtful whether that connection would have remained a secret.

BSc, PhD, MI6, IRA and the Mafia

Martyn Pritchard: Of all the characters on the drugs scene in Oxford during the early 1970s, the real mystery man had to be Howard Marks. But my singular involvement with this guy was a bust on his flat above a dress shop in the middle of the city. This was four years after he left the university. I was a member of that team, but I had left the police force by the time Marks gained international notoriety later on.

He was reputed to be a brilliant student and was always on the fringe of the Oxford scene. His business operations had kept him in the city. He was a partner in the dress shop, he ran a stamp-collecting business, a record shop, and dealt in property in a small way. He also made £3000 importing candles from the Continent during a power strike during the 1972/73 winter.

I thought it was going to be a fairly straightforward bust until I went to the briefing by a couple of Customs investigators. Then they told us our man Marks was mixed up in a £6 million smuggling racket to the States, flying cannabis in from Europe.

We were all amazed. Marks was known to be on the scene in Oxford but there wasn't a single conviction against him. And suddenly, to our embarrassment and great surprise, Howard's involved in a job this size. And there was more to come.

Reporting for the Daily Mirror, Ed Laxton knew much more about Marks than me and I knew he had an arrangement with one of the bosses at our HQ – in the same way he and I had an arrangement during Operation Julie – so it is better left to him the tell the Howard Marks story.

Mr Nice or Mr Nasty

Edward Laxton: Many thousands of words have been written by and about Howard Marks – or Mr Nice as he liked to call himself. That was the title of the first book he wrote, his autobiography. And after an early life of secretly operating as a drugs smuggler and intelligence informer, when he left prison for the last time Howard Marks became a master publicity-seeker.

He wanted to add to this image of Mr Nice, but in reality he was more suited to the title Mr Nasty. That was and still is my personal opinion. The first time his name appeared in print, the very first time he was exposed, Howard Marks was on the front page of the Daily Mirror in a report written by me. The tip-off didn't come from Martyn Pritchard – we had not met at that time – but I will explain how we put Mr Howard Marks on show.

I had a contact in Oxford who did not give me many stories, but when he did they were all big. His early tip-offs always stood up, virtually every detail proved correct. I never paid a penny for these yarns, but we enjoyed the odd drink and pleasant dinners together, courtesy of my Mirror expenses. He was a mine of information.

We met by accident one Wednesday evening in the spring of 1973. "Ah, I have been meaning to call you. Do we have time for a drink now?"

Where this particular gentleman was concerned, I was a newspaper reporter and with his prior form, there was always time for a drink.

"Keep your eye on the Old Bailey. Big drugs trial coming up and a member of the team of alleged smugglers, name of Howard Marks, will not turn up. He's on the run and young Howard has some very interesting connections."

"Never heard of him. How interesting?" I replied.

"Well, this ring exporting drugs into America was also importing guns for the IRA, and our man was being used as an informant by MI6, our intelligence service."

"Is that why he's gone missing? Did MI6 spirit him away – for obvious reasons?"

"No, no, nothing like that. They were supplying some very good quality cannabis, well-liked by the Americans who will pay handsomely for it. Their sales network is wide and has ties to the Mafia. That's who have persuaded our man to disappear."

"The Mafia?"

"That's right. Well, a character named Burton Moldese. He was suspected by the FBI of being a Mafia hitman at one time. He called on Marks, they left together, and Marks has subsequently disappeared without trace."

"So, he could be dead?"

"More likely abducted. Bail terms had him reporting to Oxford police station twice a week and he's failed four times. That's why he is unlikely to appear at the Old Bailey."

A fantastic story, from a very good source, as long as it would stand-up. As any journalist will agree, you need two sources – the first to give you the original information, the second to confirm all the facts.

It was almost too good to be true, but the story needed checking and the first check would not be difficult. The case was due to be heard at the Old Bailey "very shortly, being delayed for obvious reasons," said my man.

The Mirror had a staff reporter at the Bailey, George Glenton, so I called him at home and said, "If a drugs conspiracy case comes up and a defendant, Howard Marks, fails to show, ring me, George – or tell the desk." I figured it would not be wise to dig around too early, but if Marks missed trial, possible bingo!

Two weeks later, on a Monday evening, George called me. Howard Marks had apparently skipped bail. I had not mentioned any background to the desk, not a whiff of what might be coming. Next morning, I spoke to the news editor Dan Ferrari. "I need about three days in the clear, Dan. Not much on at the moment, anyway, but if I can stand up this yarn, I can get MI6, the IRA and the Mafia in the intro."

"Only three days?" Dan was a caustic old bugger, really good news editor and father of LBC's Nick Ferrari. Now, I laid out the background.

"Give me a ring at the end of each day, just a brief progress report. If it's there, I'm sure you will get it."

First off, that Tuesday morning, I went over to Oxford to find out all I could about Mr Howard Marks. The lady who shared a flat at Leckford Road, shut the door as soon as I identified myself. In fact, for one reason or another, a lot of people shut the door on me – physically or metaphorically. Ultimately, I needed a lot more than three days to piece it all together. And that was only the first chapter.

Marks was a financial partner in a women's fashion retailer – for a time he lived above the AnnaBelinda shop in Oxford – and I went to see Belinda. A lovely lady, who this time shut the door in a more genteel manner. But she had good reason. We'll get to that shortly.

Detective Superintendent Phil Fairweather was a very old contact and a good friend. I knew him from the Great Train Robbery 10 years earlier, when he was a sergeant. He was very senior at Thames Valley HQ now.

I phoned, mentioned the Old Bailey and we met outside Phil's local Chinese takeaway. He levelled with me straightaway, "Can't help you with this one, Eddie. We heard you were on the prowl and I had to report your approach to the ACC. Down here we're only a small cog, this one stretches a long way. To be honest, Eddie, we would be very interested in what you can turn up."

Great! Thanks, Phil, never mind the ACC. That was shorthand for "tell me what you've got and I will give you a steer if you're on dodgy ground".

He was also saying, "We'll help you if you help us." Phil

Fairweather and I had reached similar accommodations in the past. So, at the end of Day One, I phoned Dan Ferrari and reported. "We're getting there, Dan. It definitely has legs."

Of course, I went back to my original contact and he gave me two names. I already had Burton Moldese, the ex-Mafia hood. Now my contact gave me Hamilton McMillan – I would need to check on him through Balliol College – and Jim McMahon, alias Jim McCann – "Try Belfast," he said. That might attract too much attention.

Instead, I went on to the Mirror library and checked cuttings. McCann was an IRA prisoner who had gone over the wall at Crumlin Road Gaol, one of nine prisoners in a mass break-out in November 1971.

Yet another contact, with experience of drugs squad operations, checked the Criminal Records Office for me and found that McCann's file had him down as a suspected drugs smuggler – as were many in the IRA ranks, helping to finance their general activities. Now I had the IRA connection.

College records revealed Hamilton McMillan was a contemporary of Howard Marks at Balliol during the late 1960s. He had graduated and gone to the Foreign Office, where his father had served as a diplomat. I phoned the FO, but he had no listed extension. But Balliol had turned up a current address for me, in South London.

On the Thursday I knocked at that door. When it was opened, I said, "Hamilton McMillan? I'm from the Daily Mirror." Whoever it was who answered did not confirm a name, but he went a pale shade of green and closed it, very quickly.

I knocked again, and a voice said, "Please, go away." So I figured I now had a correct identity for the MI6 agent. I might not be able to use all these identities in the first story, but the acronyms MI6 and IRA, alongside 'the Mafia' would make a good read, as I had promised Dan Ferrari.

I played it straight with Customs and Excise in London, asking their Press Office to outline the case they had presented earlier that week at the Old Bailey. Very little had appeared in the daily newspapers. The court story was too obscure, the defendants who turned up had pleaded guilty, and were in court and off to prison within a couple of hours.

Customs were only too pleased to oblige. They appreciate good publicity and I was given a full background briefing... Holland, America, Ireland, lots of lovely colour. That, together with the stuff I had picked up in between the phone calls and my door-knocking, gave me plenty to write.

My progress report to Dan was delayed while I by-passed home and drove to Oxford to see Det Supt Fairweather again. I ran everything by him, the names and what they had been up to, and told him I was aiming to write it the next day, Friday, for publication on Saturday morning.

Phil gave me the nod. I had nothing that would lead to a denial and then a published correction. In fact, I was telling him stuff he didn't know. Too many different agencies were involved – the Metropolitan Police, Customs and Excise, through MI6, Interpol, the FBI. Thames Valley police were indeed, a small cog.

Chapter Twenty

The Oxford Men Go International

Martyn Pritchard: In the Thames Valley drugs squad, we thought we were pretty good at our job. Other forces, not just those across our county boundaries, asked often enough for our help. They would not invite a mug outfit on to their patch.

Howard Marks proved us wrong. We knew he was on the drugs scene and hash was his bag. But he had no convictions against his name, we had never even had him in our sights. Soon after the bust on the Oxford pad where I was involved, we were told officially that Marks was mixed up in a £6 million racket. That is a helluva lot of hash.

And to our embarrassment, we discovered he got into that heavy smuggling ring through another Oxford man – Graham Plinston, who was suspended from his college for a year after he was arrested and held in Germany on a drugs bust. Marks went over to pay his fine and get him out.

Our Oxford raid on his pad was very ordinary. The flat was clean but we took possession of some letters, accounts, airline tickets, a few scribbled notes and telephone numbers. No drugs there – and no Marks.

Knowing some of the background, it was possible to read between the lines in the letters he wrote to his live-in lover in Oxford about what he was up to. There were indications that he was loading drugs in Holland, and one letter in particular, sent from Dublin, was about landing the guns in Ireland.

Some of those letters were dated 1971, and here we were in 1974, damn near three years later, learning for the first time that Howard

Marks, a bloke on our patch, during all this time was operating as a big-time, international drugs smuggler.

I suppose MI6 had their own fish to fry and it served their purpose to let him continue with the drugs and watch McCann, the IRA man, meanwhile forgetting about co-operating with British Customs, the Central Drugs Intelligence Unit or us in Thames Valley police. Until the shit the fan.

That was at the start of the Howard Marks saga – it's funny how people from Oxford University seem to get to the top, even in the drugs world.

Official Confirmation
Edward Laxton: On the Friday morning I dictated the story from home on the phone and caught the train to London. I figured it was going to be a long day. My story would be in front of the office lawyer, a barrister and expert libel reader, and I didn't trust memos to do the job for me.

With a heavy intro like that I would rather argue personally, line-by-line if necessary, to get it through. As it turned out, the lawyer was very happy, a couple of agreed deletions and he initialled each page in red ink, indicating approval from his office.

Dan Ferrari was happy, so was the editor Tony Miles, especially after receiving a phone call with a request for a meeting at 6pm. The story was strong and it was exclusive, and scheduled for Saturday morning's splash. But the editor's visitor was aiming to keep it out of the paper.

He was the official lawyer from the Special Intelligence Service, which comprises, among other departments, the desk-bound overseers and overseas agents of MI6. If a newspaper is issued with a 'D' notice – from the Ministry of Defence – it is bound to comply and spike the story. These are rare and the SIS were not prepared on this occasion to call on their Whitehall colleagues for a 'D' notice.

So, Tony Miles was not prepared to agree to their request

that he should not publish my story. "Your lot are obviously very embarrassed to get mixed-up with a drugs smuggler, and I believe it is most certainly in the public interest for the Mirror to publish." That is apparently what he said, and the lawyer went away empty-handed.

The news editor and I were called in as soon as the man left. A bottle of champagne and three glasses were on the editor's desk. "That was really quite an experience, very enjoyable, never happened to me before," said Tony Miles.

Dan Ferrari added, "And it proves this errant reporter got it right, for once."

He chortled when he saw my face. We didn't quite finish the champagne. Dan wanted to take me over to the pub for a more personal celebration. We really had a success on Saturday morning, a big front-page splash with a turn inside. Plus, we also knew there was more, a lot more, of this fascinating yarn to come.

The story was out. I had only joined the cloak-and-dagger brigade while that was necessary, now I could make my inquiries more easily. In terms of really juicy stories, follow-ups rarely overtake the original, but Howard Marks and this £6 million racket was the exception.

It revolved around the pop scene, the mammoth overseas pop concerts. Big pop groups always like to use their own sound equipment, and those huge amplifiers are ideal for hiding a lot of cannabis. This team of smugglers were so cocky, they invented a completely non-existent band, with a phoney registered office in London, their own management company and all the trappings.

This 'band' used to obtain customs documents from Italy, Switzerland, Austria, Holland, Ireland, France, America and the UK for the temporary import and export of their sound gear. When they went on the road in Europe with their army of roadies, they insisted on having their huge amplifiers.

The amplifiers went by road from London to one of the

European countries. The so-called roadies would meet the drugs suppliers and load up. Then the equipment would be flown to the States, always to a different town where a big pop concert or festival was due to be held. A few leading bands, particularly Emerson, Lake and Palmer and Led Zeppelin, playing these concerts, were effectively used as cover.

Afterwards the equipment would be flown back to Britain to wait for the next trip. All this activity cost a lot of money – but each amplifier could hold up to 100lbs of cannabis. And they did about seven trips like this, sending anything from 14 to 23 amplifiers at a time.

When the job broke, US Customs officers reckoned 12 million dollars' worth of really good quality hash was involved, the equivalent of not less than £6 million. Howard Marks did a lot of business in London, and in Italy and Holland.

It was not his fault the operation collapsed. That was down to a 'sniffer' dog at Kennedy Airport in New York. The amplifiers were being flown from Schiphol Airport in Amsterdam to Las Vegas by Pan Am. But no direct flight meant one piece of equipment was left off the connecting flight. The dog smelled the drugs in a routine warehouse check.

By now the other amplifiers were in the air, but police at Las Vegas were tipped off and followed the guy who collected them. He realised they were on his tail, pulled into a garage and gave himself up.

It took months for American police, UK Customs, Dutch Customs and police all over Europe, to piece together this operation, but the import-export documents – and the dog – gave the game away. It was a near-perfect set-up, but then the successful smuggling operations always are, they have to be.

The financier was an American millionaire. A pair of English guys who were highly placed in the pop world – on the concert production side – ran the show this side of the Atlantic. With them were four former students at Oxford and two or three drivers, carpenters and odd-jobbers.

Many of their deals were set up in Amsterdam, a lovely city and a great shame it became the drugs capital of Europe – thanks to the notoriously lenient legal system which dispensed lighter sentences for smuggling drugs than stealing a bicycle. And not many years would pass before potted cannabis plants would be on sale at moderate prices, in garden nurseries and market flower stalls.

While police in seven different countries were looking for them, Howard and the rest of that team found out they were in trouble through a gaff on the part of someone in the American police department. Right after the bust in Las Vegas, they put out the news to the television stations.

A newsreader went on air, laughed and said, "Hey you out there, someone has just dropped 12 million bucks," and he went on to describe the big drugs bust, the sniffer dog and the trail from New York to Las Vegas.

The US. police would have rounded up a lot of people if the news had been kept secret for just a few more days. So now the main culprits are on the run. Four months later Marks was finally busted. He was back in Amsterdam again and had a little cannabis in his pocket at a party that got raided.

Had he kept quiet and maybe given an alias, a court might have fined him or passed sentence of maybe a few weeks. A little personal possession was no big deal in Holland. But Marks revealed his true identity and Interpol did the rest. He was not worried about returning to London because his fall-back story was that he was helping MI6.

He was charged with conspiracy, being part of the £6 million drugs syndicate, taken to court and remanded in custody. Then he was let out on bail because he would have to wait a while for his trial at the Old Bailey, with a £50,000 surety guaranteed by his father, a retired merchant marine captain.

He went to work on his story… the previous year in Holland, Graham Plinston had introduced him to a man who called himself Jim McMahon, who was also a smuggler. His real name was Jim McCann, an officer in the IRA Provos and an escapee from Crumlin Road Gaol in Belfast.

McMahon – or McCann – was known to be into drugs and guns, using some of the profits from the drugs to buy weapons and ammunition to send back to Ireland.

He had run a business in Dublin importing electronics equipment. But his new lifestyle on the Continent, roaring around in a Rolls-Royce, throwing lavish parties at his home in the lake resort of Loodsrecht, 12 miles from Amsterdam, and spending lots of time with dodgy characters, attracted attention from the Dutch police.

Surveillance photos were widely circulated. UK intelligence operatives soon identified McMahon as the missing man from Crumlin Road, on the run now for 18 months. More pictures were requested and showed McMahon meeting Plinston and Marks, all three together in Holland.

Back in London, the second set of photos was seen by Marks's old colleague from Balliol College, the MI6 man Hamilton McMillan, who was targeting the IRA. He identified both Plinston and Marks and planned a reunion.

An accommodation was reached. Marks would inform on Jim McMahon/McCann's weapons smuggling, which might prove useful as a fall-back cover story if he, Marks, was arrested with illegal drugs.

And that is exactly what happened. Marks was confident that when he got back to London from Amsterdam he could call on Hamilton McMillan to bail him out of trouble. He was wrong.

Who knows whether any of Marks' reports to MI6 were of any use. Certainly, they did no harm to McCann, who remained a free man and was never re-captured. Who knows if the intelligence agency had a further and wider agenda – but they were deeply embarrassed after Marks was caught, charged and bailed to appear for trial at the Old Bailey.

Marks went to see his MP, but that did him no good. He threatened MI6, saying he would blow everything but still got similar treatment. Then he made the same threats to his co-conspirators, plus the American financiers and receivers in the mammoth drugs operation.

Remember, I had explained my deal with Detective Superintendent Phil Fairweather. After my original story was published we had another meeting – Howard Marks was missing and I might discover his whereabouts first, which is exactly what happened a few months later. Anyway, Phil told me the landlady at Leckford Road had described a big man who had called for Marks on a Friday morning in early April.

"I've got to go, it's serious," Howard Marks told her and, white-faced and trembling, he left Oxford forever.

That's why police had him officially reported as 'abducted'. But by whom? If MI6 had quietly removed Marks to make sure he didn't talk in court, they weren't going to admit it. There was no phone call or anything from the IRA admitting responsibility. And if they were responsible, it was a matter of waiting for the body to turn up. They don't take prisoners, do they? That was Phil's reading of the situation.

Or maybe it was down to Marks' American connections? Police talked to his friends who told them Marks had been beaten up in London on two occasions. The American end might be concerned. If Marks started talking to keep himself out of prison, he might keep on talking. They had some hot property to protect.

Top quality cannabis, worth millions and millions of dollars, had been arriving in America from the Middle East, North Africa and the Far East, through these perfect European links. It was selling for top-dollar to the Brotherhood of Love communes, and the Californian flower power hippies. This marvellous hash was in big demand.

The obvious move was to talk to the team who had already gone from the Old Bailey to prison having pleaded guilty. Further cooperation would have a bearing on their possible parole.

An American in Brixton prison, three English guys elsewhere and an American woman in Holloway, they also had a call apparently from the same American who warned them all to keep quiet.

It took the various agencies, Customs, police in London, New York and Oxford, customs investigators in the UK and Holland, to discover that in the end, it was certainly all down to the Americans.

A long, exhausting check through files at London Airport revealed that a hood from the States, suspected by the FBI of being a Mafia former hitman, had been staying in London for two months. He went under the alias of Burton Moldese,

A photo was sent over by police in the States. The landlady in Leckford Road identified him as the man who had removed Marks, and the five in gaol also recognised the photograph. On the day Marks disappeared, airline manifests showed Burton Moldese flew from London to Milan and back again, then straight on to Los Angeles.

Howard had told a lot of his friends and his parents about his work for MI6. That's why his father stood bail surety for £50,000. Everyone in Oxford who knew him, was more than surprised when the story came out in the papers that he had disappeared. It appeared no one thought he had that much bottle.

At the time it wasn't clear whether Howard Marks was grateful for his 'abduction'. He was trying to resign himself to spending time in gaol once he accepted his MI6 overlords were certainly not making any moves to save him.

He was hoping to continue his studies for a PhD in nuclear physics while he was in gaol and had arranged for Oxford tutors to coach him by post. Apparently, he was going to ask the prison governor to have his books sent along immediately.

I went to Holland and to Ireland and talked to customs investigators who had traced seven Marks-Plinston-McCann drugs consignments. They believed four had come from Afghanistan or Pakistan, then two were shipped into Rotterdam and two into Dun Laoghaire in Dublin. Another three had reached Holland by road, from either Lebanon or Morocco.

It was all flown to America, as far as they could tell, and none found its way on to the European or UK markets. The size and number of amplifers showed the loads varied in value, between $4 million and $12 million at street-level prices in the US.

Six months after he disappeared, Howard Marks slipped back into the country. He must have crossed one of his hippy friends or contacts, as we had an anonymous tip on the Mirror news desk with enough detail to make it look genuine, plus a hideout address in London. He was here briefly to clear up his affairs.

Photographer Eric Piper was with me again and we went to an apartment in Maida Vale, West London. For the first and only time, I came face-to-face with the man and said, "Howard Marks..?"

"Who? Not me, you've made a mistake." He brushed past me, went outside and climbed into the passenger seat of a waiting white VW sports car and disappeared again – but not before Eric snapped a full-frontal picture, positively identified later by detectives in Oxford. He stayed on-the-run for another six years.

Chapter Twenty One

The 1970s Drugs Scene

Martyn Pritchard: The LSD acid tabs, amphetamines and pills of various colour and distinction, were being produced here in the UK. The increasing quantities of cannabis, cocaine and heroin were smuggled in by small operators and, later, the big syndicates.

That was the core of the drugs scene here in the 1970s and every faction was growing by the month, certainly in the Home Counties and the Thames Valley. It was more widespread too, no longer confined to the hippy communes, drop-outs, festival fans, university and college communities or wealthy party-goers.

LSD, amphetamines and a small amount of home-grown cannabis could be produced here, but the main drugs trade relied on smugglers. Demand no longer outstripped supply, market forces were controlling prices and flirting with drugs was no longer an expensive luxury.

But there were side-issues as well. Mappin & Webb, the Regent Street jewellers in London, were publicly horrified when they discovered the silver razor blades and tiny silver teaspoons they were selling on expensive chains had become upper-crust emblems of the drugs trade – for cutting the cannabis or measuring the coke snorts. These pieces of jewellery were apparently withdrawn.

I never knew Howard Marks, and as an undercover detective I dealt with some major players on the drugs scene around Oxford. But he was really big-time, an international operator. He claimed to be a great fan of soft drugs, and then the money, very big money, became the attraction.

His only good deed, as far as I am aware, was to come up with the idea that any bicycle left for a while in Oxford would not be classified as 'stolen' – it was 'temporarily borrowed' – if the cross-bar or part of the angled-frame, was painted white by the owner. Hundreds of bike-owners did that and left their machines behind when they left the university.

From everything else I heard, Howard was not a particularly wholesome character. He was very clever, he had a wide circle of so-called friends, but once he went missing, it was hard to find anyone who had a good word to say about the man.

Not Really Nice at All

Edward Laxton: Rosie Lewis, who had also been at Oxford, was a lady with whom Marks lived for five years and by whom he fathered a daughter. Rosie was the lady he left in the lurch when he disappeared from Leckford Road. She was none too pleased with his betrayal and would probably not have cast her vote for the title of Mr Nice.

Along the way Marks had married and divorced, engaged in a spot of wife-swapping and generally enjoyed a trail of romances.

After he disappeared, he went to Milan. We knew he was delivered there by Burton Moldese. What we did not know was that his sister had worked there, at a TEFAL private school – Teaching English As a Foreign Language. A year later I had a tip-off, went to Milan, traced an address and found a few eyewitnesses. But I was three weeks late and I fancied this particular contact was aware of that.

I had watched a very nervous Mr Marks Senior appearing before an Old Bailey judge, who asked if there was any good reason why Howard's father should not surrender any or all of his £50,000 bail surety.

Marks's father, Dennis, was a retired merchant marine captain, still living in the village of Kenfig Hill, South Wales, where the family grew up. His house was threatened and this world of drugs and courts and criminals was very strange to him. The boy he was so proud of when he won a place at Oxford from the local grammar school had let him down badly. Not very nice.

He was also proud to hear how Howard had helped MI6 to trap an Irish gunrunner, until that was revealed as a cover story for his drug dealings. Pretty nasty.

The judge took pity on Dennis Marks, while a barrister was pleading his case. "He knew nothing of his son's double-life and did what any father would do, coming to the boy's rescue" – or words to that effect. He kept every penny.

That same judge may have taken a different view had he known Marks Junior had gone from the Old Bailey to Oxford, on to Milan then America, where he soon connected with suppliers and buyers as the middleman again. As a fugitive from justice, Howard Marks claimed the very first deal he set up earned him £300,000.

Writing his autobiography several years later, Marks admitted, "Between 1975 and 1978, 24 loads – that's almost 23 tons, of marijuana and hashish – were successfully imported through JFK Airport in New York.

"They had involved the Mafia, the Japanese Yakuza, the Brotherhood of Eternal Love in California, the Thai army, the Palestine Liberation Organisation, the Pakistani Armed Forces and Nepalese monks.

"The total profit made by all concerned was £48 million, they all had had a good run… until the US Drug Enforcement Administration intercepted two consignments and arrested Mafia associates right there in New York."

During these years Marks used many aliases, adding one more when he bought the passport of a convicted American killer, Donald Nice, an ideal name for his self-portrayal as a loveable rogue. 'Mr Nice' became his new persona and he was soon rising to the very top in the world of high-quality soft drugs.

In 1979 he linked up with Colombian cannabis dealers and

that year imported 50 tons of cannabis into the UK, enough to supply the entire British market for almost a year. Twelve months later Marks, back in England, walked into a trap and was arrested by UK Customs officers for his part in importing £15 million of cannabis. He was caught with a lot of incriminating evidence, plus £30,000 in cash.

Back at the Old Bailey and defended by Lord Hutchinson QC, Marks pleaded not guilty and the court heard his six-year-old MI6 defence. The jury believed him, he was acquitted but found guilty of using false passports.

Sentenced to two years, he was released after five days – Marks had spent months in prison on remand awaiting trial – and that counted towards his sentence.

Marks was immediately re-arrested by Customs for the 1973 escapade – when he first disappeared and went on the run – but following a plea-bargain and the threat to re-run the MI6 defence, he served just three months of a three-year sentence.

Throughout the 1970s, Howard Marks led a charmed life. Though several months were spent in prison cells, they were minimal compared with all of his gaoled associates in 1974, and a reasonable return for the estimated £2 million a year he was earning.

Into the 1980s, a free man and no longer 'Wanted – a Person of Interest', Marks settled in Majorca, but he was soon running a multi-faceted business empire, which included drugs smuggling, on a massive scale.

Yet another estimate... for some years he was suspected of supplying one-sixth of the entire global market in soft drugs. Marks was laundering his money through Chinese Triads in the Far East, and in Europe and America through a travel agency, a paper mill, a wine importer, a secretarial service and a water-freight company.

He would marry again, to Judy Lane, and they had three children, and along the way he met international playboy and conman

Lord Tony Moynihan. They went into business together and that led to his eventual downfall.

Lord Moynihan, the third baronet, inherited his title, married five times and ran a seedy operation in the Philippines, bars, brothels and massage parlours, heroin-dealing, until a coup ousted the dictator Ferdinand Marcos in 1986, and his protector fled.

The playboy peer was now vulnerable and targeted by Scotland Yard and the DEA, who offered him immunity from arrest if he wore a secret tape recorder. He met Howard Marks, offering to sell him a small island in the Philippines, where all the land could be turned into a cannabis farm to produce his own marijuana.

Tony Moynihan was very much the black-sheep of his family. His great-grandfather won a VC during the Crimea campaign, while his grandfather was an eminent surgeon in London. His half-brother Lord Colin Moynihan − another Oxford graduate − won an Olympic silver medal for rowing, later becoming a Conservative MP and Minister for Sport.

Back in Majorca, DEA agent Craig Lovato set up Operation Eclectic and finally pulled in Howard and Judy Marks. Simultaneous arrests were made in America, England, Holland, Pakistan, the Philippines, Spain, Switzerland and Thailand.

The couple spent many months in prison, in Barcelona and Madrid, before Lovato had them extradited to stand trial in Florida. Lord Moynihan was the chief prosecution witness, his wire-tap transcripts and the statements of two more former criminal conspirators − Ernie Combs, from the Brotherhood of Eternal Love, and brother-in-law Peter Lane, both bargaining for reduced sentences − were part of a 140-page dossier.

Faced with such compelling evidence, Marks pleaded guilty and was gaoled for 25 years for racketeering. He was sent to Terra Haute, a State Penitentiary in Indiana, one of the six most secure prisons in the country, and with the very worst reputation − for gang rape and violence.

Marks claimed he remained on good terms with the inmates, who regarded him as 'charming, British and eccentric'. He also became the prison's 'in-house lawyer' and part-time teacher with small classes of inmates, helping him to earn an early release.

Judy was waiting for him, they moved back to Majorca for a while, but in 2005 they split up, leaving her to bring up the children.

Out of prison, Marks turned to new revenue-streams, writing his autobiography in 1996 under the title Mr Nice – later turned into a film with actor Rhys Ifans in the lead. He did some acting, singing, more writing and a string of stand-up, one-man theatre appearances, An Evening with Mr Nice.

He also stood for Parliament in four different constituencies and constantly campaigned for the legalisation of cannabis. He called his last book, published the year before he died, Mr Smiley – My Last Pill and Testament.

Seven years in a Florida state penitentiary and three years in different prison cells in England, Holland and Spain, is a tall price to pay for any kind of fame... or fortune. More years on the run, strange hiding places and forking-out regular ransoms to guarantee his freedom, hardly led to any peace-of-mind or a permanent and stress-free lifestyle.

No one disputes his claim to have made £30 million out of drug smuggling, but Howard Marks was penniless, and virtually friendless, in the end. He suffered for 15 months with terminal cancer and died, aged 70, in April 2016.

Chapter Twenty two

A Dedicated Bunch of Detectives

Edward Laxton: Martyn Pritchard was undoubtedly a dedicated copper, a low-key version of the US undercover detective Frank Serpico, who exposed police corruption in New York and whose life-story was turned into a top-selling book and award-winning film.

In Busted, Martyn's original biography, he named and thanked 50 of his fellow drugs squad officers for their friendship and support in doing and enjoying the job. They managed to do both in the many years I witnessed them in action.

One Saturday evening I went into one of my local pubs in South Oxfordshire, The Cherry Tree, and was surprised to see a few non-local but fairly familiar faces. These were drugs squad detectives gathering to raid a fancy-dress party. Consequently, the police officers were also in fancy dress.

Their leader was Mick Strutt, who, hilariously, had bought a dress from an Oxford charity shop, donned a wig and borrowed a few accessories from his wife, Heather, another CID officer. "Talk to me on Monday, dear boy," he said and disappeared.

A large, nearby house in our rural village, was leased to six post-graduate students. Their thinly veiled invitations left no doubt about the central theme for the party – which attracted the uninvited attention of the drugs squad. They busted a number of party-goers, all charged with possession of various drugs.

Here was a classic example of introducing some lighthearted humour into an otherwise serious police operation. Their activities at some of the Free Festivals were similar, a great laugh – but they got the job done at the same time.

With just over eight years' service, Martyn quit. He knocked the police as he told his story, yet he enjoyed the job, thrived on the personal challenge it provided and loved the freelancing aspect of his career in the drugs squad.

Further testament to his vocation came from some of the men and women he busted, charged and took into court. Later, a few became friends, very few remained enemies. Martyn was sad to leave the force, but a uniform and an eight-hour shift could not compete with those happy, hippy, free-wheeling days. EL

LOOKING BACK... AND AHEAD

Martyn Pritchard: Now it's all over. My patched-up jeans, the torn T-shirts – in fact, all my old hippy gear except my combat jacket – have been burned. My hair has been cut and I shower or have a bath every day. Luxury!

All I have left of my years undercover on the drugs squad (DS) are the memories of the good times, the great officers I worked with. But there were a few regrets, like the junkies we didn't get off the hook, the youngsters who went too far and couldn't kick the habit, the busts that went wrong, the pushers that walked away, and the kids that died.

However, you always remember the good times, the junkies that did give up drugs and how we helped them get a hospital bed and possibly saved their lives. I recall the days and nights of obs, boring and sometimes frustrating, freezing cold or boiling hot in the cars and vans, but those I remember best are the ones that paid off.

A lot of you reading this will no doubt come to different conclusions. Some will say, "Ah ha! We always said the police abused their powers." Well, I can assure you we never abused the powers given to us. We may sometimes have gone to the outer limits of the law, but we never went beyond them.

When we tapped phones, it was done with permission from the

Home Office – there was no other way we could get the information we needed. And what we heard was never evidence in court, so phone taps alone never sent anyone to prison.

When we held our clients in the cells we often lied, as they lied, and let them think we knew far more about them and their activities than was really so, but we had often followed and observed these people for weeks or months. Keeping close to the scene and with our instinct and experience, we knew what was going down.

Everyone is innocent until proved guilty, so knowing and proving are two different things. I don't think setting a few verbal traps to get the proof was a bad thing. Law enforcement in this country is not carried out by secret service agents, but by coppers who use their common sense. We were handpicked volunteers who had had to pass a rigorous board to get into the drugs squad, but common sense was vital, as it is in so many walks of life.

We put ourselves about and knocked off kids on small possession charges not because we wanted to, nor because they were the people we were really after. We had to make sure our drugs scene was kept under some sort of control. And all the time our work would lead us on, up the ladder to the pushers. They were always our main target.

Looking to the future, I would like to see a National Drugs Squad set up, like the DEA in America. Customs and police should work together, instead of having one side whose interest is only in the illegal importation. The Central Drugs Intelligence Unit should be operational instead of merely an intelligence source, and I bet they won't last long. [Martyn was right. The CDIU was scrapped in 1988, replaced in 1992 by the National Drugs Intelligence Unit. Eventually, in 2013, the National Crime Agency became responsible for coordinating intelligence for organised crime in general: money laundering, people trafficking and slavery, cyber-crime, child sexual exploitation... and drugs.]

Operation Julie brought together a hardcore of drugs squad

officers. We had experts in surveillance and undercover work, along with others who were skilled in obtaining obscure information, which helped us to build our intelligence index. And they were all of them absolutely dedicated.

When it dispersed late in 1977, six out of 26 resigned and only four remained as operational drugs squad officers. Most of the very senior police officers across the country looked down their noses at the DS. We were an embarrassment. Civil servants at the Home Office had much the same view.

As for the junkies… I would not join the 'legalise drugs' lobby, no way, but let me say this: in my opinion, the guy with a little cannabis who goes home, listens to his stereo music and turns on with a joint, isn't doing any harm.

But if you legalise cannabis, what happens? For so many, it's the easy entry to the wider and more dangerous hard-drugs scene.

The weak characters start with a little smoke. They are then persuaded to sniff a little coke, and then it's using the needle. They think they haven't made it until there are track marks all up their arms.

Drugs abuse can and does kill. OK, the counter-argument points out that hard drinking does the same. But do any of us know an alcoholic in their early twenties who is dead or dying?

As for myself, I have 'kicked it' too. I enjoyed the work and I loved the challenge. Belonging to the drugs squad was special, a member of an exclusive club of professionals. Make no mistake, I loved the life and I wouldn't have missed it for the world. But I could not go back to being an ordinary copper after that experience.

I was a uniformed sergeant at Slough. As well as ordinary working, most sergeants have a particular responsibility in the nick as well – the stolen bicycles book, lost property book, things like that. At Slough my responsibility was bollards.

Police traffic bollards. I had to look after the bollards book, check them in and out and make sure we didn't lose any. Bollards!

I didn't see the likelihood of much adrenalin pumping at the prospect of losing one or two bollards. They said bollards to me… and I decided to say something similar by way of a reply. And I quit the police.

Edward Laxton: Martyn went on to run a pub in the Midlands and then went back to South Wales where he died, suffering from diabetes, in the mid-90s.

Also by Mirror Books

One Last Job

Tom Pettifor and Nick Sommerlad

**Branded 'The Master' and 'a Gentleman Thief',
this book tells the extraordinary life story of Brian Reader,
Britain's most prolific old-school crook.**

The iconic £14million Hatton Garden raid of 2015 has already entered criminal folklore. This book cuts through the myth to document the astonishing true-life story of its elderly mastermind, Brian Reader.

Gang insiders, family, friends and detectives talk for the first time about Reader's six-decade career, from mixing with the Krays and the cream of the London underworld to an ill-fated collaboration with violent gangster Kenny Noye.

It reveals the Hatton Garden gang's links to an unsolved gangland murder, bent cops, police supergrasses and an alleged establishment cover-up. The book also includes new details about Basil, dubbed The Ghost after he became the only gang member to escape justice.

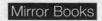

Also by Mirror Books

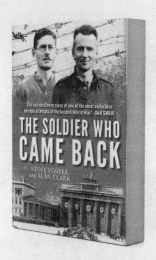

The Soldier Who Came Back

Steve Foster with Alan Clark

Northern Poland 1940. At the Nazi war camp Stalag XX-A, two men struck up an unlikely friendship that was to lead to one of the most daring and remarkable wartime escape stories ever told.

Antony Coulthard had a first-class honours degree from Oxford. Fred Foster, was the son of a Nottinghamshire bricklayer. This mismatched pair hatched a plan to disguise themselves as advertising executives working for Siemens. They would simply walk out of the camp, board a train - and head straight into the heart of Nazi Germany.

Their route into Germany was one that no one would think to search for escaped PoWs. This audacious plan involved 18 months of undercover work. They set off for the Swiss border taking notes of strategic interest while drinking beer with Nazi officers, just yards from Hitler's HQ.

But when they reached Lake Constance, with Switzerland within their reach, Antony crossed over into freedom, while Fred's luck ran out. What happened to them next is both heartbreaking and inspiring.

Mirror Books